Editor's w

EDITOR
MAX FRASER

ASSISTANT EDITOR
JESSICA KNOWLES

SUB EDITOR
ELLEN HIMELFARB

DESIGN
RICHARD ARDAGH STUDIO

COVER DESIGN
PETER CRAWLEY

PUBLISHER
MAX FRASER

CONTRIBUTORS
SIMON ALDERSON
GEMMA BELL
PATRICK CLAYTON-MALONE
NAOMI CLEAVER
SHERIDAN COAKLEY
YVONNE COURTNEY
TOM DIXON STUDIO
BRENT DZEKCIORIUS
ADAM HILLS
BENJAMIN HUBERT
HETTIE JUDAH
LINA KANAFANI
KIT KEMP
MARINE MALAK
HANNAH MARTIN
HUGH PEARMAN
BRADLEY QUINN
LIBBY SELLERS
ANNE SOWARD
JONATHAN STEPHENSON
SEAN SUTCLIFFE
KATIE TREGGIDEN
JALI WAHLSTEN

Dedicated to Arthur Fraser
& Frederick Lockie

We welcome feedback and
recommendations:
info@londondesignguide.com

PUBLISHED IN 2011
BY SPOTLIGHT PRESS

Welcome to the 2
only publication c
destinations. Buoy
I approached this totally updated and rewritten edition with the
same dedication to accuracy and detail as the first. I personally
visited each featured shop, dealer and gallery, evaluating all aspects
of the experience to impart an honest, unbiased review. The
exhaustive research will appeal to design authorities, enthusiasts
and novices alike.

It never ceases to amaze me – a born and bred Londoner –
just how vast this cosmopolitan city has become. I still find the
variety of offerings overwhelming and the task of tracking them
down daunting – though it has been rewarding. For this edition
I navigated more than 600 miles of road to reach 200 businesses
before editing down my final selection to the finest 138. In many
spots I highlighted my favourite finds, and shared them with you
in the new 4x4 section.

To help you work through the material, I've divided the city
into design-heavy neighbourhoods and marked each featured
destination on a map. Each chapter includes a walking tour tailor-
made by a resident stylemaker, so you can see things from a local
perspective. And in case you're carrying this with you on the road,
I've added 'eat and drink' suggestions to the end of every chapter,
selected with the design-savvy visitor in mind.

You'll also find ten featured essays by London design
professionals, each discussing a different facet of the industry, be it
production, retail, communications, collecting, even salvage. These
critical analyses give us all a better understanding of the industry
and its workings.

London Design Guide is a snapshot of the design scene today,
a practical resource from cover to cover. It'll get you out of the
house and into the streets to experience the places where creativity
plays a vital role. This world-class city has a world of good design
on offer: explore it, debate it, praise it and, by all means, denounce
it. But above all: make it your own.

Max Fraser

BOCCI 28
28 by Omer Arbel
Standard Fixtures and Custom Chandeliers
LED | Xenon | Halogen
www.bocci.ca
+44(0) 7794 587 325
saleseu@bocci.ca

GUIDELINES AND CRITERIA

The definition of 'design' in this guide refers to three-dimensional objects in the broadest sense, and furniture, lighting, ceramics, glass, textiles and tableware more specifically. The focus is on contemporary design, but we've also included vintage originals. New to this edition are shops selling contemporary prints and graphic art. The guide reviews businesses open to the public, so it doesn't include references to studios, or interior and architecture practices.

We have chosen to exclude the following: shops devoted to 'permanents', such as bathroom and kitchen appliances, tiles, flooring, light fixtures, etc; office-furniture showrooms; shops with stock comprising more than 50 per cent clothing; businesses with an 'appointment only' opening policy; businesses that are utterly unbearable to deal with (you know who you are). In very few cases, there are exceptions to this criteria.

London's boundary is defined by the M25 orbital motorway. No neighbourhood was predetermined – all were defined after we had researched, visited and approved every place. We defined each area by the high concentration of design activity within it, afterwards adding recommendations for the *Eat & drink* sections concluding each chapter. The maps that open each chapter are illustrative and include streets that are relevant to the entries in the guide. We recommend carrying a comprehensive street map for a greater overview.

Most importantly, no person or business has paid to be included in the editorial portions of this guide, nor can any exert pressure on us to tailor the reviews. Research visits were anonymous and unannounced to ensure a genuine customer experience. Clothes worn were casual with no outward display of wealth.

Now that's clear, please enjoy!

Contents

Why London Now?

*W*hether or not you agree with all those published rankings of the world's best cities to live in, there's no escaping the fact that London continually rates highly on the global stage. It's considered by many to be Europe's central meeting point, and indeed visitors from around the globe flock to the English-speaking megacity for business, leisure and a dose of culture. Steeped in history on the one hand, London never sits still on the other, and progress marches on unabashed.

The sprawling capital is spread over a whopping 600 square miles. This mass is home to a multicultural mix of young hopefuls and families, all attracted to London for the financial prospects and the tolerance of new values. International influences have infused the very fabric of the city, stimulating the masses across every pursuit, from cuisine, theatre, film and festivals to art, architecture and, of course, design.

When it comes to the creative industries, our cultural melting pot gives individual practitioners a certain freedom of thought and expression. There's an open-minded attitude towards new ideas and a willingness to explore and challenge the status quo – often with a healthy dose of irony and humility.

Every year established London-based designers are joined by a flurry of new design grads, many of whom studied in top local colleges and are fired up to bring fresh energy to the commercial and cultural sectors. These talents have endured years of hardship brought on by the high cost of living – the main drawback of living in one of the world's most expensive cities. Still they want to make a go of it here and persevere with an attitude that if you can survive here, you can survive anywhere.

There's no escaping the fact that jobs are few and far between these days; economic turbulence has taken its toll on employment. The burden of a fickle income stream coupled with high overheads tends to weed out those independent contractors who are half-hearted about the industry. The ones who are prepared to make a go of it understand that hard work is key, and that being simply 'good enough' is, well, not good enough.

There is a multidisciplinary nature to survival here: you need to develop a multichannel portfolio of activity to diversify your risk. Within the industry this gives rise to a culture of collaboration.

The most highly developed talents merge together and give rise to strong conceptual unions, the output of which manifests in many varied permutations. The annual celebration of these collaborations comes in September during the London Design Festival, when events, exhibitions and installations pop up across the capital. The festival has gained traction over the years, attracting more members of the public who have become increasingly design literate, and garnering support and endorsement from our politicians, who have demonstrated their awareness of the industry's economic contribution.

Barely a week goes by without a festival to celebrate some cultural niche in one form or other. Dwarfing them all in 2012 are the Olympic Games, the Holy Grail of cultural events worldwide. When London won its bid to host them back in 2005, we were oblivious of the impending financial crisis. The event comes at an extraordinary cost (approximately £7.5 billion), which many feel the city can ill afford. Nonetheless the excitement around the games will surely provide a welcome boost to the country's morale at this time of economic uncertainty.

The development of the Olympic Park on post-industrial wasteland in east London has been a positive regenerative exercise for a neglected corner of the city. It has given rise to stadia, housing, sculpture and landscaping by homegrown architects and designers. It has created an entirely new neighbourhood, which most assumed would be impossible in a city already so built up. The 500-acre site is a very vivid reminder of London's constant expansion and morphing, while its neighbourhoods fluctuate and gentrification sets in.

It is often those working in the creative industries who discover and nurture cheaper, less developed parts of the city. Attracted by affordable rents, they tend to give rise to exciting and unusual interventions. Eventually, the element of 'cool' they bring attracts investment, bringing with it the inevitable property hikes that so ironically squeeze them out eventually. Areas like Clerkenwell, Islington, Shoreditch, and now Hackney and Dalston have all undergone such transformations. This is the recognised reality of London's constant shift. There is no room for complacency here. In such a hotbed of energy and ideas, the process of reinvention never sits idle. For the gangs of individuals driving such change, this city of 7.8 million residents acts as a perfect playground.

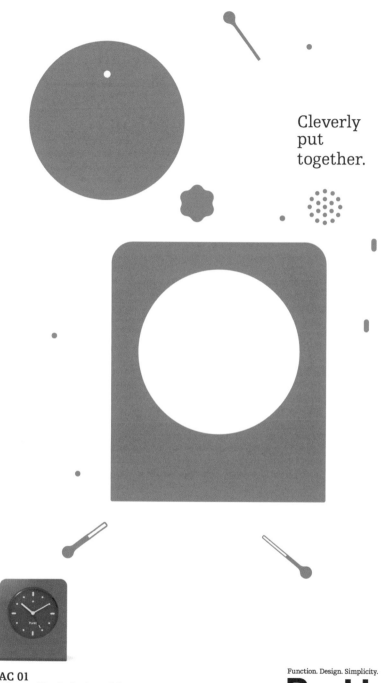

Cleverly
put
together.

AC 01
Alarm Clock designed by Jasper Morrison
punktgroup.com

THE STATE OF RETAIL

In the process of compiling this guide I've visited more than 200 stores in person, covering great distances across London's shopping districts. I've spoken with numerous storeowners and staff, many bemoaning the current state of retail. Yes, while many paint a positive picture of unusually strong sales, others struggle to conceal their business woes.

The economic downturn is widely blamed for consumer gloom, and government austerity measures are understandably making people nervous about financial security. For many people, purchasing non-essential items is something to be postponed.

Even in good times retailers in the capital have battled with climbing rents and stinging business rates. But now suppliers are contending with increasing costs for raw materials, transportation and basic utilities. As such, consumer prices are being forced up and profit margins are taking a hit. Even established chains are defaulting, no longer able to sustain enough volume to bolster their bottom line. Habitat is one of the more significant casualties.

Consumers must also contend with the paradox of too much choice. Londoners have little time to wade through all the stuff on the streets – so much of it derivative. So they turn to the Internet for simplicity. With even big brands selling direct online, the role of the traditional retailer is increasingly sidelined.

Store owners talk about the Amazon Effect: shoppers browsing in store then finding it cheaper online. (A positive consequence of this sees foreign buyers ordering from the UK, taking advantage of the weak pound.) To compete, retailers have continually slashed prices in the hope that customers will commit to their offerings before searching elsewhere. This can be off-putting, however; not everyone wants to shop in a sea of discounts, mediocre visual merchandising and despondent staff.

All these factors paint a pretty depressing picture. That said, the hardest hit seem to be the big-brand businesses – those that have lost the vision and integrity of the original founder and follow an army of managers and bureaucrats. Smaller, independent retailers seem to be thriving as discerning customers seek out the unusual, unwilling to settle for the commonplace. Such storeowners are injecting a strong point of view into their offerings, hoping that punters are prepared for the hunt (and prepared to pay a bit more for something a bit less

ubiquitous). Shoppers seem less interested in acquiring mere 'stuff', but more interested in acquiring individuality. They're buying less, but better. These independent retailers seldom attract the masses. Nor are they trying to. Often confined to small spaces, characterful shops are curated by passionate owners who strive for stock that's not widely available, so their style and content are followed by a niche – in some cases a profitable niche. They're often operating with limited cash assets, so they have to remain nimble and open to change, shifting and altering displays regularly to remain fresh and appealing to loyal customers. They're on email and social media to keep their target audience in the loop, regardless of their geographic location. This guide is dominated by such independent stores, many of which, thankfully, seem to have remained buoyant.

Unfortunately, rent increases are a scourge for such shops. Just as the independents play a part in gentrification, they also dig their own graves as landlords hike up rents disproportionately. I've heard stories of 40 per cent rises, a nail in the coffin for most small businesses. As they fall, mainstream retailers take over, contributing to the homogeneity of our high streets. Many long-standing independents I've spoken to have one thing in common: they opted to sidestep rent and bought their properties outright.

The ones that don't make it leave empty storefronts and create a dispiriting eyesore on our shopping streets. Still, there are plenty of enterprising individuals willing to take advantage of the vacancies and transform such spaces with temporary 'pop-up shops', as they are commonly referred to. They last only a few days to several months, but these interventions usually come with a healthy dose of theatre, free as they are from the mundane realities of retail. As the name suggests, they simply pop up with little notice, surprising passers-by and whipping up word-of-mouth excitement. People travel especially to visit such places, eager to experience the frenzy and buy while it lasts. This sort of sensational retail injects energy back into shopping and reminds us of the pleasure that comes with physical, tactile interactions – a pleasure that, despite the multiple advantages, can never be replaced by the Internet.

As human beings, we respond well to sensory stimuli and we flock to places that titillate them all simultaneously. Struggling retailers would do well to remember that.

#Just say HELLO!

At the tender age of 17 I worked in the designer menswear departments at Harrods every Saturday. On training day we watched the induction video featuring owner Mohamed Al Fayed, who announced something that has always stuck with me: "You are the ambassadors to my business."

That remark has repeatedly echoed in my mind while putting together this publication. I've been subjected to various degrees of unacceptable service – even at the city's most influential boutiques. After I started noticing it, I was amazed how many places failed at the basic courtesies. Surely good service is one of the crucial components of successful retail. Incensed, I'd often return to the office and recount my stories, exclaiming: 'How difficult is it to JUST SAY HELLO?!' And so this public plea to join my *Just Say Hello* campaign was born.

It's pretty straightforward: all I'm looking for when I enter a retail establishment is a handful of basics: a hello, eye contact and, ideally, a smile. Yes, it's as simple as that. It's probably going too far to ask me how I am. Yes, I know you'll be there if I need your help. And, no, I don't want to be referred to as your 'mate'.

You'd be amazed at how many assistants I found affixed to their computer screens, too engrossed to look up. Others chatted amongst themselves, oblivious to the fact that they were recounting their weekend escapades to the entire store. A classic is for staff to look you up and down and make an immediate judgment. Big mistake. At Harrods I learned quickly that the people you wouldn't expect to spend often spend the most.

Retailers must wake up to their lacklustre staff and realise it's not enough to carry a product that sells; you need to keep customers coming back. So many places seem to sell the same stuff anyway that great service is likely to be the deal-breaker. And if shoppers feel they've been treated better than they expected, there's a higher chance they'll return.

This is particularly crucial today as the retail environment struggles under a weak economy and competition becomes ever more rife. The ingredients that make up customer loyalty are fickle and transferable; they need to be nurtured and massaged wherever possible. In fact, succeeding at customer service takes more than simply saying, 'Hello.' But that's certainly a good start.

Join our campaign to stamp out bad and encourage good service. Whichever you encounter, share it on Twitter using the hashtag #JustSayHello

RUCHÉ one-arm sofa with table. Design: Inga Sempé.
Catalogue: www.ligne-roset-westend.co.uk

STAYING HOME IS THE NEW GOING OUT to A FANCY PLACE.

Ligne Roset Westend

23/25 Mortimer Street - 0207 323 1248
ligne-roset-westend.co.uk

contemporary furniture, lighting,
rugs and objects for the home

BEAUTIFUL STATEMENTS. ligne roset®

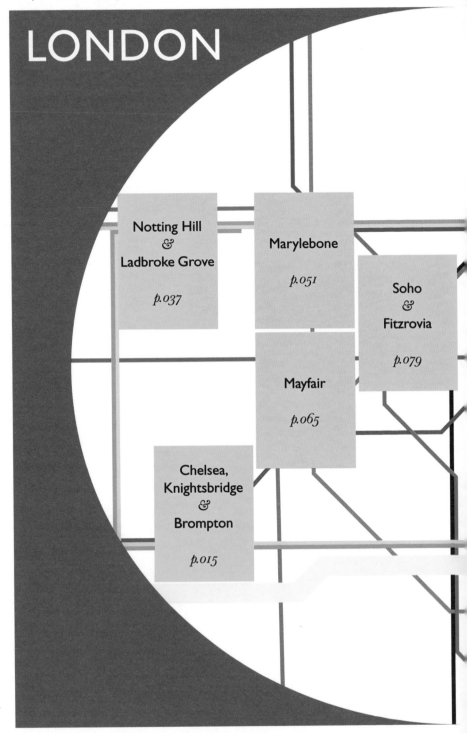

LONDON

Notting Hill
&
Ladbroke Grove

p.037

Marylebone

p.051

Soho
&
Fitzrovia

p.079

Mayfair

p.065

Chelsea,
Knightsbridge
&
Brompton

p.015

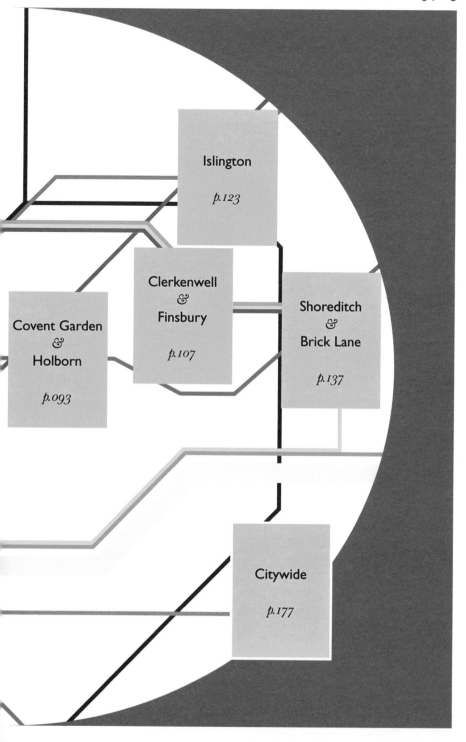

Islington

p.123

Clerkenwell
&
Finsbury

p.107

Shoreditch
&
Brick Lane

p.137

Covent Garden
&
Holborn

p.093

Citywide

p.177

**Earls Court
London
20 – 23 September 2012**

100%**design**®
100%**futures**®
100%**materials**®

See inside today's brightest creative minds at 100% Design

4 days, 400 world-class exhibitors. Source new products for projects and find the latest furniture, lighting, textiles and accessories. Connect with the best under one roof and enjoy workshops, seminars, trails and events. Whether you're looking for cutting-edge products, innovative materials, fresh talent or great inspiration, you'll find it at 100% Design.

Live and breathe the interior landscape at the UK's leading interior design show.

Register now for entry:
www.100percentdesign.co.uk

Imagined by: Peter and Paul · Inspired by: Amy Levinson Design · Andy Murray · Atelier Areti
Carlo Borer · Dare Studio · Design Virus · G Squared Art · Jeongwon-il · Normann Copenhagen
Philip Watts Design · Sandin & Bulow · Stuart Akroyd · Suck UK · Westergaard Designs

Chelsea, Knightsbridge & Brompton

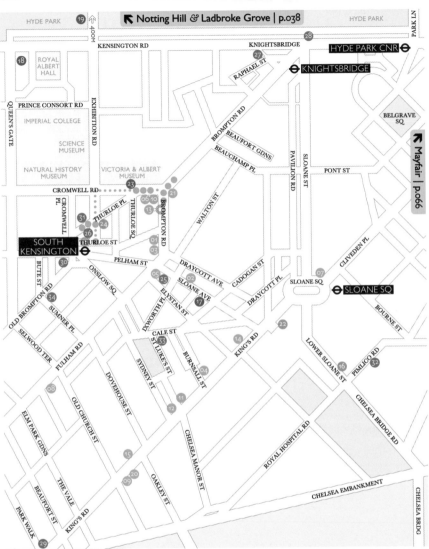

↑ Mayfair | p.066

● Design galleries & institutions
● Design shops & C20th vintage
● Design bookshops

● Eat & drink
  (pp.032-033)

••• Take a walk route

Chelsea, Knightsbridge & Brompton

TAKE A WALK WITH

*Lina Kanafani**

I'll start with the deliciously retro Gessler at Daquise Polish restaurant (20 Thurloe Street). The restaurant launched in Warsaw in 1938 and came to London decades ago to serve hearty meals in a friendly, old-fashioned setting. Impressively, it's withstood South Ken's massive modernisation. Opposite are the V&A Reading Rooms (8 Exhibition Road), a haven for avid readers complete with a bar for the perfect mix of culture and consumption. Round the corner; at 29 Thurloe Place is the Japanese restaurant Tombo, immaculately designed and ideal for casual, affordable dining. The Sampler, a sophisticated wine shop where you can enjoy tipples of expertly chosen wines, is across the road.

Heading up Cromwell Road, be sure to visit the magnificent V&A museum, a must for designers and art-lovers especially. A cultural hub, it boasts a huge permanent collection and puts on fascinating temporary shows.

Across the road on Thurloe Place was once an array of specialist 19th-century shops selling silver, jewellery and antiques relating to the museum collection. Today only two landmarks remain: the silversmith M.P. Levene and Robert Frew, specialising in fine and rare books, prints and maps. They're worth a visit before time takes its toll and they disappear without warning. If you like that kind of thing, head down the road to James Hardy & Co (235 Brompton Road), a silversmith and diamond merchant established in 1953. Vacant now it retains its original Victorian shop fittings and picture window. Today the space is used for temporary exhibitions.

Head back to Brompton Quarter, past kitchen suppliers Divertimenti and the design boutique Skandium. The road bends left to reveal an array of unusual shops like Few and Far. Next door is the delicious Brasserie Cassis, serving light lunches and more serious suppers.

The final destination before reaching my shop Mint (2 North Terrace) is The Garage (1 North Terrace). It's an empty but alluring space that has become a landmark showcasing design events year-round. Exhibitions there are part of Brompton Design District's ongoing promotion of the area.

* Owner of Mint mintshop.co.uk

01 B&B ITALIA

- 250 BROMPTON ROAD SW3 2AS
- 020 7591 8111
- BEBITALIA.COM
- MON-SAT 10-6, SUN 12-5
- SOUTH KENSINGTON

02 BISAZZA

- 60 SLOANE AVENUE SW3 3DD
- 020 7584 8837
- BISAZZA.COM
- MON-SAT 10-6
- SOUTH KENSINGTON

Italian furniture company B&B Italia has nurtured its image of sophistication and refinement ever since Piero Ambrogio Busnelli formed it in 1966. Today the company can boast a strong international presence, and a reputation for style and quality in modern home furnishings.

The London flagship occupies an enormous space at Brompton Cross, the heartland of upmarket Chelsea. The cavernous, 120-metre-deep, cathedral-like showroom is the result of a collaboration between pioneering architects John Pawson and Antonio Citterio. Together they converted a former car showroom into a bright, slick contemporary environment with monumental windows that frame some meticulously styled displays. Plenty of passers-by would be intimidated by the grandiose modernity on show, but they shouldn't let that put them off going in and having a good look around.

What they'll see is a large proportion of the brand's home collections, updated regularly and complemented by the slightly more bourgeois offerings from sister brand Maxalto. Neutral colours dominate, an ideal palette for B&B's modern, aspirational, yet comfortable pieces.

Working with some of the leading designers from around the world, the Busnelli family has consistently invested in design knowhow and worked tirelessly on its brand communication. This dedication and tenacity has sustained the brand's status at the top of the high-end furniture game.

The extraordinary potential of glass mosaic tile is taken to an extreme by Bisazza, the Italian producer founded in 1956. The company has since positioned itself firmly in the luxury design sector with trailblazing presentations at design events around the world. Working in partnership with a number of dynamic design talents, this enterprising outfit has proven that mosaic tiles are a versatile decorative addition to public and private interiors, and even exteriors.

So just what can be achieved with a swathe of small square tiles? Bisazza's London flagship will show you. The store – designed by the Bisazza Design Studio under the direction of architect Carlo Dal Bianco – was conceived as a series of environments over two floors. They display a selection of patterns and pieces from the *Home Collection*, including mosaic-clad furniture and objects by leading talents such as Tord Boontje, Alessandro Mendini and Studio Job. More recently Bisazza launched a bathroom division called *Bisazza Bagno*, with debut collections by Jaime Hayon and Marcel Wanders.

As intimidating as it is to enter this showroom, remember: You're the customer. Whatever you're considering – be it classic patterning or something more vivid or even bespoke – a staff member here can talk you through the design options. Get chatting and you'll realise there are endless opportunities to consider, from the sublime to the ridiculous. Tilework is always going to be unique to your own space, so the Bisazza environment is effectively a place of inspiration, a place for awakening a customer's imagination.

03 BOFFI CHELSEA
254 BROMPTON ROAD SW3 2AS
020 7590 8910
BOFFI-CHELSEA.COM
MON-SAT 10-6
SOUTH KENSINGTON

04 CHRISTOPHER FARR
6 BURNSALL STREET SW3 3ST
020 7349 0888
CHRISTOPHERFARR.COM
MON-FRI 10-6
SLOANE SQUARE

Showrooms for 'permanent' appliances (kitchens, bathrooms and the like) fall outside the editorial remit of this guide, but Boffi is an exception, primarily because it gives us a chance to marvel at some of the finest modern design on the continent. The Italian manufacturer's 600-square-metre Chelsea space lives up to expectations, displaying that exquisite detailing, tactile quality, refined craftsmanship and solid construction the name is famous for.

A palette of white and grey dominates along with stainless steel, wood and irresistible Corian; right angles are occasionally balanced by curvy taps and rounded baths and basins. The beauty is in the minimalist aesthetic, which conceals the precision detailing and extraordinary functionality. Such perfection doesn't come cheap but will nevertheless last a lifetime.

The kitchen is not only functional, but also satisfies our appetites for culinary creativity; it's a place to experiment and perfect flavour combinations to sample and enjoy. The bathroom is not only a space for daily ablutions, but also a private spot for introspection, calm and replenishment. Many of us take these components of the home for granted – that is, until we're presented with more indulgent alternatives. Boffi's showroom is one such place where we can admire what could be.

One-time artist Christopher Farr began a career in the rug field in 1988, dealing in antique decorative and tribal floor-coverings. It wasn't long before he was able to transfer his skills as a painter to rug design and, in so doing, attract the attentions of the design community. His acceptance was reinforced a few years later when he collaborated with textile and fashion designers from the Royal College of Art on an exhibit called *Brave New Rugs*. The show helped Farr establish the lowly rug as a medium for contemporary expression… and build a name for himself in the process.

Since then Farr and business partner Matthew Bourne have commissioned a number of designs from a diversity of artists, designers and architects alike – names like Romeo Gigli, Kate Blee, Allegra Hicks, Tony Bevan, Ilse Crawford, Timorous Beasties, Michael Young, John Pawson and Andrée Putman. They've contributed all manner of styles, from soft and subtle to geometric, bold and decorative. Meanwhile, a textile business, featuring bold prints and textural weaves, has sprung up.

The quiet, slightly cluttered office showroom off the King's Road is where clients can view the plethora of designs and samples and meet to discuss individual requirements. Each rug is made to order, so you can discuss your preferred size, colourway and textural nuances before the weaving begins – in Turkey, by traditionally skilled weavers. To learn more about the process, treat yourself to some time wandering around and chatting to the friendly team.

THE CONRAN SHOP

- MICHELIN HOUSE, 81 FULHAM ROAD SW3 6RD
- 020 7589 7401
- CONRANSHOP.CO.UK
- MON-FRI 10-6, WED-THU 10-7, SA 10-6.30, SU 12-6
- SOUTH KENSINGTON

The Conran Shop's infamous founder, Sir Terence Conran, has always had a knack for finding great London buildings to convert. His keen eye for old spaces with character triggered him to restore Michelin House, the 1911 headquarters of the eponymous tyre company. In 1987 he opened the landmark as a hub for contemporary homewares at a time when there was little competition.

Since then, London's appetite for design has grown immeasurably, thanks in part to Conran's reputation for design-led projects and his promotional skills. The city's now-mature industry is testament to Conran, and the Michelin House location is still a mainstay in the capital.

The Conran Shop sells a well-edited selection of products for the home, a combination of modern classics and cutting-edge releases from around the world – much of which is gathered together in the windows along the Sloane Avenue side of the store. These expert windows make a bold impact, so be sure to admire them and get a sense for the feel of the store before heading in.

The ground floor is dedicated to larger furnishings, and in the vast basement you'll find everything else: lighting, tableware, kitchenware, accessories. It's an unusual approach; the other stores often demote furniture to quieter areas with less footfall. Perhaps putting the big-ticket items by the foyer sets a high-end tone for the store and creates an aspirational benchmark for visitors.

Conran's mission has always been to make good design more accessible and more appealing. While his stores (see also Marylebone, p.055) offer top-spec sofas, chairs, beds, tables and lighting,

they have always been careful to offer alternatives that don't cost a fortune. They also manage to steer many practical items away from the mundane. 'All I've ever wanted from life are plain, simple, useful products,' Conran has said. The sentiment is there in the *Well Considered* range of simple, affordable, own-brand designs.

The mini-emporium at Brompton Cross continues to attract a loyal following among gift-givers and home-design addicts alike. Unlike so many other home stores in the post-recession retailscape, Conran refreshingly avoids cheapening his offer or compromising on quality.

06 CREST LIVING

📠 AT FEW AND FAR, 242 BROMPTON RD SW3 2BB
📞 020 7225 7066
🔗 CRESTLIVING.CO.UK
🕐 MON-SAT 10-6, SUN 12-5
⊖ SOUTH KENSINGTON

07 DAVID MELLOR

📠 4 SLOANE SQUARE SW1W 8EE
📞 020 7730 4259
🔗 DAVIDMELLORDESIGN.COM
🕐 MON-SAT 9.30-6, SUN 11-5
⊖ SLOANE SQUARE

The newly established retail arm of Crest Contract Interiors shows a diverse collection of first-rate European furniture and lighting at its Brompton showroom. Despite – or perhaps owing to? – the quality content on the floor, it's rather hidden in the basement space of Few and Far (p.023), so you won't notice it at street level.

Head past the colourful curiosities at Few and Far and descend the stairs for a contrasting take on contemporary living. Crest offers a more brand-driven version of the future, which is organised in tableaux incorporating seating and dining options, all illuminated by decorative wall, table and pendant lighting.

Excellence is evident across all the products on display, from pioneering furniture brands like Thonet and Artifort and contemporary lighting counterparts Pallucco and Metalarte. However – and this is typical of so many businesses that expand from the serious and rather stark world of commercial interiors – Crest's stylists often forget to soften the aesthetic with a few human touches for the domestic market.

Industry types will be familiar with the design provenance of the brands and designers carried here, but I always try to put myself in the shoes of a layman visiting for the first time. And I suspect that, beyond the obvious beauty of the individual items here, visitors may not truly appreciate their relevance. I myself left feeling that there was something missing: some sort of compelling explanation for the pieces chosen for sale and the connections between them.

I must admit: I really enjoy exploring kitchen and tableware shops. It never ceases to amaze me how many implements have been invented to facilitate the joyous task of food preparation and cooking. That said, it's amazing how many wares don't satisfactorily fulfil their functional promise, which is why I usually head to the David Mellor shop in Sloane Square, as I know their selection has been vigorously assessed.

Mellor's designs take pride of place on the ground floor, overseen by helpful and informed staff. If you need any other kitchen paraphernalia, the basement space houses a perfectly curated selection of internationally sourced equipment to meet the greatest culinary expectations.

Why do I have such faith? Well, David Mellor (1930-2009) was one of the UK's leading designers, a distinction that goes back to when he was elected Royal Designer for Industry in 1962. He was responsible for designing some major civil interventions, including the British traffic light, but he is perhaps best known for his classic cutlery, still produced at his factory near Sheffield. Throughout his life, his eye for design and attention to detail were honed to perfection and, as such, his output was widely admired by loyal followers. Now overseen by his son, Corin, this exemplary British brand has been given a new injection of energy.

08 DE PARMA

- 247 FULHAM ROAD SW3 6HY
- 020 7352 2414
- DEPARMA.COM
- MON–SAT 10–6
- SOUTH KENSINGTON

09 DESIGNERS GUILD

- 267 & 277 KING'S ROAD SW3 5EN
- 020 7351 5775
- DESIGNERSGUILD.COM
- MON–SAT 10–6, SUN 12–5
- SLOANE SQUARE/SOUTH KENSINGTON

Fulham Road's exclusive antique dealers have made space for De Parma, a design gallery selling covetable furnishings and *objets*. Owner Gary De Sparham first blended into the neighbourhood with his traditional European antiques, but more than a decade ago he branched out into his ultimate passion: 20th-century design.

His current space is three years old and its clean white interior seems smart and fresh in this upmarket area. Don't be put off by the pristine surroundings, though. The friendly staff will welcome you, offer their service, then, if you wish, leave you alone to browse their tidy displays. They include a whole lot of Italian design from the 1930s through to the 1960s: a pair of mahogany-framed armchairs by Franco Albini; low chairs by Ugo Cara; a red serpentine-shaped sofa by Ico Parisi; and dozens of sculptural lights in all shapes and sizes.

Without a doubt my favourite piece on a recent visit was a bronze 1930s cuboid ceiling light from France, an Art Deco triumph from Ruhlmann. It sat in contrast with a pair of bulbous 1988 *Embryo* chairs by Marc Newson. It was interesting to see a fairly recent design make it into De Parma, but it makes perfect sense now that Newson has become so collectible.

Whatever you're after, you can rest assured it will be in good condition; the gallery has its own workshop, which sympathetically repairs and refurbishes where necessary.

If you're ever in need of cheering up, the blast of colour that hits you upon entering Designers Guild should do the trick. Set up in 1970 by textile queen Tricia Guild – who has never been shy about using shocking colour, pattern and texture – this London flagship is the ultimate showcase of her trademark bold style.

The first thing I noticed on my last visit was an energetic 'hello' from a smiley staffer. That put me in the mood to like the place, so I sauntered around the multilevel emporium admiring the styled-to-a-T room sets, featuring vintage furniture reupholstered in fresh new fabrics (the full range of which are displayed next door). Other leading brands, including Knoll, Vitra, B&B Italia, Fritz Hansen, Moroso and Cappellini, complement the on-trend look.

Plenty of natural light floods the store and brings the high-impact colour to life. And the visual stimuli don't end there, thanks to the plethora of accessories in store, including tableware, ceramics, blankets, cushions and rugs.

A definitive female slant prevails at Designers Guild, which is only heightened by the mainly female staff and clientele. Whether or not you subscribe to the message of its aesthetic, you have to celebrate any business that encourages people to embrace colour in their homes. If there were an anti-bland movement in existence, you could bet that Tricia Guild would be leading it.

10 FEW AND FAR

➤ 242 BROMPTON ROAD SW3 2BB
☎ 020 7225 7070
⬈ FEWANDFAR.NET
🕐 MON–SAT 10–6, SUN 12–5
⊖ SOUTH KENSINGTON

It takes nerves of steel and serious conviction to open retail premises in London. Such are the pressures of high rents, fickle consumers and generally tough trading conditions. Defiant of such hurdles, Priscilla Carluccio opened Few and Far in 2008 with plenty of skills amassed from creative positions at The Conran Shop (pp.020 & 055), Habitat (p.084), Heal's (p.085) and, more recently, the Carluccio's restaurant chain.

Answering to no one here on Brompton Road, she has ploughed her energy and ambition into a very personal shopping experience that operates far from the faceless monotony of much retailing today. In many respects her aim is to return to the core values of shopkeeping, where a distinctive product is married with impeccable standards, and where customers feel well served and inspired.

Carluccio travels the world to source her inimitable pieces: antiques, tableware, toys and jewellery from Europe and colourful pieces from Morocco, Mongolia and India. She hunts down stuff you won't find anywhere else in London – a rare skill in the Internet age. So you won't find any designer names or brand logos here, only homemade tags with references to provenance and unusual production techniques.

The results are eclectic, to say the least, a rich visual treat. There's something of the bazaar here, meaning what stands out for me and someone else may differ. Carluccio transforms the space and the merchandise regularly, styling theatrical window displays according to the theme of the season. Such an intensive approach succeeds at keeping the customer experience fresh with each visit. Whatever your impression of Few and Far, you must admit you truly get a feel for the owner's point of view here. At a time when homogeneity pervades the retail landscape, a point of view is something to be celebrated and supported.

13 MINT

🏠 2 NORTH TERRACE SW3 2BA

📞 020 7225 2228

↖ MINTSHOP.CO.UK

🕐 MON–SAT 10.30-6.30, THU 10.30-7.30

⊖ SOUTH KENSINGTON

Mint is one of a kind. It's no surprise it is regularly selected as one of the best design shops in the world. This has nothing to do with size or grandeur but can rather be attributed to the fact that the shop is guided by owner Lina Kanafani, whose personality and point of view are uniquely distinctive. Kanafani couldn't be happier than when she is sourcing original furnishings, lighting, ceramics, glass, textiles and *objets*. Whatever the item, she and her team always manage to create stunning compositions in this South Ken store.

Located a stone's throw from Brompton Road, the shop offers an experience unlike anything else in London. The modest façade gives way to a beautifully textured interior and an ever-evolving selection of designs by big name designers as well as newly graduated talents. In this respect there is no hierarchy. The message is that all genres and styles should coexist solely on the merits of their design.

Curiosity gets the better of you when you browse the ground floor space and the cosy basement level. Even industry types find things they've never seen before. A longtime supporter of new talent, Kanafani picks through graduate exhibitions and shows all over the world for her treasures. She always listens to her instincts and simply introduces what she loves to Mint. She takes a passionate approach that is irresistible to her loyal customers.

Without consciously trying, Mint sets the trends that other retailers try to follow. But the reality is: no one could replicate her distinctive style. This fact will always distinguish Mint from the others. If your budget doesn't measure up, you can always nab a special gift or home accessory from the collection of young designers. But if you can afford to bring more Mint into your home, there's an interior design consultation service available.

15 POLIFORM

🏠 278 KING'S ROAD SW3 5AW
📞 020 7368 7600
🔗 POLIFORMUK.COM
🕐 MON–SAT 10–6
🚇 SLOANE SQUARE

16 POTTERTON BOOKS

🏠 93 LOWER SLOANE STREET SW1W 8DA
📞 020 7730 4235
🔗 POTTERTONBOOKSLONDON.COM
🕐 MON–SAT 10–6, SUN 11–5
🚇 SLOANE SQUARE

High-end Italian manufacturer Poliform can boast a similarly high-end showroom on this upmarket stretch of King's Road. Set in a minimal Cubist Paolo Piva-designed building, the vast showroom is the ideal clean backdrop for the company's refined living solutions. You get your first look from the pavement through the floor-to-ceiling windows: slick orchestrated "rooms" designed with Poliform's upholstered furniture and storage solutions, commissioned from the world's leading design talents.

Poliform has a history in cabinetmaking that spans 40 years. In that time it's supplied a discerning customer, the kind who is attracted to purity of design. This sort of furniture does not rock the boat – it projects a modern aesthetic that rarely deviates from its muted palette. I often find it strange that showrooms like this don't attempt to soften their look, or add small flourishes that reflect the way people really live. I crave texture, colour, natural and human touches to counter-balance the tailored formality. I have the same reaction when I visit the space of kitchen brand Varenna, which shares this Chelsea space.

I suspect any flourishes might risk distracting the customer from the core collections. Perhaps the on-site design service can better communicate how the furniture would feature in a real home.

Potterton Books is a long-established specialist bookseller of new titles and rare, vintage and out-of-print books from around the world. For more than 25 years the business has stocked a comprehensive selection of titles on interior design, architecture, fine and decorative arts, fashion, design, photography and culture. Leadership has come from the HQ in North Yorkshire, and branches have opened in both New York and Los Angeles, but this small shop is London's first edition, strategically located around the corner from Chelsea's Pimlico Road interiors and antiques district.

While Potterton stocks a wide selection of specialist genres, its forte is sourcing in- and out-of-print titles for discerning customers and collectors. Bookworms, rejoice: if you're sure you've spotted a certain publication before but can't remember the title or author, chances are the knowledgeable staff here will be able to track it down. This service is a favourite with regular customers, whether private homeowners, collectors, interior designers or dealers.

The intimate boutique is lined with shelves of titles organised according to genre. New titles and unusual finds are stacked up on the central table or along the curved feature wall, which gives casual browsers a great selection of glossy tomes from which to choose. If you're looking for one, every book here is a conversation piece.

(17) RABIH HAGE

- 69-71 SLOANE AVENUE SW3 3DH
- 020 7823 8288
- RABIH-HAGE.COM
- MON–SAT 10–6
- SOUTH KENSINGTON

(18) ROYAL COLLEGE OF ART

- KENSINGTON GORE SW7 2EU
- 020 7590 4444
- RCA.AC.UK
- DAILY 11–5.30 (DURING EXHIBITIONS)
- HIGH STREET KENSINGTON / SOUTH KENSINGTON

Paris-trained architect Rabih Hage is an entrepreneurial character on the London design scene, working as he does as an interior designer, gallerist and advisor to collectors. His base is in Sloane Avenue, where he has had a design gallery since 2002. In tandem he runs a successful interior-design studio from his lower-ground office, as well as the burgeoning online design think tank, www.detnk.com.

It was Hage who helped forge the turbulent 'design art' movement that has exploded in recent years. Collectors have been attracted to his functional objects, all of them imbued with some combination of rare materials, unusual forms and specialist skills, and this has seen some living designers become collectible stars, a status previously enjoyed only by visual artists.

Hage seeks out talents from all over the world and showcases their work in his Chelsea gallery. His enthusiasm surges when he encounters a new talent whose work he can feature and skills he can nurture. Over the years, he has showcased the light alchemy of Paul Cocksedge; the scavenged constructions of Karen Ryan; and the tech-genius of Moritz Waldemeyer and Assa Ashuach. Foreign names include Matali Crasset, Aki Kuroda, Gaetano Pesce, Piet Hein Eek and Johnny Swing. Between exhibitions, the space features a mix of works from the aforementioned names and others as well.

Because of the gallery's upmarket location, passers-by may feel too intimidated to browse. But I can assure you that the friendly staff, even the personable and chatty owner himself, welcomes all visitors.

Widely reputed to be one of the most influential postgraduate universities of art and design in the world, the Royal College of Art specialises in teaching and research across the disciplines of fine art, applied art, design, communications and humanities. If you've ever wondered who's shaping the way we live our lives today, there's a good chance that alumni from this college have been involved. Indeed you'll recognise household names from the graduate rolls: James Dyson, Thomas Heatherwick, David Adjaye, Zandra Rhodes, Philip Treacy, David Hockney, Tracey Emin, and even Ridley Scott.

The college's main building is located next to Albert Hall in Kensington Gore and serves as a base for hundreds of talented students. The galleries and lecture theatres are frequently used for a lively programme of exhibitions, events, symposiums and talks by leading figures in the worlds of art and design. Staged either by the RCA itself or a combination of external partners, these activities are often open to the public.

An annual highlight includes the RCA Secret fundraising exhibition, for which invited artists, students and alumni transform blank postcards into works of art, which are then sold anonymously for £45 apiece. In June the highly anticipated graduate Summer Show provides a unique opportunity for the public to buy or commission work from emerging talents before the galleries and collectors snap them up.

The RCA doesn't operate on a regular schedule, so it's not advisable to simply turn up. Be sure to check the RCA website for event details before making the journey.

19 SERPENTINE GALLERY

🏠 KENSINGTON GARDENS W2 3XA
📞 020 7402 6075
➤ SERPENTINEGALLERY.ORG
🕐 DAILY 10–6
⊖ KNIGHTSBRIDGE/SOUTH KENSINGTON/LANCASTER GT.

20 SIGMAR

🏠 263 KING'S ROAD SW3 5EL
📞 020 7751 5801
➤ SIGMARLONDON.COM
🕐 MON-SAT 10–6, SUN 12–5
⊖ SLOANE SQUARE/SOUTH KENSINGTON

Since opening in 1970, the Serpentine Gallery has emerged as one of Britain's best-loved galleries, having staged pioneering exhibitions of modern and contemporary art by more than 1,500 artists, architects and designers, including well-known talents like Dan Flavin, Bridget Riley, Damien Hirst, Ellsworth Kelly, Cindy Sherman, Wolfgang Tillmans and Richard Hamilton.

While the core activity in this Grade II-listed former tea pavilion is the appreciation of art, the gallery has also flirted with design as a subject medium. The 2010 *Design Real* exhibition, curated by German designer Konstantin Grcic, was the gallery's first exhibition devoted entirely to contemporary design and explored everyday mass-produced items and their impact. I do hope they continue to integrate such design-led content into future exhibition schedules.

During the summer months the Serpentine Gallery's annual Pavilion is a unique and enormously popular project. Each year the gallery, taking advantage of its grounds, asks an internationally acclaimed architect (one who has yet to complete a structure in England) to build a temporary pavilion. Recent honourees have included giants like Zaha Hadid, Oscar Niemeyer, Toyo Ito, SANAA, Jean Nouvel, Rem Koolhaas and Peter Zumthor. The pavilions host a busy calendar of events, film screenings, talks and concerts that draw huge crowds.

The gallery closes for periods between exhibitions, but its popular bookshop, operated by Koenig Books (p.099), remains open regardless. If you visit, be sure to work in a stroll; the gallery is beautifully sited at the centre of Hyde Park.

Nestled among the upmarket offerings of King's Road is Sigmar, an outlet with a subtle street presence but a strong purpose. It was founded in 2004 by Nina Hertig and Ebba Thott, a decorative-arts dealer and interior designer who share a love of fine craftsmanship.

There's little this enthusiastic duo don't know about 19th- and 20th-century Modern and, as such, they have a clear vision for this small shop. Selling vintage alongside the new, they aim to unite function, beauty and craft with quality, longevity and soul. Each piece, sourced from across Europe, tells a story and celebrates the thought and skill that went into its making.

With a popular interior design business tucked away in the basement, it is at street-level where you can explore hard-to-find treasures like a rare 1952 Belgian wardrobe by Willy van der Meeran; a 1950s Danish wicker armchair by Jørgen Bækmark; midcentury sculptural solid-brass hooks from Austria; and a black metal and brass floor lamp by Kaare Klint, who designed in Denmark in the 1940s.

The new pieces fit the bill and feel right at home here – including exquisite lighting and glassware by Michael Anastassiades and newly imported solid-wood stools and tables by Danish legend Nanna Ditzel.

Tactility and patina are pretty much guaranteed at Sigmar, as are highly personal service and passionate storytelling – which is why a visit to this shop should be a top priority.

21 SKANDIUM

📍 245-249 BROMPTON ROAD SW3 2EP
📞 020 7584 2066
↖ SKANDIUM.COM
🕐 MON-SAT 10-6.30, THU 10-7, SUN 11-5
⊖ SOUTH KENSINGTON

Following in the footsteps of Skandium's successful Marylebone store (p.058), the Brompton Quarter location was a no-brainer. In recent years this area has supported the emergence of a number of design stores, and Skandium's arrival on this prominent corner in 2005 marked a significant step forward for the company and the neighbourhood.

Window displays draw the eye straight into this immense store, which houses an impressive product range of not only Scandinavian Modernism but, more recently, international pieces that share the aesthetic.

The shop's visual clarity transcends the merchandise. Most designs boast confidence of form, material honesty and quality. Who can resist the warmth of a beech *Wishbone* chair by Hans Wegner? The ultimate lounge chair, the *PK22* by Poul Kjærholm? The handmade birch light shades by Seppo Koho? Or the angular *w101* task lamp made from biodegradable paper by Claesson Koivisto Rune?

The background shade here is earthy, with most of the larger furnishings made from natural materials in natural tones. The accessories bring in the colour: tableware by iittala; vacuum jugs from Stelton; bold textiles from Marimekko.

Owners Magnus Englund, Chrystina Schmidt and Christopher Seidenfaden always handpick everything in store and remain vigilant in their scrutiny of new stock. Unconcerned with fickle trends, the trio instead choose to align themselves with quality and longevity in the belief that good design stands the test of time. The integrity of their approach, coupled with an

infallible attention to detail, has earned Skandium its place in London's retail establishment.

② TASCHEN

- 📍 12 DUKE OF YORK SQUARE SW3 4LY
- 📞 020 7881 0795
- ↖ TASCHEN.COM
- 🕐 MON-TUE & THU-FRI 10-6, WED & SAT 10-7, SUN 12-6
- ⊖ SLOANE SQUARE

As a child, Benedikt Taschen had a bit of a thing for art books. He sensed at a tender age that books could open doors to different worlds. His frustration at the high price of many niche titles led him to assess alternative publishing models as he grew up, with the aim to make such books more affordable and accessible. More than 30 years later: mission accomplished. His publishing business has brought coffee table tomes within arm's reach of the masses.

In more recent years, TASCHEN has embraced retail and opened dedicated stores in major cities around the world, London included. The Chelsea store, outfitted by French design maverick Philippe Starck, houses a bookstore and a gallery stocking the company's entire range of books covering art, photography, architecture, design, fashion, film, travel, pop culture and sex.

The bookshop is conducive to a leisurely browse, with books displayed on abstract tree-trunk stands and windows dressed in billowing white drapes. In the basement, a small gallery brings together prints and photographs, complemented by some of TASCHEN's high-end limited-edition titles. With a choice of titles to satisfy most people's cultural curiosity, TASCHEN manages to successfully stick to its credo: 'Don't underestimate or bore your audience.'

VICTORIA AND ALBERT MUSEUM

CROMWELL ROAD SW7 2RL

020 7942 2000

VAM.AC.UK

DAILY 10–5.45, FRI 10–10

SOUTH KENSINGTON

The suitably regal Victoria and Albert Museum is one of the most impressive cultural beacons of London. It was established following the success of the Great Exhibition in 1852 with the mission to make art available to all and to inspire British designers and manufacturers. Without a doubt the museum continues to follow its mandate, attracting several million visitors every year.

The collections span over 2,000 years of human creativity, in virtually every medium and from many parts of the world. The diversity of the exhibits is awe-inspiring: painting, sculpture, architecture, ceramics, furniture, fashion, textiles, photography, glass, jewellery and metalwork.

My current favourites include the recently renovated Contemporary Ceramic galleries, mindboggling in their diverse content. The ornate, high-ceiled spaces are gloriously tranquil and flooded with natural light. Visitors wander around with a look of amazement on their faces, dazzled by such a thorough repertoire – including comprehensive displays of cups, saucers, beakers, vases, jugs, vessels, plates and figurines. Be sure to check out *Swarm Study / III* by rAndom International, a stunning, site-specific interactive installation hovering over a nearby staircase.

It's worth getting hold of a museum map when you arrive and manoeuvering your way through the vast building to your chosen starting point, from which you can then meander back. Pass through the special exhibition of the day, which could cover anything from design and fashion to photography and architecture. To celebrate London's Olympic Games, throughout 2012 the museum is staging a number of

exhibitions that will showcase the best British creative talent. Then, towards the end of 2012, the museum will launch the Furniture Galleries.

Navigating this much content, it's easy to become complacent, but I would urge you not to. Should you feel your energy levels start to wane, you can always refuel at the café, rest your feet in the popular central garden or browse the comprehensive bookshop.

Or, if you're not up for a day-long visit, pop in for an hour: it's free. Either way, I find each visit helps to rejuvenate my mind. For this I am grateful, as I suspect it will take me a lifetime to properly absorb all the museum's delights.

24 V&A READING ROOMS

- 8 EXHIBITION ROAD SW7 2HF
- 020 7225 0594
- VANDAREADINGROOMS.CO.UK
- DAILY 10.30-8
- SOUTH KENSINGTON

If ever you needed to be reminded of the joys of browsing a boutique bookstore, you could get your cue at the V&A Reading Rooms, a local offshoot of the infamous Victoria and Albert Museum (opposite). Located on the newly pedestrianised Exhibition Road, this small space cleverly blends an eclectic array of titles with a wine bar. This way, you can take time to flip through a shortlist of books over a glass of wine before you decide to buy.

As so many mainstream bookshops dumb themselves down with novelties and toys, more and more bookworms are craving a return to the small, independent store, the kind where you know an individual has personally assessed and endorsed every title. In this respect, the Reading Rooms have hit the nail on the head.

And they've gone one step further. Rather than categorising titles by the usual genres, they've opted to mix them up under a different set of criteria. For example, in the shelves facing the bar, titles falling within the bracket of 'fictions', 'histories', 'narratives' and 'theories' are merged with 'facts', 'foods', 'myths' and 'poems'. In the second room, 'people', 'places' and 'styles' are married with 'loves', 'pleasures', 'shocks' and 'sounds'. Not immediately obvious, such groupings make you spend more time browsing and picking up publications that you might not otherwise encounter.

Dotted about the shop are chairs and stools on which you can perch with your chosen title and calmly peruse. In a strange way the intimate scale of the rooms – outfitted with high ceilings, bay windows, original cornicing and warm

lighting – makes you feel as though you've been invited to access a friend's home library. Amid the frenzy of life in London, consider this to be a rare place where you can enjoy time with yourself.

But please: don't exploit the fact that you can stay for hours while enjoying drinks and a nibble. After all, the Reading Rooms are in the business of selling books. Perhaps you'll be inspired to buy after hearing that every purchase here supports the V&A Museum.

LDG

Eat & drink

Great for... classic French with a British twist

BIBENDUM [PICTURED]

Elegant dining room serving classic French dishes with British influence. Original setting in the iconic Michelin House with stunning stained-glass windows. Stunning Art Deco architecture. Ground-floor Oyster Bar nice for a seafood platter and quick glass of wine.

MICHELIN HOUSE, 81 FULHAM ROAD SW3 6RD | 020 7581 5817 | BIBENDUM.CO.UK

Great for... authentic tapas 26

CASA BRINDISA

Traditional Spanish tapas. Popular walk-in warren on different levels. Tapas bar and ham-carving counter. Good choice of sherries and Spanish wines.

7-9 EXHIBITION ROAD SW7 2HE
020 7590 0008 | BRINDISA.COM

Great for... classic French bistro 27

CHABROT BISTROT D'AMIS

Casual French bistro hidden down a Knightsbridge alley – but could be in Paris. Dark, intimate interior with smart waiters serving classic French dishes. Comprehensive wine list.

9 KNIGHTSBRIDGE GREEN SW1X 7QL
020 7225 2238 | CHABROT.CO.UK

Great for... watching chefs at work 28

DINNER BY HESTON BLUMENTHAL

Smart yet pricey fare by food alchemist Heston Blumenthal. Menu inspired by historic British gastronomy with the chef's signature flourishes. Book a table near the kitchen for in-progress views.

MADARIN ORIENTAL HYDE PARK, 66 KNIGHTSBRIDGE SW1X 7LA
020 7201 3833 | DINNERBYHESTON.COM

Great for... dumplings & pan-Asian treats

EIGHT OVER EIGHT

Asian-inspired menu, including dim sum and sushi. Modern interior with Eastern influences. Dark-wood floors and chairs contrast with white tablecloths, pale walls and oriental lampshades. Smart location for a memorable meal.

392 KING'S ROAD SW3 5UZ | 020 7349 9934 | RICKERRESTAURANTS.COM

Great for... Scandinavian treats (30)

MADSEN

Modern Scandinavian interior for lovers of
Nordic cuisine. Danish owners give bias to their
country for traditional dishes revived with modern
flourishes. Popular with Scandi Londoners.

20 OLD BROMPTON ROAD SW7 3DL

020 7225 2772 | MADSENRESTAURANT.COM

Great for... a tipple of wine (31)

THE SAMPLER

Fine-wine shop rewriting the rules with
machines that help you taste before you buy.
Not your usual stuffy wine store. A fun pre-
dinner spot.

35 THURLOE PLACE SW7 2HP

020 7225 5091 | THESAMPLER.CO.UK

Great for... local Italian (32)

TINELLO

Buzzy Italian with plenty of contemporary
influences in the menu. Smart location
attracts elegant clientele. Bare red-brick walls
and low-key lighting creates an understated
environment – unlike elsewhere in Chelsea.

87 PIMLICO ROAD SW1W 8PH

020 7730 3663 | TINELLO.CO.UK

Great for... relaxed lunch (33)

TOM'S KITCHEN

Casual, all-day brasserie-style venue.
Traditional British and French cuisine
with emphasis on local and seasonal
ingredients. White-tiled walls, industrial
pendant lights, scrubbed-wood tables.
Relaxed, unpretentious but rather pricey.

27 CALE STREET SW3 3QP

0207 349 0202 | TOMSKITCHEN.CO.UK

Place to sleep?
NUMBER SIXTEEN FIRMDALE.COM

DESIGNING

DESIGN

'I am an industrial designer.' That's what I say when somebody asks me what I do. This is normally met with raised eyebrows, followed by questions about industrial equipment. It's true to say that industrial design is not fully understood in comparison to, for example, graphic design. Industrial design is the design of anything three-dimensional that is often industrialised or manufactured in at least batch production. However, the role of the designer is far more complex than merely designing the object.

To work successfully as an industrial designer requires expertise or knowledge across a broad range of areas and an understanding of the various stakeholders involved in the process. It's commonplace for the design process to start with a pure conceptual idea or an insight into the needs of a user, which forms the structure of a project. Then the conventional process of determining a balance between form, function, sustainability and longevity proceeds.

However, to get a product through to production requires several more steps beyond these conventions and involves the designer validating and proving the necessity for the product. This means you become a marketeer for the client, by benchmarking and positioning your project on the current and future markets. You become a sourcing agent, dealing with factories, production and schedules. This process can be incredibly demanding, but in order to ultimately drive a product through to the consumer, these become the responsibilities for the industrial designer in the 21st century.

Such efforts are particularly necessary when designing furniture and lighting – especially when the deal is based on royalty payments rather than a fixed fee. The enormity of the workload is often carried out several years prior to a product hitting the market and generating income. After the initial design concept has been approved by a client, the process of actually earning money from a product can take anywhere from two to five years. Therefore, as

> "...glamorous appearances can be deceiving: it can be incredibly difficult to build a business around a new design. In fact, many products never make it past the prototype stage."

a designer, the more you can prove, source and validate to guarantee a product's industrialisation, the better.

The designer will often launch a new product at a large design exhibition (the world's most notable takes place each April in Milan). Thousands of new products are launched at these fairs, but glamorous appearances can be deceiving: it can be incredibly difficult to build a business around a new design. In fact, many products never make it past the prototype stage.

The best approach is to believe in your own value and see past the hype. A lot of people will ask you to work without considering the value of your time. As such, it's important to bring a level-headed business mind to the discussions around designing something new or working with a brand you respect. Setting some rules for yourself regarding your day rates and your workload – as well as learning when to say no – is critical.

The conflict between the reality of business and the prestige of design is particularly true at the beginning of your career. You need to be prepared to invest huge amounts of time and money into building prototypes and participating in exhibitions before you start making any substantial returns. If you're lucky, you may win awards and get press attention in this period, too. Awards can get you noticed by the right people, who may give you the opportunity to design for their brand, gallery or home.

The best way to generate a working business in design is to create products for the right reasons. Designing products that are truly new and relevant is the most challenging part but should remain the primary focus. If you can avoid creating objects that simply adhere to the latest trends and focus instead on a considered approach to adding value and longevity to your designs, this will stand you in good stead as an industrial designer. At least it's a good place from which to start.

BENJAMIN HUBERT IS AN INDUSTRIAL DESIGNER
benjaminhubert.co.uk

Neo-Mio by Nigel Coates

Limited edition of 12. Size: 1000 x 850mm. Handblown in Murano, Venice

Vessel Gallery

114 Kensington Pk Rd W11 2PW   T +44 (0) 207 727 8001   www.vesselgallery.com

Notting Hill
& Ladbroke Grove

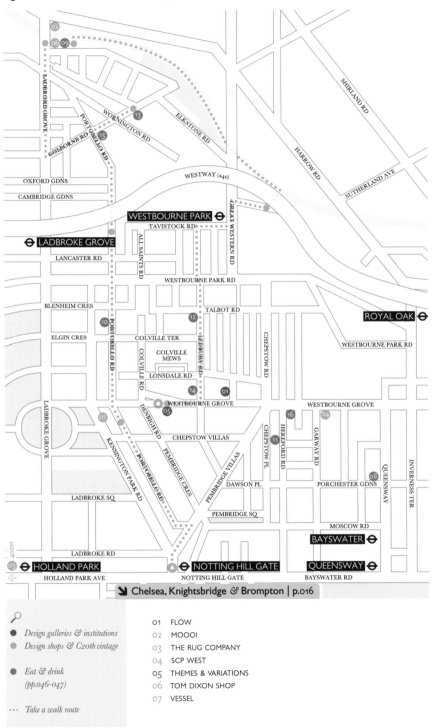

⊖ LADBROKE GROVE
WESTBOURNE PARK ⊖
ROYAL OAK ⊖
BAYSWATER ⊖
⊖ HOLLAND PARK
⊖ NOTTING HILL GATE
QUEENSWAY ⊖

↘ Chelsea, Knightsbridge & Brompton | p.016

Design galleries & institutions

Design shops & C20th vintage

Eat & drink
(pp.046-047)

••• Take a walk route

01 FLOW
02 MOOOI
03 THE RUG COMPANY
04 SCP WEST
05 THEMES & VARIATIONS
06 TOM DIXON SHOP
07 VESSEL

Notting Hill
& Ladbroke Grove

TAKE A WALK WITH

Tom Dixon Studio *

From Notting Hill Gate station, follow the signs to Portobello Road and Portobello Market, always a source of inspiration and a good place to wander on a Friday morning. Keep an eye out for the Russian doll specialist, and The Grain Shop (No 269) for takeaway vegetarian food. Eventually you'll reach the dynamic and imposing Westway, an elevated carriageway that runs over the north end of the market. Locals, from skateboarders to gourmet butchers, set up in its cavernous concrete underpass.

Further up the way you'll reach vibrant Golborne Road. If you fancy something sweet, turn right to Lisboa Patisserie (No 57); if not, turn left. At Ladbroke Grove take a right and walk along this long, straight thoroughfare for a good ten minutes until you reach the Grand Union Canal. Stand on the bridge over the canal and look to your left; you'll spot Tom Dixon's converted water tower, still a work in progress. To your right is Portobello Dock, our base since 2009. We've transformed what was once Richard Branson's music-recording studio into a design store selling our own designs as well as other global artefacts. Located above the shop with a terrace overlooking the water is Dock Kitchen, where chef Stevie Parle is inspired by everything from Milanese markets to Sri Lankan delicacies.

From Portobello Dock, drop down onto the canal towpath and patiently follow the canal east until you reach Great Western Studios, a base for many young artists and sculptors. Catch one of their open studio weekends, an art-bingo night or a temporary exhibition.

From here join Great Western Road, pass Westbourne Park station and turn right into Tavistock Road. Snake through the residential streets of Notting Hill until you reach Westbourne Grove. At No 231 is Themes & Variations, selling an expertly curated collection of coveted modern furniture. In a central island in the street is the Public Toilet, a landmark in itself. In reaction to the council's lacklustre proposal, local residents commissioned the structure by architect Piers Gough. It now serves as a flower shop, featuring green glazed tiles and a station-style clock.

Compiled by staff at Tom Dixon Studio tomdixon.net

 FLOW

1-5 NEEDHAM ROAD W11 2RP

020 7243 0782

FLOWGALLERY.CO.UK

MON–SAT 11–6

NOTTING HILL GATE

A stone's throw from fashionable Westbourne Grove, Flow is calm and light filled. Founder Yvonna Demczynska, who opened the gallery in 1999, represents more than 100 artisans, home-grown and international, who work across the disciplines of ceramics, glass, paper, wood, textiles, metal and jewellery.

The feeling at Flow is totally unlike any shop of mass-market items. The tranquil main space, flooded with natural light from the skylights, celebrates tactile, original handmade artworks – both functional and non-functional – exhibited on large, round plinths. Highlights for me include ethereal porcelain vessels by Henk Wolvers, folded and reformed porcelain tableware by Benben Li, textured-glass vases by Edmond Byrne, intricately cut paper artworks by Claire Brewster and simple beech and ash jugs by Hans-Henning Pederson.

Demczynska travels extensively in order to fill her programme of six exhibitions a year. What she finds she groups in different themes: heritage, collective, even colour. Indeed on my visit she was running an exhibition that explored the different ways current artists use the colour blue. Whatever it is she settles on, she always chooses work she personally admires and would like to own herself. The gallery's strong raison d'etre, and the stories behind each piece, lend the gallery an extra dimension. And they may go some way to explaining Flow's devoted following – shoppers who buy into these more unusual, beautiful and collectible objects for their homes.

02 MOOOI

🖃 THE WHITE BUILDING, 555 HARROW ROAD W10 4RH
📞 020 8962 5691
↖ MOOOI.COM
⊕ MON-THU 9-5 (BY APPOINTMENT ONLY), FRI 10-5
⊖ KENSAL GREEN

When Dutch brand Moooi launched in 2001 the design industry was dazzled by its daring collections of playful yet exclusive furniture, lighting and accessories. In contrast to so many other serious top-end producers, Moooi's founders – designer Marcel Wanders and entrepreneur Casper Vissers set about creating 'a serious company with a smile'.

The company is named after the Dutch word for beautiful (mooi) with the third 'o' representing added beauty value. This slightly tongue-in-cheek approach translates to the output; everything has a quirk that imbues it with extra charm. Wanders has a dry sense of humour, which you'll notice in his own designs as well as those he selects from his pool of talented contributors. The look is 'neo-baroque', infused with a new, modern form.

Having developed a faithful UK market, Moooi chose to open a flagship in this auspicious canal-side location in 2010, in partnership with resin-flooring manufacturers Senso. The Grade II-listed stucco White Building has 250-square-metres of floor space, with naturally lit, white showrooms leading off the main hallway.

They like their black and white here. In one display a round black *Container Table* is flanked by a set of soft, puffy black *Monster Chairs* by Marcel Wanders and illuminated by a white spider-like articulated hanging *Dear Ingo* centrepiece light by Ron Gilad. In a separate room an all-white *Paper Floor Lamp* by Studio Job lords over the iconic black leather-upholstered *Smoke chair* by Maarten Baas, the ceiling peppered with multiple *Raimond* pendant lamps by Raimond Puts. And on it goes with flamboyant presentations of the extensive catalogue of lighting, furnishings, storage, rugs and accessories by such talents as Jurgen Bey, Jasper Morrison, Ross Lovegrove, Bertjan Pot, Nika Zupanc, Kiki van Eijk and Front.

A large percentage of Moooi's UK turnover is generated from commercial interiors, and this showroom purports to serve the contract market. So be warned: this isn't a shop as much as a showcase for the Moooi collections. Should you wish to purchase something, staff will direct you to your nearest retailer.

03 THE RUG COMPANY

- 124 HOLLAND PARK AVENUE W11 4UE
- 020 7229 5148
- THERUGCOMPANY.INFO
- MON–SAT 10–6, SUN 11–5
- HOLLAND PARK

Christopher and Suzanne Sharp founded The Rug Company in 1997, and originally focused on vintage Armenian, Berber, Persian and Turkish carpets in addition to their own designs. It was in 2000 that they began working with popular stylemakers and launched the *Designer Collection*, which comprises an enviable array of rugs by some top names in fashion and furniture design. Today the latter category includes Tom Dixon, Barber Osgerby, Ron Arad, Committee and Jaime Hayon, who share the honour with such fashion labels as Alexander McQueen, Paul Smith, Vivienne Westwood, Matthew Williamson and Diane von Furstenberg.

Take a peek at The Rug Company's price list and you'll understand why the Sharps chose this location, flanked as it is by affluent Notting Hill, Kensington and Holland Park. Most of the rugs are priced in the thousands of pounds, and my instincts prompted me to find out why. Without hesitation a staff member switched on to my questions, clearly primed to communicate the story to each visitor.

The rugs are all made from the wool of Tibetan sheep reared on remote pastures at an altitude of more than 10,000 feet. The wool is coarse, lustrous and of high-tensile strength – ideal for rug-making. The fleece is processed in Nepal, dyed and knotted by skilled Tibetan refugees in the Kathmandu Valley, where the traditional techniques have been practiced for many generations (with the exception of the Swiss aniline dyes, introduced for accurate colour matching and a wider palette). A single rug takes a staggering four months to complete.

'Artwork for the floor' is one way of describing these contemporary rugs. The majority are neatly piled in a stack, but two staffers happily folded back each selection so I could view it. I was sold on the rugs before I learned about the *Boutique Collection* of handmade cushions and wallhangings made with similar levels of craftsmanship.

The Sharps are aware their creations are an investment, so they offer free consultations and home visits as well as a bespoke service. Having cultivated a loyal customer base in London, they've gone on to open stores around the world. There are 17 in total, with more being planned.

04 SCP WEST

🚪 87 WESTBOURNE GROVE W2 4UL

📞 020 7229 3612

↖ SCP.CO.UK

🕐 MON 10-6, TUE-SAT 9.30-6, SUN 11-5

⊖ BAYSWATER/QUEENSWAY

05 THEMES & VARIATIONS

🚪 231 WESTBOURNE GROVE W11 2SE

📞 020 7727 5531

↖ THEMESANDVARIATIONS.COM

🕐 MON-FRI 10-1, 2-6, SAT 10-6

⊖ NOTTING HILL GATE

In 2007 the original east London headquarters of design purveyor SCP (p.153) gained a sibling on the other side of town. The new outpost, situated on a busy stretch of Westbourne Grove, is a 200-square-metre corner plot housing SCP's tantalising array of furniture, lighting and accessories. With massive windows, the store benefits from plenty of natural light that bathes the product displays within and lures in passers-by.

Much of the content comes from SCP's extensive catalogue of modern sofas, chairs, tables and storage and toes the signature functionalist aesthetic. The company's owner, Sheridan Coakley, commissions some of the finest British talents and is widely acknowledged to be one of the country's most respected manufacturers and suppliers of contemporary design. When he began incorporating lighting and accessories into his line-up Coakley began embracing products from other brands that lend this shop a well-rounded appeal.

It's by no means intimidating here. Shoppers with varying budgets – from gift-seekers to those kitting out an entire house – will find something that's accessible. As the rising rents of the past decade have pushed other design stores out of this neighbourhood and replaced them with upmarket fashion boutiques, SCP represents a beacon of hope for contemporary furniture and lighting in Notting Hill. So it's most certainly a welcome tenant on this side of town.

Dealer Liliane Fawcett has been trading her collection of postwar and contemporary design in this lofty space for nearly three decades. She converted this former garage in the early '80s, back when Westbourne Grove was certainly nothing to write home about. Fawcett's prescience paid off. Today there is a plethora of high-end fashion boutiques around to complement her high-end collectibles gallery.

Fawcett steers the emphasis here towards Scandinavian and Italian decorative arts and furniture by a wide range of artists from the past and present. She knows what sells, so things come and go and it's impossible to predict what will be displayed at any given time. On my visit, a 1970s black marble table by Angelo Mangiarotti caught my eye, as did an enormous 1950s desk by Osvaldo Borsani. There was a 1988 gold-leaf *Crown* chair by Tom Dixon displayed near some *Arsos* vases by Alessandro Mendini and a slick silver *Hyperfast* vase by Cedric Ragot. The gallery has a longstanding relationship with the Fornasetti Studio, so you can always bank on there being some signature designs in its popular black-and-white illustrative style.

The success of Themes & Variations is largely down to the confident individuality of its owner, who simply buys distinctive pieces she likes. She has a loyal following supported by an international clientele looking for something precious and unique. And she delivers, with an intriguing selection of curiosities, most of which are wise investments for the future.

06 TOM DIXON SHOP
- PORTOBELLO DOCK, 344 LADBROKE GROVE W10 5BU
- 020 7183 9737
- TOMDIXON.NET
- MON-SAT 10-6, THU 10-7, SUN 11-5
- LADBROKE GROVE/KENSAL GREEN

Fans of the furniture and lighting produced by British design hero Tom Dixon will be delighted they can now source it all in one place. Dixon's official flagship – the only one in the world – popped up two years ago in a converted Victorian goods carrier on the Grand Union Canal. You can find Dixon's entire collection here, but you can't reach it easily via public transport, so the HQ remains something of a destination. When you get close, follow the walkway off Ladbroke Grove and take the stairs down to the showroom – or head straight ahead to Stevie Parle's popular Dock Kitchen for a bite to eat. En route to the shop you'll pass a series of alcoves overlooking the water, treasure troves featuring styled displays of Dixon's greatest offerings.

Dotted around the vaulted showroom are groupings of furniture from the latest collections illuminated by clusters of lights – be they Dixon's now iconic *Mirror Ball*, his brass *Etch* or the chunky *Pressed Glass* pendants. You may also spot the odd prototype; with the company's head office so close by, new designs are often trialled here.

Other international designers get an outing here too, in displays curated by Dixon himself. The *Scrapwood* collection of furniture by Dutch designer Piet Hein Eek stands out; it's accessorised with blankets by Spanish producer Teixidors; ceramics by Danish potter Gurli Elbækgaard; and leather vessels by Simon Hasan. The roster of talents is changed up quarterly to revive the look of the place. This should give visitors a good reason to come back regularly.

07 VESSEL

114 KENSINGTON PARK ROAD W11 2PW
020 7727 8001
VESSELGALLERY.COM
MON–SAT 10–6
NOTTING HILL GATE

When it comes to contemporary tableware
I think it's fair to say that Vessel is a leading
authority. Since 1999 owners Nadia Demetriou
Ladas and Angel Monzon have sold some of the
finest ceramics and glassware from around the
world – and they've received critical and industry
recognition for doing so. Pure and functional
Scandinavian design sits alongside flamboyant
art glass from Italy and other gems from the UK,
Holland, France, Germany and Japan.

The cosy boutique is like a gallery,
uncluttered by the irresistible displays of crockery,
stemware, cutlery, candleholders, vases and
captivating *objets*. The ground floor space is where
the more functional and accessible designs – by
well-known producers such as Stelton, iittala,
Orrefors, Venini, Salviati, Rosenthal and Bitossi
– create a welcoming atmosphere. There's limited
space up here, though the owners have access to a
broad number of suppliers, so it's worth chatting
to the informed staff should you be hunting for
something specific. They'll be more than likely
able to fulfil your request.

Vessel's bold, exclusive, attention-grabbing
centrepieces tip it into gallery domain. The shop
has always embraced the finest crafted art-
glass and studio ceramics, staging breathtaking
exhibitions throughout the year along thematic or
experimental lines. In the past it has launched the
first range of homewares by minimalist architect
John Pawson, and debuted UK ceramicist Ted
Muehling's porcelain range for Nymphenburg
Porzellan. It's also produced several showcases of
limited-edition glass by Swedish sensation Lena
Bergström and continually brings producers

together with designers for the creation of new
works exclusive to Vessel. Such initiatives have
seen Vessel move into the realm of extraordinary
lighting installations – a side of the business set
to grow. The owners' passion for such artwork is
contagious – you really won't go wrong to view
their portfolio of represented artists and designers
to discover more than what's on display.

Whatever the pricepoint (accessible to eye-
wateringly expensive), Vessel manages to appeal
without compromising on quality and beauty.
Service is always personal and attentive, and
advice is informed and considered – which might
go some way to explaining the steady return of
Vessel's loyal customers.

LDG

Eat & drink

Great for... long lunches 08

LE CAFÉ ANGLAIS
Classic Anglo-French menu. Grand, 1920s-style room divided into two by the sweeping-arc silhouette of a beige-leather banquette. High ceilings with imposing Art Deco lights. Enticing dining experience overall.
8 PORCHESTER GARDENS W2 4DB
020 7221 1415 | LECAFEANGLAIS.CO.UK

Great for... alfresco lunch 09

DOCK KITCHEN [PICTURED]
Experimental kitchen changes menu daily. Uses seasonal ingredients and global culinary influences. Light-filled Tom Dixon-designed interior. Great spot on Grand Union Canal with peaceful outdoor dining area.
PORTOBELLO DOCK, 344 LADBROKE GROVE W10 5BU
020 8962 1610 | DOCKKITCHEN.CO.UK

Great for... people watching 10

ELECTRIC BRASSERIE
Classic brasserie and bar next to Electric Cinema. Cosmopolitan menu and atmosphere. Brown-leather banquettes and chrome tables. Popular with Notting Hill residents.
191 PORTOBELLO ROAD W11 2ED
020 7908 9696 | ELECTRICBRASSERIE.COM

Great for... best of British 11

HEREFORD ROAD
Onetime Victorian butcher's shop, now popular neighbourhood spot. Classy, American-style leather booths. Distinctly British menu. Good spot for a romantic dinner.
3 HEREFORD ROAD W2 4AB | 020 7727 1144 | HEREFORDROAD.ORG

Great for... gastronomic dinner

THE LEDBURY

Elegant, smart culinary gem. Quality French cuisine. Strong wine list. Modern-chic interior. Outdoor patio area great in summer. Pricey.

127 LEDBURY ROAD W11 2AQ

020 7792 9090 | THELEDBURY.COM

Great for... sweet treats

LISBOA PATISSERIE

Traditional Portuguese café/patisserie. Trying the Pasteis de Nata, famous Portuguese custard tarts, is a must. Popular and slightly shabby local institution in the shadow of iconic Trellick Tower.

57 GOLBORNE ROAD W10 5NR | 020 8968 5242

Great for... take away salads and cakes

OTTOLENGHI

Chic café with exciting takeaway menu. Mediterranean cuisine with North African spices. Finest raw ingredients. Chic all-white decor. Heaven for all types, vegetarians included.

63 LEDBURY ROAD W11 2AD | OTTOLENGHI.CO.UK | 020 7727 1121

Great for... pizza

PIZZA EAST PORTOBELLO

Sister restaurant to original outpost in Shoreditch. Occupies a restored Georgian pub. Stripped-back, textured interior with old industrial furniture and fittings. Popular.

310 PORTOBELLO ROAD W10 5TA

020 8969 4500 | PIZZAEASTPORTOBELLO.COM

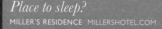

Place to sleep?
MILLER'S RESIDENCE MILLERSHOTEL.COM

PRODUCING

DESIGN

As I walk the aisles of graduate design exhibitions, I have a wonderful sense of excitement, hope and youthful enthusiasm: so many talented, young designers poised to take on the world. I wish I could give them all jobs, but I can't. We're a small furniture maker, and when I recruit I look for very specific qualities. Producing design requires a delicate balance of harnessing creative talent, then rationalising, engineering and evaluating designs for manufacture. If we do it well, we end up with desirable, useful, well-made products. If we do it badly, we're left with styled nonsense.

Sketching is a brilliant tool and good designers use it effectively to quickly convey the spirit and look of an object. A simple model or 3D sketch helps designers tackle some basic issues of structure, proportion and stability. I enjoy working with designers who master these basic skills, and I find them a much quicker route to a prototype than the sometimes-sterile CAD models. They're also a good indicator the designer is going to take a hands-on role: getting involved in the workshop; making hammer-and-nails full-size mock-ups; working with us to resolve the technical challenges and balance them against the visual issues.

The best designers we work with also have a very real awareness of commercial considerations – they'll know the cost implications of their choices. Also, what size does it come in? How strong is it? What finishes can be achieved? There's a lot to know, and while we can bring this knowledge to the table, it's exhausting to have to explain things that a designer should already know (worse still to have to argue the point when basic knowhow should make the answer clear). I firmly believe that a year spent at the workbench is a huge asset to any designer. There's so much to be gained by knowing your materials and respecting the mindset of the maker.

Having worked through sketches and models to our satisfaction, we can begin the

"Producing design is much more about grit, dust and perseverance than it is about cocktail parties in Milan"

expensive business of prototyping. Manufacturers invest huge amounts of money getting from this stage to the final product, so it's a significant act of faith in the designer we're called to make. If we're lucky, we'll get a satisfactory prototype on first or second try. (Chairs may take more attempts to resolve the ergonomics, structure and upholstery.) By the time a product is ready for production, the designer will have invested many workshop days and the maker will have invested five to ten times the product's unit price. So no one can take the process lightly.

Only now do we start the real making. Final specifications, clear drawings, jigs, CNC programmes and cutting sheets are vital for smooth production. Once we start cutting the wood, metal, plastic or fabric, we're finally underway. When we've completed the first batch, we can begin the final part of the design process: an evaluation and review. Again the designer plays a central part in this; we're still a team.

Then there's the whole route to market – in itself an enormous and potentially costly stage that includes photography, marketing, press, exhibitions and sales. Again, the designer can really help. The product is going to carry his name, so to have his personality attached will carry the product further and faster.

If we've all done our jobs at every stage of production, the designer will start to receive his hard-earned royalty payments and the maker will embark on the road to recovering his investment. Producing design is much more about grit, dust and perseverance than it is about cocktail parties in Milan, but for the designer/maker partnership it has very real and tangible rewards – and we love it.

Oh, and one final tip for designers working with woodworkers: wear dust-coloured clothing.

SEAN SUTCLIFFE IS CO-FOUNDER OF ENGLISH FURNITURE MAKER
BENCHMARK *benchmarkfurniture.com*

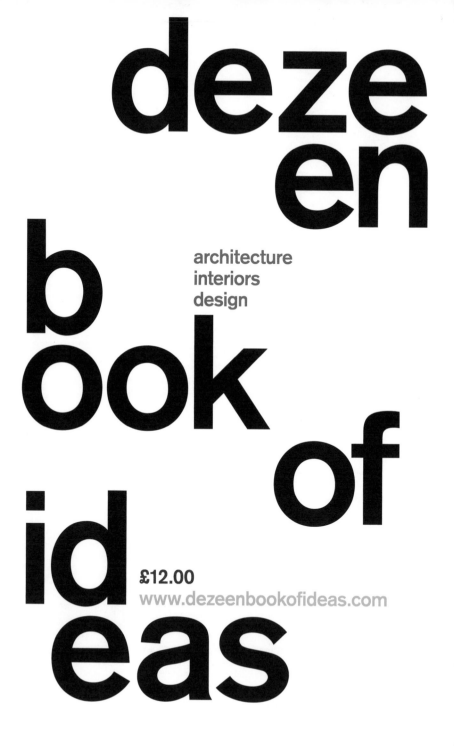

Marylebone

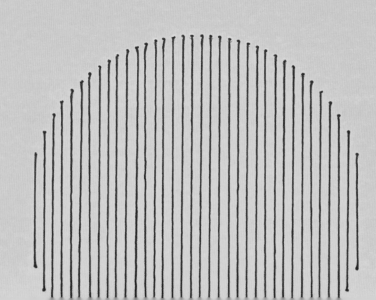

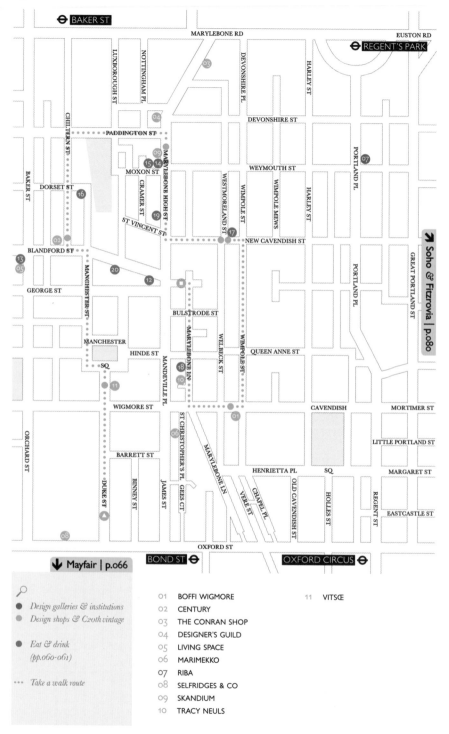

BAKER ST

MARYLEBONE RD

EUSTON RD

REGENT'S PARK

Soho & Fitzrovia | p.080

Mayfair | p.066

BOND ST   OXFORD CIRCUS

Marylebone

*Jali Wahlsten**

The enormous department store Selfridges & Co is a good place to start. This place has all kinds of great products under one roof, including one of London's best selections of international magazines. Take the Duke Street exit and head to the Vitsœ showroom for a taste of Dieter Rams's iconic 606 shelving systems. The displays here are always immaculate and the rotating exhibitions are expertly curated.

Cross over Manchester Square and take Manchester Street towards Chiltern Street. This charming road is set to become a true West Marylebone destination, with an André Balazs hotel rumoured to be opening in the former fire station. Opposite the fire station at No 8 is the smart menswear boutique Trunk Clothiers, which carries some hard-to-find international brands.

Keep heading north. At Paddington Street turn right and continue on to Marylebone High Street. Allow yourself some time to browse and enjoy the mood at the beautiful Daunt Books (No 83). For a one-stop shop of the best Scandinavian design, be sure to pop in next door at Skandium (No 86).

Continue down the High Street and take a left into New Cavendish Street, towards residential East Marylebone. You'll see the local branch of Nordic Bakery tucked away at the corner of Westmoreland Street. On the same corner is Roger Pope & Partners, an optician with an impressive selection of eyewear.

Take Wimpole Street south towards Wigmore Street. Over the next couple of blocks you'll sense a different London made up of slightly taller and very elegant residential buildings that remind you you're in a wealthy, cosmopolitan city. On Wigmore Street be sure to visit the boutique of fashion designer Margaret Howell – not only a beautiful space but also an excellent showcase for her good-quality, refined collection. In addition to her fashions you'll see a selection of Ercol furniture, vintage tableware and books.

To complete the walk, continue west along Wigmore Street until you spot Marylebone Lane on your right. Meander along and visit the little, independent boutiques before recharging with a meal at Le Relais de Venise L'Entrecôte, where they serve some of the best steak frites in London.

* *Owner of Nordic Bakery nordicbakery.com*

01 BOFFI WIGMORE
25 WIGMORE STREET W1U 1PN
020 7629 0058
BOFFI.COM
MON-SAT 9.30-5.30
BOND STREET

02 CENTURY
58 BLANDFORD STREET W1U 7JB
020 7487 5100
CENTURYD.COM
TUE-SAT 11-5
BOND STREET/BAKER STREET

When it comes to kitchens and bathrooms, Wigmore Street has established itself as something of a hub. It sealed its status in the summer of 2011 when it attracted leading Italian brand Boffi to the block by Wigmore Hall – quite a coup, considering the gloomy economy, even despite the success of Boffi's first UK showroom in Chelsea (p.019).

The voluminous space is painted in shades of grey, against which Boffi displays its splendidly crafted modern kitchens, bathrooms and wardrobe systems. A former bank, the two-storey showroom retains a number of original period features, including super-thick vault doors in the basement. Boffi's creative director, Piero Lissoni, embraced these characteristics when he embarked on the renovation.

We tend not to include the 'permanents' of the home – kitchens and bathrooms in particular – in this guide (see p.003 for our criteria) but I feel compelled to make an exception here. After all, the high-end craftsmanship inherent in Boffi's designs is something to be marvelled at and enjoyed, constructed as they are to the highest standards using sumptuous materials and timeless detailing. Boffi cuts no corners and works with leading designers including Marcel Wanders, Naoto Fukasawa, Claesson Koivisto Rune, Claudio Silvestrin, Norbert Wangen and Lissoni himself to ensure quality and perfection prevail. These attributes will pretty much guarantee the brand will be around for years to come.

When you get there, don't be startled to find a hairdresser, who shares the tiny two-storey premises with Century. Owner Andrew Weaving keeps a few vintage furnishings and accessories up there, too, but displays most of his 'modern retro' items in the intimate basement.

Weaving's area of expertise is American and British retro furniture, with choice lighting, accessories and textiles added to the mix. On my visit I enjoyed plenty of vintage Ercol and other British classics, such as a G Plan glass-topped coffee table, a Gordon Russell sideboard and an Ernest Race dining set. It was a treat to find a rare Heywood Wakefield dresser alongside more familiar American offerings from Charles and Ray Eames, plus lighting from George Nelson.

Vintage textiles from talents like Lucienne Day, Barbara Brown, Marion Mahler and Allan Walton help soften the space, as do retro-inspired ceramics by American potter Jonathan Adler and wall sculptures by Curtis Jeré.

It's a relief to find that the small Century hasn't been crammed with too much merchandise. If you're hunting for something in particular, Weaving may have it in storage or is likely to know where to source it – after all, he's a published authority on Modernism. As is always the case when selling originals, stock fluctuates, so it's worth popping back every so often to see what other gems may have arrived.

03 THE CONRAN SHOP

- 📫 55 MARYLEBONE HIGH STREET W1U 5HS
- ✆ 020 7723 2223
- ➘ CONRANSHOP.CO.UK
- 🕙 MON-WED, FRI 10-6, THU 10-7, SA 10-6.30, SU 11-5
- 🚇 BAKER STREET

04 DESIGNERS GUILD

- 📫 76 MARYLEBONE HIGH STREET W1U 5JU
- ✆ 020 3301 5826
- ➘ DESIGNERSGUILD.COM
- 🕙 MON-SAT 10-6, THU 10-7, SUN 12-5
- 🚇 BOND STREET/BAKER STREET

Sir Terence Conran, legendary founder of The Conran Shop, has always had a knack at finding and renovating characterful buildings and transforming them into enticing shopping or culinary hotspots. This former stable at the north end of Marylebone High Street is no exception. Today the three-storey space houses Conran's reputed home store.

Customers travel to Marylebone specially to visit The Conran Shop; it's a reliable outpost for gifts up to entire home fit-outs. While quite large, the store refrains from offering too much choice, which makes browsing easy and unstressful. Furnishings for every area of the home are covered here; stock comprises a mix of classic bestsellers, recognisable brands and some previously unseen and own-brand offerings.

The selection here strives to meet Sir Terence's criteria for good design: timeless modernity, simple forms and comfortable functionality. All three floors – each covering a different area of the home – manage to adhere to these qualities. The shop has become a good guide to the style zeitgeist without playing lip service to fashion-led trends. But while I value this attitude to retail, I occasionally crave a few fanciful flourishes or surprise additions. As it stands, the directional product ranges, imaginative merchandising and rotating displays keep customers coming back for more.

This store opened on bustling Marylebone High Street in 2010, London's first Designers Guild satellite (read about the Chelsea flagship on p.022). Tricia Guild has steered this business since founding it in 1970, and built up a strong following among those drawn to her bold and colourful textile and wallpaper designs.

These designs are brought alive in the interior settings mounted here in Marylebone. Guild has never been afraid to create confident statements with the aim to inspire customers to use colour in combination. She often focuses on one particular colour, creating alluring displays comprising objects sharing a similar or contrasting palette. This is likely to involve a mix-and-match approach with new and vintage furnishings, lighting and accessories – all of which are available to buy.

While her aesthetic may trigger a love-or-hate reaction, Designers Guild manages to remain contemporary without being garishly modern. Sure, it's fair to say it's rather girlie overall. Others might describe it as 'homely', which can be no bad thing. Everything in store is super-styled, with the attractive staff and gentle soundtrack creating an air of calm – so calm, in fact, that I could have quite easily indulged in an afternoon nap on one of the inviting display beds.

LIVING SPACE

- 55 BAKER STREET W1U 8EW
- 020 7731 1180
- LIVINGSPACEUK.COM
- MON-SAT 10-6, SUN 12-5
- BAKER STREET

MARIMEKKO

- 16-17 ST CHRISTOPHER'S PLACE W1U 1NZ
- 020 7486 6454
- MARIMEKKO.COM
- MON-SAT 10-6.30, THU 10-7, SUN 12-5
- BOND STREET

This central London location is the third from Living Space, purveyor of slick European furniture. But unlike the Islington and Fulham sites, the Baker Street showroom focuses on kitchen and wall-storage designs from Italian brand Lago, along with some complementary pieces by other producers.

The minimal grey and white space operates around three small "rooms": a kitchen, bedroom and living area. They feature the *Air* series of beds and couches with clear-glass bases that seem to float above the shop's wooden floor. The focus, however, is on Daniele Lago's *Compositions*, a shelving range designed to be built up and customised. Customers can choose a colour, finish and combination of parts to create their own one-of-a-kind library or storage system.

Living Space also carries televisions and speakers by Loewe and bright floorwear from Kymo to add a touch of warmth to the space. But the most charming feature is the *Biblioteca Lago*, a range of vintage Italian books, ranging from Pinocchio to the story of Pope Giovanni XXIII, spread around the shop.

The overall look of the space is contemporary Italian: minimal, slick and, some might say, slightly clinical. Of course, the product is well made and will appeal to those with little tolerance for clutter in their homes.

Founded in 1951 by visionary textile designer Armi Ratia and her husband Viljo, Finnish brand Marimekko has grown significantly since its early fame in the swinging '60s. Back then, the bold, colourful designs adorned the sexy dresses and interiors of a liberated generation, embodying the free spirit of the era. The brand gained global repute and is now a publicly traded company with more than 1,000 retailers worldwide.

I suppose such growth has been good for the brand, although I think Marimekko needs to be careful about how much it diversifies. Currently the company designs and manufactures clothing, decorative textiles, bags and myriad accessories. "Each individual Marimekko product," its materials say, "must earn its own design value and express Marimekko's lifestyle concept". Whether or not you agree, Marimekko has successfully introduced the brand to a wider audience by offering a variety of accessible price points.

You need to see a large swathe of each fabric to appreciate the graphic impact of the print. This small London store has a good selection of the most popular patterns, available to purchase by the metre. Hanging on a wall, on its own or in a frame, a piece of fabric offers a striking and less-permanent alternative to wallpaper. If you're seeking some vivid colour to accent your interior, Marimekko may be the place for you.

07 RIBA
🖅 66 PORTLAND PLACE W1B 1AD
📞 020 7580 5533
↖ ARCHITECTURE.COM
🕐 MON-SAT 10-5
⊖ GREAT PORTLAND STREET

08 SELFRIDGES & CO
🖅 400 OXFORD STREET W1A 1AB
📞 0800 123 400
↖ SELFRIDGES.COM
🕐 MON-FRI 9.30-10, SAT 9.30-9, SUN 11.30-6.15
⊖ BOND STREET/MARBLE ARCH

The Royal Institute of British Architects (RIBA) champions better buildings, communities and the environment through architecture. Supporting more than 40,000 members, it is the UK's major body for architecture, design education and professional development, providing the standards, training and recognition (with its Stirling Prize) for the industry. With help from the government the institute works to improve the architectural quality of public buildings, new homes and communities. Residents can use RIBA's records and listings to help themselves locate the ideal architect for their private project.

RIBA was founded in 1834 for 'the general advancement of Civil Architecture'. One hundred years later the London headquarters opened, a classic Art Deco showpiece designed by George Grey Wornum. The Portland Place landmark still stands proudly today, hosting a variety of activities and services for its members; it can also be hired for events by the public.

Within its various soaring galleries you can attend a rotating programme of exhibitions that covers every angle of building design throughout the year. On the ground floor, the RIBA Bookshop operates as a valuable resource for all the latest books, contracts and forms on architecture, design and construction. Upstairs is the library, holding one of the most comprehensive collections of architectural books, periodicals, drawings, photographs, models and archives in the world. But if all that is industry overload for you, you can also enjoy a meal in the stunning café and restaurant, or meet a friend for a drink and snack in the ground floor bar.

Back in 1909 the entrepreneur Gordon Selfridge believed that a grand, modern department store should be as important to public life as a historic landmark. And so Selfridges & Co was born, bringing its undeniable grandeur to London's Oxford Street. Today his eponymous retail emporium has achieved both a global reputation and institutional presence in central London. Its very existence attracts hordes of customers to the thoroughfare – although Oxford Street is now arguably far less grand.

You'll find the main entrances behind a stately columned façade. They plunge you into a world scented by perfume and cosmetics – a busy environment I choose to escape, either for the nearby Food Hall or Wine Shop.

The basement level focuses on contemporary interiors, starting with a kitchen department featuring a worthy selection of accessories and tableware; Italian brand Alessi has a concession here, and Scandinavian design is well represented by Skandium and Design House Stockholm. Alas, the best Selfridges has to offer is overwhelmed by all that 'other stuff' department stores feel they must bring to the table.

Taking a lift to the fourth floor lets you bypass fashion for the furniture emporium. Since introducing bland high-street brands like Bo Concept, Natuzzi and Loft Living, the floor has lost a lot of its spark – even the lighting section suffers due to overcrowding. If it leaves you cold, too, retreat back into the basement, where you can seek respite in the quieter, more comprehensive bookshop.

09 SKANDIUM
🚩 86 MARYLEBONE HIGH STREET W1U 4QS
📞 020 7935 2077
🔗 SKANDIUM.COM
🕐 MON-SAT 10-6.30, THU 10-7, SUN 11-5
🚇 BAKER STREET/BOND STREET

10 TRACEY NEULS
🚩 29 MARYLEBONE LANE W1U 2NQ
📞 020 7935 0039
🔗 TN29.COM
🕐 MON-FRI 11-6.30, SAT-SUN 12-5
🚇 BOND STREET

In 1999, Skandium began life on Wigmore Street with a clear vision: to bring the best Scandinavian design to Marylebone. The retailer single-handedly brought together the finest furniture, lighting, accessories and textiles from the biggest Nordic talents, from 20th-century design masters or their contemporary heirs. The Marylebone flagship has since become an anchor on the street and a leader of London's design scene.

The lofty, two-storey space sells a mix of enduring midcentury classics by the likes of Aalto, Jacobsen, Saarinen, Franck, Wegner and Kjærholm and more current designs by Claesson Koivisto Rune, Harri Koskinen, Lena Bergström and Matti Klenell. The abundance of natural light on the ground floor provides a fresh backdrop against which the kitchenware, glass, ceramics, books and accessories are displayed. Larger furnishings, lighting and textiles live downstairs in the basement.

The collection is comprehensive but not overwhelming; each piece is given enough space to properly catch and hold your attention. Under no illusion that the merchandise is cheap, Skandium's owners have always understood the value of employing approachable and knowledgeable staff to assist customers in making suitable choices. After all, when you're buying designs that are made to last, well-informed decision-making is of paramount importance.

I seldom wax lyrical about women's footwear. But, truth be told, I could happily engage in conversation about Tracey Neuls's studio. Her shoes, to me, feel more like crafted objects than just containers for the feet.

The Canadian-born talent has been designing women's footwear in the UK since she launched the TN_29 label in 2000. She opened her shop five years later on peaceful Marylebone Lane, a backstreet that always captivates me with its playful window displays. Neuls's windows are some of the best. Strictly speaking, shoe shops are outside the editorial remit of *London Design Guide*, but this boutique's idiosyncratic approach makes it an exception to the rule.

Neuls often collaborates with other artists and such unions manifest themselves in the store design. Shoes are displayed like installations, dangling from the ceiling, perched atop stools or even integrated into a dining-table setting. Neuls's unconventional way of merchandising encourages customers to view the shoes from all sides, which gives them a sense of stellar craftsmanship she brings to each design.

Her designs emphasise texture, pattern, unusual stitching, moulding and intricate embossing on the sole; they're really like 3D artworks, influenced by Neuls's inquisitive mind. A timeless individuality pervades her shoes, whether they be from the premium Tracey Neuls collection or the more accessible TN_29 range.

The service here is personal and attentive – and often accompanied by fresh coffee and baked bread. Who else makes shoe-shopping such a welcoming experience for women and their men?

11 VITSŒ

3-5 DUKE STREET W1U 3ED

020 7428 1606

VITSOE.COM

MON-SAT 10-6

BOND STREET

In 1960, a 28-year-old German designer by the name of Dieter Rams designed a shelving system for Danish furniture entrepreneur Niels Vitsœ and German furniture-maker Otto Zapf. The result was *606 Universal Shelving System*, a fully modular system of aluminium tracks that supports shelves, cabinets and a table. More than 50 years later, this design can be found on the walls of some of the world's finest institutions, stores, even homes. And on plenty of normal ones, too.

Shelving is not something one would envisage getting excited about. And a shop dedicated entirely to shelving is not my idea of riveting retail. But all credit to Vitsœ... I'm hooked. This company produces a flawless product like no other on the market. The fact it's still in production today is validation.

The Duke Street location was built in 1928 as two separate stores. It served as office space for 60 years before Vitsœ restored it to its original glory. The company made best use of the intimate warrens and high-ceilinged rooms, where the shelving configurations are displayed.

Discreet, adaptable and timeless are the right words to describe the product. Like many of the best ideas, it focuses on functional simplicity. It is made up of a handsome set of components that lock together and are easily moved, repaired, altered or updated as needed – like a kit of parts. By virtue of this flexible system, you're in full control of the configuration, so you can start small and add to it as life demands. In Vitsœ's own words: 'It is a furniture system made to transcend the

temporary interpretations of fashion and style and instead offer a neutral canvas on which to paint a colourful life.'

So much design today inflicts rigidity onto our lives, meaning products must be replaced when our circumstances change. Vitsœ preaches against such built-in obsolescence with its ethos: live better, with less, that lasts longer.

LDG

Eat & drink

Great for... unpretentious haute cuisine

L'AUTRE PIED
Modern European bistro serving high-calibre dishes. Informal, bustling atmosphere with modern chinoiserie surroundings. Unpretentious, without tablecloths or fancy silverware. Imaginative, well-considered flavour combinations.
5-7 BLANDFORD STREET W1U 3DB | 020 7486 9696 | LAUTREPIED.CO.UK

Great for... quality British fare

CANTEEN [PICTURED]
Stunning canteen-style resto on busy thoroughfare. Superb ingredients, no-nonsense menu. Postwar feel with relaxed, intimate atmosphere. Ask for a booth.
55 BAKER STREET W1U 8EW | 0845 686 1122 | CANTEEN.CO.UK

Great for... cheese lovers 14

LA FROMAGERIE
Dedicated dairy, deli and café. Stylish and unconventional with communal eating. Ideal for indulgent lunch or early-afternoon snack. Tantalisingly rich flavours with aroma of freshly baked bread.
2-6 MOXON STREET W1U 4EW
020 7935 0341 | LAFROMAGERIE.CO.UK

Great for... quality meat 15

GINGER PIG
Proper traditional butcher selling proper quality meat. Produce comes from their own farms. Daily menu of cooked take-home meals. Treat yourself to the aged steak.
8-10 MOXON STREET W1U 4EW
020 7935 7788 | THEGINGERPIG.CO.UK

Great for... local gatherings 16

HARDY'S
Intimate, earthy neighbourhood restaurant in quiet Marylebone. British classics and modern European dishes complement with intriguing wine list. Honest cooking popular among locals.
53 DORSET STREET W1U 7NH
020 7935 5929 | HARDYS-W1.COM

Great for... discreet café catch-up

NORDIC BAKERY

Contemporary café serving simple sweet and savoury Nordic goods. Calm atmosphere with Minimalist Scandinavian interior. Highlights are the sticky cinnamon buns and great coffee.

37B NEW CAVENDISH STREET W1G 8JR

020 7935 3590 | NORDICBAKERY.COM

Great for... the perfect cup of tea

PAUL ROTHE & SON

British treasure in Marylebone, established in 1900. Family-run. Serves a wide variety of teas and no-nonsense English food. Great selection of jams and relishes for sale. Polite and welcoming, attracting all sorts.

35 MARYLEBONE LANE W1U 2NN | 020 7935 6783

Great for... flavour combinations

THE PROVIDORES AND TAPA ROOM

Formal dining room upstairs, casual tapas café downstairs. Asian-fusion cuisine with New Zealand twist. Always packed: expect to queue. Makes for a fun culinary romp.

109 MARYLEBONE HIGH STREET W1U 4RX

020 7935 6175 | THEPROVIDORES.CO.UK

Great for... a taste of the country

ROGANIC

Sister restaurant to L'Enclume in Lake District. Two-year London pop-up restaurant celebrating seasonal British ingredients in a simple, modern interior.

19 BLANDFORD STREET W1U 3DH | 020 7486 0380 | ROGANIC.CO.UK

SELLING

DESIGN

When twentytwentyone began trading in 1996, the business of selling design was quite different. The demand came from a narrow band of curious yet informed individuals spread thinly across the world.

Knowledge and understanding has developed with time. We fielded many enquiries relating to the work of Charles and Ray Eames when we hosted an Eames exhibition in 1997. It was our aim to convince people they were a husband and wife team of unsurpassed talent. Today Eames is a household name.

As the market has matured, more retailers have started representing international brands as an agent or distributor. Others have produced their own collections. A market for collectible design has emerged, with limited-edition creations taking their place in rarified, gallery settings. The passage to growth is certainly one of trial and error.

The design market is now much larger, with retailers in most cities and a strong online presence. It continues to evolve, and the retail rules are still in flux. Our experience at twentytwentyone is by no means a template for selling modernism. Our desire to select designs that stimulate and offer longevity remains core to our business. Any retailer's collection should reflect its personality, and combine with other collections to offer a cohesive cross-section of functional designs. Communication is an essential tool; we conceive exhibitions and events to start a dialogue among our customers and ourselves. These macro-scale techniques are reflected and balanced on a micro-scale through in-store displays.

Our culture has grown increasingly focused on brand names and consumer buying patterns are becoming indiscriminate. We are obsessed with the latest and the supposed best. To foster more measured decision-making, design retailers need to convey their enthusiasm for and knowledge of good design – indeed, they've got the deepest understanding of materials,

> "To foster more measured decision-making, design retailers need to convey their enthusiasm for and knowledge of good design."

processes and history, so only they can properly communicate the complexity, value and stories behind those products.

The public's growing appetite for design is increasingly fed by the Internet, which bestows upon us greater flexibility in locating, buying and selling design. The virtual marketplace has provided manufacturers and designers with a forum to showcase their creations to wider audiences. And to retailers it has given the freedom to engage with a wider customer base that might never be able to simply walk in the door. Embracing the online market is essential, and a carefully curated selection is an asset that will positively reward retailers.

The Internet has become a powerful medium for both selling and communicating. But it's also created its share of turmoil. It's become a tool for marketing unlicensed design by less-principled, profit-driven retailers. Easy sourcing, made possible by the Internet, has simplified the acquisition process and allowed some lazy, copycat retailers to create identikit products for the middle market. Deep discounts by online merchants have further cheapened the work of true designers.

These practices are jeopardising online design retail, driving it towards the world of fast fashion and white goods. It's debatable whether such models for short-term gain are sustainable. E-commerce is an essential element in successful design retailing, but it should be treated with respect.

The merits of traditional retail remain convincingly high, but it is vital to employ contemporary mediums to reach new markets and new generations. Bricks and mortar retail can and must continue to foster an emotional connection with design – after all, don't we all want to touch, experience and bond with well-conceived products, and ask questions of those selling them to better understand their attributes?

At the essence of good design is the thoughtful evolution of process to create the best possible solution. The same can be said of good design retail.

SIMON ALDERSON IS CO-OWNER OF MODERN DESIGN RETAILER TWENTYTWENTYONE *twentytwentyone.com*

HANNAH MARTIN

ICONIC FINE JEWELLERY LONDON EC1
WWW.HANNAHMARTINLONDON.COM

Mayfair

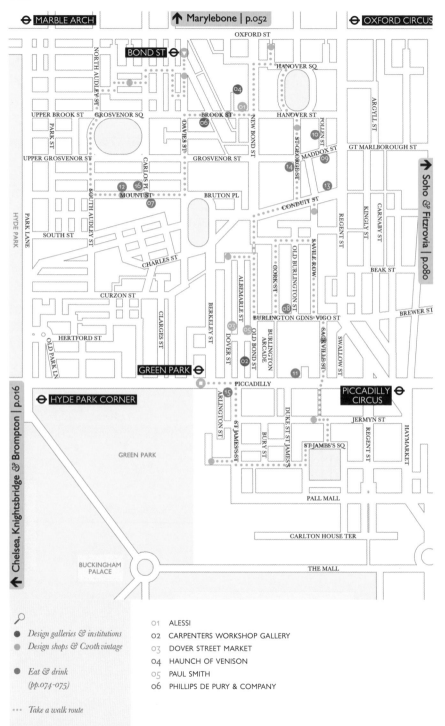

OXFORD ST

BOND ST

HANOVER SQ

04

01

BROOK ST

06

HANOVER ST

NORTH AUDLEY ST

UPPER BROOK ST

GROSVENOR SQ

PARK ST

DAVIES ST

NEW BOND ST

ST GEORGE ST

10

POLLEN ST

ARGYLL ST

GT MARLBOROUGH ST

UPPER GROSVENOR ST

GROSVENOR ST

MADDOX ST

09

CARLOS PL

14

13

12 16

MOUNT ST

07

BRUTON PL

CONDUIT ST

CARNABY ST

KINGLY ST

REGENT ST

BEAK ST

SOUTH AUDLEY ST

SOUTH ST

HYDE PARK

PARK LANE

CHARLES ST

CURZON ST

CLARGES ST

HERTFORD ST

BERKELEY ST

ALBEMARLE ST

CORK ST

SAVILE ROW

OLD BURLINGTON ST

08

BURLINGTON GDNS VIGO ST

05

DOVER ST

OLD BOND ST

02

BURLINGTON ARCADE

SACKVILLE ST

SWALLOW ST

BREWER ST

GREEN PARK

11

PICCADILLY

OLD PARK LN

HYDE PARK CORNER

15

ARLINGTON ST

GT ST JAMES'S ST

DUKE ST ST JAMES'S

BURY ST

ST JAMES'S ST

ST JAMES'S SQ

PICCADILLY CIRCUS

JERMYN ST

REGENT ST

HAYMARKET

GREEN PARK

PALL MALL

CARLTON HOUSE TER

BUCKINGHAM PALACE

THE MALL

🔍

● *Design galleries & institutions*

● *Design shops & C20th vintage*

● *Eat & drink*
  (pp.074-075)

••• *Take a walk route*

01   ALESSI
02   CARPENTERS WORKSHOP GALLERY
03   DOVER STREET MARKET
04   HAUNCH OF VENISON
05   PAUL SMITH
06   PHILLIPS DE PURY & COMPANY

Mayfair

TAKE A WALK WITH

*Brent Dzekciorius**

Step out of Bond Street station and head to Grays Antique Market on Davies Street for a gander at its diverse collections of fine antiques, jewellery and vintage fashion. To the west is Brown Hart Gardens, a street-level garden refashioned in 1903 into one of Mayfair's most beautiful architectural features: an elevated, paved Italian garden complete with domes and neo-Baroque pavilions at either end. Continue through Grosvenor Square to the eponymous Mount Street Deli where you can take away a toasted brioche to enjoy in peaceful Mount Street Gardens. Outside The Connaught Hotel, look for the ethereal Silence water feature designed by Tadao Ando.

For lunch, head to Brook Street for a traditional Japanese at Ikeda, renowned for its Iberico pork and Kabu nosenmai zuke. If you're a fan of traditional teas, try a cuppa at Postcard Teas on Dering Street, more than two centuries old. Otherwise, head to Condé Nast Worldwide News on Hanover Square, a shop selling all the publisher's magazines. Nearby, you can see artworks by Matthew Barney, Urs Fisher and Raymond Pettibon at Sadie Coles (4 New Burlington Place), then snake through to Sprüth Magers (7A Grafton Street) for the latest creations by John Baldessari, Sterling Ruby and Kenneth Anger.

Swing past the high-end jewellers of Old Bond Street to London's art gallery capital, Cork Street, before exploring the famous tailoring street of Savile Row. Further on, at Sackville Street, you'll spot Sotheran's, the longest established antiquarian booksellers in the world. Fans of bespoke shoes should cross Piccadilly to Jermyn Street for John Lobb, showcasing the art of traditional shoemaking.

To wrap up, walk through St James's Square and along Duke Street. On the other side of St James's Street, near St James's Palace, you'll come upon Dukes Hotel, where, at the hotel bar, you can enjoy an aperitif or, more specifically, London's finest martini (this is where Ian Fleming was moved to immortalise the 'shaken, not stirred' drink). If you're hungry, there are plenty of great dining options around here, otherwise head home from Green Park tube.

*Director of Retail Operations at Phillips de Pury phillipsdepury.com

01 ALESSI

22 BROOK STREET W1K 5DF

020 7518 9091

ALESSI.COM

MON-SAT 9.30-6.30, THU 10-7, SUN 12-6

BOND STREET

No European brand has been more dedicated to adding character to your household than Italian stalwart Alessi. The company's distinctive catalogue colourfully covers every room of the house, from the kitchen to the dining room, the bathroom and lounge. Family-run since 1921, Alessi has garnered a global reputation under the creative direction of Alberto Alessi, who invests in leading design talents to create an ever-expanding collection of iconic designs.

The London showroom's high-end location is just moments from the exclusive shopping thoroughfare of New Bond Street, but Alessi's three-storey flagship is thankfully devoid of the retail snobbery so prevalent in the area. Take a quick glance at the stuff and it is clear why: there's a distinct mischievousness to almost everything – particularly the playful plastic homewares by Stefano Giovannoni that implore customers not to take life too seriously.

Despite Alessi's popular appeal, design purists tend to baulk at the gimmicky nature of some of its ranges, and there's a chasm between the smiley-faced trinkets and the refined stainless-steel pieces that make up a major part of the label's offering. Still, the latter designs, be they functional or purely sculptural, are undeniably striking. Visit the Brook Street HQ and you can't avoid Nigel Coates's sensual *Big Shoom* centrepiece, nor the faceted *Orloff* bowl by Patricia Urquiola.

When it comes to designers, the world's finest have worked with the brand – from Italian masters like Alessandro Mendini, Ettore Sottsass, Achille Castiglioni and Aldo Rossi to international stars Michael Graves, Philippe Starck, Jasper Morrison, Marc Newson, Naoto Fukasawa and David Chipperfield. Whether or not these names mean anything to you, chances are you'll be drawn in by their (relative) affordability. And there's something for everyone, whatever your needs and style, whether you're looking for a gift or treating yourself. We agree with Alberto Alessi when he says that Alessi's products 'somehow make commonplace gestures more pleasing, more straightforward and more personal'.

02 CARPENTERS WORKSHOP GALLERY

- 3 ALBEMARLE STREET W1S 4HE
- 020 3051 5939
- CWGDESIGN.COM
- MON-SAT 10-6
- GREEN PARK

Carpenters Workshop Gallery has successfully embraced and become a key player in the burgeoning market for high-end design that converges with sculptural art. Founded in 2006 by French duo Loïc Le Gaillard and Julien Lombrail, the gallery began life in – you guessed it – an old carpenter's workshop in Chelsea. A couple of years later, as the gallery matured, it graduated to a second space in Mayfair, at the centre of London's fine-art scene and only moments from the Cork Street establishment.

The gallery has tapped into the growing lust among art collectors for strikingly contemporary design (and capitalised on their disillusionment by the out-of-control art market). Featured works have been created with an element of functionality in mind but undertaken without constraints – resulting in designs that push materiality to extremes in concept, form or construction. This burgeoning genre has been dubbed 'design art', a rather lacklustre term despite the magnificence of some of the product.

Housed in a classic Mayfair terrace, the gallery itself isn't huge but the simple white interior helps give the illusion of space. One-off and limited-edition works are given pride of place, either in solo or group exhibitions. Carpenters supports up-and-coming designers (or 'artists', as they prefer to call them), such as rAndom International, Vincent Dubourg, Sebastian Brajkovic, Charles Trevelyan, Pablo Reinoso, Robert Stadler and Lonneke Gordijn & Ralph Nauta – each one of whom is carving out his own appeal among the collectors. But there are more established names here, too.

The smart neighbourhood combined with the slick, professional space and high price points may make this gallery intimidating to enter. The package concoction doesn't bode well for footfall, but I will always encourage readers to have a look around, regardless of their intentions. During my most recent visit the place lived up to the gallery stereotype: I was totally ignored on entry, then while browsing and again when I left. Complacency, snobbery – call it what you will – may be unnecessary, but they shouldn't get in the way of your enjoyment, especially when such fine works are on show.

⓸ DOVER STREET MARKET

🏠 17-18 DOVER STREET W1S 4LT

📞 020 7518 0680

⬆ DOVERSTREETMARKET.COM

🕐 MON-WED 11-6.30, THU-SAT 11-7, SUN 12-5

⊖ GREEN PARK

As a rule we don't include fashion boutiques in this guide. But I'm making an exception for Dover Street Market, which has turned the age-old concept of the polished mono-brand flagship on its head to become a one-of-kind retail destination. The high-fashion megastore displays a unique combination of fashion and bespoke visual merchandising over six floors in a converted Georgian building. It is the brainchild of Comme des Garcons' Rei Kawakubo, who has injected her strong personal vision into this 'atmosphere of beautiful chaos'.

True to the latter part of its name, the interior is rough and deliberately unfinished – though by no means haphazard or unconsidered. Couture and high fashion are presented like art on unusual displays comprising old corrugated-metal and wood huts; red-painted steel hanging racks and scaffolding-pole booths. The result is a cross between high-end boutique and raw exhibition space – though it even nods to its previous life as an office block.

Dsm sets itself apart from other high-fashion retailers by mixing its founder's own collections with those of other prominent figures, cultivating an atmosphere of collaboration and creative fusion rather than one of designer rivalry. Along with fashion Dsm highlights quirkier items, like a vending machine dispensing T-shirts and glass cabinets stuffed with sculptural animal skulls. Then there are the always-changing installations, curated by artists and film and theatre designers invited to put their stamp on the existing spaces.

Taking into account the sheer size of the 'market' and the big-name designers on show (Celine, Lanvin and Jill Sanders are just a few), a visit can seem overwhelming. However I love that the selection is well edited – the cream of the fashion crop monopolising every level. If you're still intimidated, take the lift to the top floor and refuel at Rose Bakery.

04 HAUNCH OF VENISON
6 HAUNCH OF VENISON YARD W1K 5ES
020 7495 5050
HAUNCHOFVENISON.COM
MON-FRI 10-6, SAT 10-5
BOND STREET

After years lodging in spaces at the back of
the Royal Academy of Arts, this decade-old
gallery recently returned to the magnificent,
old Mayfair courtyard for which it was named.
Some of today's leading contemporary artists are
showcased here (and at the New York exhibition
space): Enrico Castellani, Richard Long, Patricia
Piccinini, Joana Vasconcelos, Tom Wesselmann,
Jésus Rafael Soto and Uwe Wittwer among them.
The three-storey Georgian townhouse has been
refreshed with a pristine white backdrop to show
these big names in the best light.

Over the past few years, art collectors have
expressed interest in acquiring design. Some
serious enquiries have prompted Haunch of
Venison to look into suitable living designers with
whom they could work and tentatively approach
this relatively new domain. Curator Rachael
Barraclough heads up the design division and has
so far embraced the edition works of Thomas
Heatherwick, Stuart Haygarth and the duo
Edward Barber and Jay Osgerby.

Designers normally constrained by functional
requirements are free, with a gallery, to take
their work into new areas of experimentation,
and concentrate on craft skills, new materials
and processes that would be prohibitive in the
world of mass production. The results are often
spectacular, so be sure to keep an eye on the
website for forthcoming shows.

05 PAUL SMITH NO 9
🡒 9 ALBEMARLE STREET W1S 4HH
📞 020 7493 4565
🡔 PAULSMITH.CO.UK
🕐 MON-SAT 10.30-6, THU 10.30-7
⊖ GREEN PARK

Paul Smith is respected the world over for adding a distinctive twist to quintessentially British fashion. The designer cites inspiration from the most unexpected of places – indeed it's on his travels that he picks up the multicultural influences that fuel his designs. But he also has an insatiable appetite for collecting 'things'.

It was only a matter of time before he would open a shop for his things, which is exactly what he did in Mayfair in 2005. At this corner shop he brings together a varied selection of original antiques, objects, art and curiosities from around the world with no obvious theme, era or genre. The result is a rather odd mix yet one that commands your attention.

The shop consists of two rooms, each with a different look and atmosphere. Enter the larger of the two and you'll get an ever-changing selection of furniture, displayed in a simple arrangement against pastel-painted walls. On my visit I spotted an enormous handcrafted cherrywood studio desk designed by American Michael Coffey in the 1970s. On its surface was a selection of classic stainless-steel tea and coffee pots by Arne Jacobsen for Stelton, recently updated with brightly coloured handles by Paul Smith himself, in celebration of the designs' 50th anniversary. Beside them were some vibrant bowls and containers from the same *Cylinda* range.

Another piece that caught my eye was a 1950s bureau designed by the legendary American postwar optimist Raymond Loewy, made from wood with a writing tablet that folds down to reveal a striking blue interior. A 1970s chest of drawers simply clad in brushed steel was a slick

addition to an overall collection that, generally, doesn't shy away from decorative flourishes.

A cosy room at the back of the shop, with its distressed plaster and vintage wallpaper, is home to a mismatched yet simply arranged collection of smaller tabletop items, as well as art, vintage jewellery, books, magazines and other intriguing oddities. Scattered throughout the shop are various ornate chairs and sofas, each given a new lease of life with signature Paul Smith fabrics.

Displays change regularly as the one-off pieces sell. So fans of Smith and collectors alike should make return visits.

06 PHILLIPS DE PURY & COMPANY

- 45-47 BROOK STREET W1K 4HN
- 020 7318 4010
- PHILLIPSDEPURY.COM
- MON-FRI 10-6
- BOND STREET

In June 2011 the well-known auction house Phillips de Pury & Company opened an exhibition and retail gallery in Mayfair to complement its sizable headquarters and sale rooms at Howick Place in Victoria (p.192). The space is used to showcase highlights of all the house's auction sales – including Contemporary Art, Design, Photography and Jewels.

The double-fronted space adjoins the famously upmarket Claridge's Hotel, so it seems the house is clearly aiming to tap into the wealthy Mayfair market and its foreign counterparts who shop on busy Brook Street. It is just this sort of clientele who will likely go in for the collectible, high-value pieces that preview here prior to their sale under the hammer at Howick Place.

The space isn't huge – just big enough for a few quality-not-quantity selling exhibitions throughout the year. The debut was *Linda McCartney: Life in Photographs*, which featured 26 photographs taken by Paul McCartney's late wife from the '60s through the '90s. Then stylist and designer Faye Toogood showcased her third collection of furniture and objects, *Delicate Interference*, during 2011's London Design Festival.

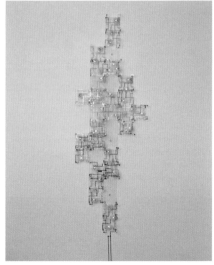

The company continues to explore today's leading designers at occasional pop-up-shop events selling studio-based product and furniture design; artist multiples; editions; and printed matter. These ensembles showcase the creative talents of such achievers as Max Lamb, Nendo, Bertjan Pot, Massimiliano Adami and Peter Marigold before they reach the collectible status reserved for the auction room.

LDG

Eat & drink

Great for... meat lovers

ALLENS

Mayfair's oldest butcher operating since 1830. Suppliers to smart London eateries like The Wolseley and Cecconi's. Traditional: sells only finest-quality cuts.

117 MOUNT STREET W1K 3LA
020 7499 5831 | ALLENSOFMAYFAIR.CO.UK

Great for... a Bellini at the bar

CECCONI'S

A beacon of London's Italian-dining scene, from Soho House Group. Studioilse design: black-and-white-striped marble floors and bright-green leather chairs. Instant classic. Famous for truffle risotto and draught prosecco.

5A BURLINGTON GARDENS W1S 3EP
020 7434 1500 | CECCONIS.CO.UK

Great for... Michelin bargain lunch

HIBISCUS

Haute cuisine at a reasonable fixed price for lunch. Subdued interior with oak paneling and white linen gives explosive dishes centre stage.

29 MADDOX STREET W1S 2PA
020 7629 2999 | HIBISCUSRESTAURANT.CO.UK

Great for... refined flavours

POLLEN STREET SOCIAL

Masterful cooking from chef Jason Atherton, professionally served in elegant, light-filled setting. Popular for its original and elaborate flavour combinations. Culinary gem.

8-10 POLLEN STREET W1S 1NQ
020 7290 7600 | POLLENSTREETSOCIAL.COM

Great for... dining in ornate surroundings

RESTAURANT AT THE ROYAL ACADEMY [PICTURED]
Benefits from ornate institutional interior with original elaborate features. British menu from Peyton & Byrne served in Tom Dixon-designed space.
ROYAL ACADEMY OF ARTS, BURLINGTON HOUSE, PICCADILLY W1J OBD
020 7300 5608 | ROYALACADEMY.ORG.UK

Great for... seafood

SCOTT'S
Glamorous seafood restaurant and Mayfair institution that opened as an oyster warehouse in 1851. Fresh fish prepared simply and presented beautifully. Oak-panelled dining room and magnificent green onyx-topped bar.
20 MOUNT STREET W1K 2HE
020 7495 7309
SCOTTS-RESTAURANT.COM

Great for... Champagne afternoon tea

SKETCH
Large venue offering extravagant dining experience at the Lecture Room or cosy afternoon break at the Parlour. The Gallery adds site-specific video installations to the mix. Futuristic East Bar. Witty, elegant and refreshingly individual. Check out the toilets. Open late.
9 CONDUIT STREET W1S 2XG | 020 7659 4500 | SKETCH.UK.COM

Great for... modern European

WILD HONEY
High-quality Euro dishes with English touches. Elegant oak-paneled room with ornate plaster mouldings and original fireplace. Noisy during the week; more relaxing at weekends.
12 ST GEORGE STREET W1S 2FB
020 7758 9160 | WILDHONEYRESTAURANT.CO.UK

Great for... people watching

THE WOLSELEY
Classic all-day restaurant inspired by Europe's grand brasseries in a former 1920s car showroom. Marble floors, pillars and archways. Ideal for breakfast or afternoon tea, but packed whatever the hour.
160 PICCADILLY W1J 9EB
020 7499 6996 | THEWOLSELEY.COM

Place to sleep?
THE CONNAUGHT HOTEL THE-CONNAUGHT.CO.UK

IDENTIFYNG

DESIGN

As a teenager I was a letterpress printer and typographer. Examining typography and the quality of lines in printed matter fascinated me. I was always seeking the best possible spacing, the best arrangement of letters and images. And I would cast a sharp eye over the paper quality, the impression of the ink… Every last detail mattered intensely.

Thirty years later my daily work involves exhibiting and selling midcentury vintage furniture by Dutch, Danish and American designers; reissuing classic pieces by Danish-American designer Jens Risom; and promoting contemporary pieces by young furniture-makers.

Whether I'm selling classic items or reissues, for me all these are equally significant and worthy of scrutiny. I apply the same attention to detail when selecting items for sale as I once did with letterpress printing. I want every dovetail to be as near perfect as possible, the inside of a drawer to be lined with the most appropriate material. I love beautifully constructed things, whether they're handmade or mass-produced. I hate rushed work. If you're going to live with a piece of furniture, you want it to be well made inside and out.

One of the most interesting changes in the retail of well-designed furniture over the past few years? Consumers will now mix old with new without hesitation. As Jens Risom has said: 'Good design means that anything good will go well with other equally good things – contemporary or traditional.' The complication here is with the arrival of fakes: convincing reproductions produced without the permission of the designers or their heirs. You may find the 'look' of a PK27 by Poul Kjærholm, which is captivating. And if the fake looks the same and costs a quarter of the authorised version, well, why not? But originals and authorised reissues have so many subtle elements to them. They may

"...we can experience the best of the past while simultaneously exploring a modern future tied to our requirements for function, rather than being a slave to nostalgia or fashion."

not be immediately obvious to us, subtle aspects that don't reveal themselves at first sight, but they're important, informed decisions made by the designers – who, in the words of Malcolm Gladwell, have put in their '10,000 hours'.

Although I also work as a gallerist, the arena of 'design-art' doesn't really interest me. Just because an artist chooses to make a table, that doesn't validate him as a designer (unless he happens to be trained in furniture design). Let's not be afraid of function. Design is not about trends and fashions; it has to be studied and practised in order to develop. It takes commitment, ingenuity and clarity to be successful. But we're all part of it to some extent. And the less we spend on cars and electronic gadgets, the more we can spend on our basic daily furniture. As such we can experience the best of the past while simultaneously exploring a modern future tied to our requirements for function, rather than being a slave to nostalgia or fashion.

The process of design is always developing; the variations are endless, the solutions infinite. No designer can ever ultimately conclude his investigations. That's why the door is wide open for contemporary designers to continue the exploration of furniture making. And why, if we can't afford Modernist classics for our tiny, overpriced London apartment, we can look at the work of young designers, trust our instincts and make some personal choices that don't have the endorsement of time.

This takes us back to the importance of function – a timeless quality and an informed way to judge contemporary design. Don't fall into the glossy magazine trap of pursuing 'style' or you'll soon find your home misses out on functionality, a daily requirement for leading a comfortable human life. The best young designers are exploring function beyond form. In the words of Jens Risom, 'Furniture is not sculpture, nor is a particular design created only for visual appearance. Furniture clearly satisfies all requirements: it should be used, enjoyed and respected.'

JONATHAN STEPHENSON IS A TYPOGRAPHICAL DESIGNER AND OWNER OF ROCKET GALLERY *rocketgallery.com*

THE
LONDON
DESIGN
FESTIVAL

Soho & Fitzrovia

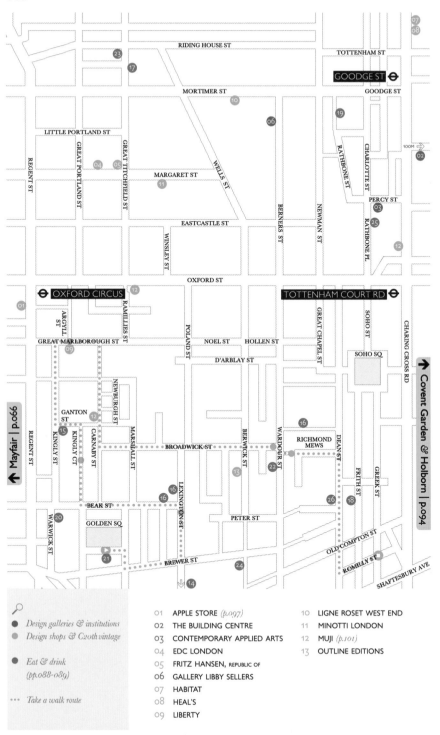

RIDING HOUSE ST
TOTTENHAM ST
MORTIMER ST
GOODGE ST
GOODGE ST
LITTLE PORTLAND ST
MARGARET ST
PERCY ST
EASTCASTLE ST
REGENT ST
GREAT PORTLAND ST
GREAT TITCHFIELD ST
WINSLEY ST
WELLS ST
BERNERS ST
NEWMAN ST
RATHBONE ST
CHARLOTTE ST
RATHBONE PL
OXFORD ST
OXFORD CIRCUS
TOTTENHAM COURT RD
Covent Garden & Holborn | p.094
ARGYLL ST
RAMILLIES ST
POLAND ST
NOEL ST
HOLLEN ST
GREAT CHAPEL ST
SOHO ST
CHARING CROSS RD
GREAT MARLBOROUGH ST
D'ARBLAY ST
SOHO SQ
Mayfair | p.066
NEWBURGH ST
GANTON ST
MARSHALL ST
BROADWICK ST
BERWICK ST
WARDOUR ST
RICHMOND MEWS
DEAN ST
FRITH ST
GREEK ST
KINGLY ST
KINGLY CT
CARNABY ST
LEXINGTON ST
PETER ST
REGENT ST
BEAK ST
WARWICK ST
GOLDEN SQ
OLD COMPTON ST
BREWER ST
ROMILLY ST
SHAFTESBURY AVE
100M

Design galleries & institutions

Design shops & C20th vintage

Eat & drink
(pp.088-089)

••• Take a walk route

01 APPLE STORE *(p.097)*
02 THE BUILDING CENTRE
03 CONTEMPORARY APPLIED ARTS
04 EDC LONDON
05 FRITZ HANSEN, REPUBLIC OF
06 GALLERY LIBBY SELLERS
07 HABITAT
08 HEAL'S
09 LIBERTY

10 LIGNE ROSET WEST END
11 MINOTTI LONDON
12 MUJI *(p.101)*
13 OUTLINE EDITIONS

Soho & Fitzrovia

*Bradley Quinn**

I like to start the day near my home at Nordic Bakery, a place where I can unpack my laptop and catch up on email while eating breakfast in the slick Finnish interior. The tableware and furniture here are classics from designers such as Kaj Franck, Alvar Aalto and Ilmari Tapiovaara. From there it's a short walk to Skk Lighting on Lexington Street, where lighting designer Shiu-Kay Kan sells his own work and funky lighting from other designers. A few blocks to the west, tucked away in a courtyard off Carnaby Street, is Kingly Court, housing more than 30 boutiques in a three-storey open-air complex.

Luxury department store Liberty – Soho's only one-stop shop for fabric, lighting and home accessories – is a couple of hundred metres to the north. From there I usually head east along Broadwick Street, popping into Broadwick Silks to see what's new in textile design; it even has its own production facility, where it can fashion bespoke fabrics for a wide range of design applications. On the other side of the street, Agent Provocateur's window displays always stop me in my tracks. The fantastic fetish fashion is not for the faint of heart, and the oddly angled sofas and chaises in the window reveal new ways of making your partner comfortable at home.

Crossing Wardour Street, I enter The Soho Hotel from the back entrance, hidden behind The Ship pub. The hotel was conceived as a design destination, combining avant-garde design with quirky vintage finds and cutting-edge contemporary art. The cocktail selection at the hotel bar is served up in true style, making it a great place for an afternoon drink or a sundowner. Leaving the hotel from the main entrance, I head south on Dean Street and turn left into Romilly Street, where the revamped Kettners boasts one of the coolest bar interiors in the area. Designed by Ilse Crawford and kitted out with pieces from top European designers, its Apartment Bar is a great place to end a long day.

*Design author and journalist

THE BUILDING CENTRE

📍 STORE STREET WC1E 7BT
📞 020 7692 4000
🔗 BUILDINGCENTRE.CO.UK
🕐 MON-FRI 9.30-6, SAT 10-5
🚇 GOODGE STREET

CONTEMPORARY APPLIED ARTS

📍 2 PERCY STREET W1T 1DD
📞 020 7436 2344
🔗 CAA.ORG.UK
🕐 MON-SAT 10-6
🚇 TOTTENHAM COURT ROAD

With a title like London Design Guide, it's perhaps obvious that we would take an interest in the built environment of this great city. The enormity of London makes it a full-time job to keep up with developments across the metropolitan sprawl. One place where one can stay abreast of such progressions (or monstrosities, as the case may be) is The Building Centre, established in 1931 as an independent forum for providing information to the construction industry.

It is in this building that the organisation New London Architecture is based. NLA debates issues facing architecture, planning, development and construction in the capital. They stage a programme of exhibitions, conferences and lectures on the Centre's ground floor, a public space that welcomes anyone willing to learn about the major developments across all 33 boroughs. Changes are plotted onto a giant scale model of central London that dominates the foyer. It's a superb overview I could spend hours studying.

Beyond the exhibition space is a bookshop full of titles on architecture, sustainability, construction, contracts and pricing – which may come in handy if you're considering home improvements or a self-build. Visit the Information Centre for further advice or browse the permanent trade show, where you can learn about some of the latest innovations in building materials.

Founded after the Second World War as the Crafts Council of Great Britain, this organisation went through various guises before renaming itself Contemporary Applied Arts. Its remit is to champion and promote British craftsmen and women, which it has succeeded in doing since 1995 here at its West End gallery. This is London's largest applied-arts gallery, representing more than 300 ceramicists, glass blowers, jewellery designers, metalworkers, textile designers and woodworkers.

Having work represented in a central London location is ideal for members, as it widens the audience for local crafts. There's a lot to be said for the power of association, with each practitioner sharing a democratic exhibition platform to mutual benefit. As a visitor, you can happily browse the rich pickings knowing some of the finest new craftwork often debuts here.

Of course CAA celebrates the expression of human imagination and the skill invested in it, so it's natural that visitors react differently to each piece. You'll feel differently about an unaffordable, collectible piece of art than you will about a practical, affordable homeware or design. And that's a good thing.

CAA's lower level houses member works accompanied by a selection of topical books and magazines. The bright space upstairs plays host to a changing programme of solo, mixed and themed exhibitions, often curated externally.

EDC LONDON

- 20 MARGARET STREET W1W 8RS
- 020 7631 1090
- EDCLONDON.COM
- MON-SAT 10-6
- OXFORD CIRCUS

FRITZ HANSEN, REPUBLIC OF

- 13 MARGARET STREET W1W 8RN
- 0844 800 8934
- FRITZHANSEN.COM
- MON-SAT 10-6.30, SUN 11-5
- OXFORD CIRCUS

European Design Centre has been based on Margaret Street for several years, selling high-quality contemporary and classic pieces from – you guessed it – a wide variety of European brands. Up the road, the business also runs a mono-brand showroom for high-end Italian manufacturer Minotti (p.087).

In 2010 EDC took a directional plunge into retail with the opening of this 200-square-metre showroom. Having worked with most of the continent's leading furniture brands for many years, they now aim to deliver an environment that mixes and matches complementary designs from these producers, with an eye to putting 'the fun back into furniture.'

Agreed, the furniture industry can take itself ever so seriously, often pushing a polished, slick aesthetic to people who would prefer a more relaxed environment to tie in with their lifestyle. In fairness to EDC, the showroom has made an effort to create comfortable, personal room sets dressed with softening touches like flowers and 'lifestyle accessories' (their words, not mine). And the space is revamped quarterly to inject new energy into the displays.

EDC deals with more brands than I care to mention, so it's well worth chatting to staff if you're hunting for something special. The effort taken here is valiant, but without significant footfall EDC needs to strive for a distinctive, inimitable edge to get the punters in the door.

When it comes to the world's leading furniture brands, Danish manufacturer Fritz Hansen would have to be near the top of the list. Established in 1872 in Copenhagen by its namesake, a cabinetmaker, the business quickly won favour within the country's prestigious interiors industry. In the 1930s, the company invested its knowhow in steam-bending beech, which soon became their speciality and gave rise to the *Ant* chair in 1934, followed in 1958 by the instant classic *Series 7* chair, both by Arne Jacobsen. The business has enjoyed considerable growth since the midcentury, and continues to produce many of the 20th century's most iconic furniture designs.

Surprisingly, Fritz Hansen has never had a dedicated London retail space. In September 2011, however, the brand joined forces with their strongest champion, the retailer Skandium (pp 028 & 058), to open a store that combines the Fritz Hansen product with other, complementary Scandinavian lighting and accessories. This was an informed decision, seeing as mono-brand stores can be rather dull. Along with classic items from iittala, Georg Jensen and Louis Poulsen, Skandium's owners have introduced a selection of vintage Scandinavian ceramics and glass with a bias towards Danish collectibles.

On going to press, the Fitzrovia shop was still under construction, so I can only speculate on the customer experience. However, the reputations of both Fritz Hansen and Skandium precede them, and I expect this new launch will be a significant addition to London's design scene.

06 GALLERY LIBBY SELLERS
🚩 41-42 BERNERS STREET W1T 3NB
📞 07774 113 813
↖ LIBBYSELLERS.COM
🕐 TUE-SAT 11-6
⊖ GOODGE STREET

07 HABITAT
🚩 196-199 TOTTENHAM COURT ROAD W1T 7PJ
📞 0844 499 1122
↖ HABITAT.CO.UK
🕐 MON-WED & FRI 10-7, THU 10-8, SA 9.30-7, SU 12-6
⊖ GOODGE STREET

In 2007 this former Design Museum curator launched herself onto the burgeoning design-gallery scene. Sellers's strategy was to 'pop up' in temporary locations across Europe, creating a platform for conceptual and progressive designs by the continent's most engaging young designers. Such talents have included the likes of Fabien Cappello, Stuart Haygarth, Simon Heijdens, Julia Lohmann and Peter Marigold, each of whom infuses strong conceptual ideas into unique or limited-edition designs.

During the gallery's nomadic years, Sellers was able to gauge the market and assess the best path for growth, which would ensure a strong direction when her permanent gallery did eventually open in Fitzrovia in September 2011. The 170-square-metre gallery benefits from an alluring front window, through which passers-by can admire the show – exhibitions change several times a year and range from single-designer shows to group and themed exhibitions.

The space is white-walled with high ceilings, a simple backdrop against which each piece can shine. There's also a 'jewel box' space: a small, separate room flooded with natural light from a pitched-glass roof. Here, Sellers supplements her own agenda with a changing programme of temporary installations.

The high-end market for collectible design demands a fine balancing act between idea, story, skill, material, craft and presentation. As a former curator, Sellers acutely considers these points. Her talents for assessing such merits will quickly establish Gallery Libby Sellers as an integral part of London's design and gallery scene.

In 1964 Terence Conran was a bold design entrepreneur eager to move Britain's interior options away from dark and chintzy and towards a brighter, simpler, more affordable modern aesthetic. His founding of Habitat back then represented a seismic shift in our understanding and appreciation of contemporary design. A new generational style was born – one that we perhaps take for granted today, what with the myriad imitation stores flogging the 'designer' dream.

With such competition stealing away market share, Habitat has certainly had to adapt over the years. It operates in a tricky realm – offering neither the cheapest nor the most exclusive items. So how does Habitat succeed commercially in the middle ground while still maintaining quality and making a difference? Well, with difficulty it turns out. Recently we sadly witnessed the closure of all Habitat's UK stores, apart from its e-commerce platform and three prime spots in London. In 2012 Habitat's new owner, Home Retail Group, plans to launch Habitat 'shop in shop' concessions within its Homebase stores.

For many, Habitat's near demise in the UK signifies the end of an era. As we went to press, Home Retail Group was promising to invest in the London stores, recognising that the remaining locations need to improve rather than slowly decline into middle-market mediocrity. For the in-house design team, now's the time to carve out a strong point of view to lure in new customers and keep existing ones coming back. That'll carry the brand into a progressive moment in its history.

Habitat's other London stores are located in King's Road and Finchley Road.

08 HEAL'S
- 196 TOTTENHAM COURT ROAD W1T 7LQ
- 020 7636 1666
- HEALS.CO.UK
- M-W 10-6, TH 10-8, FR 10-6.30, SA 9.30-6.30, SU 12-6
- GOODGE STREET

09 LIBERTY
- GREAT MARLBOROUGH STREET W1B 5AH
- 020 7734 1234
- LIBERTY.CO.UK
- MON-SAT 10-9, SUN 12-6
- OXFORD CIRCUS

Heal's turned 200 last year. Once a mere bed maker started by John Harris Heal, the business evolved into a leading homewares retailer under the eye of Sir Ambrose Heal, who headed it from 1913 through 1959. It was Heal's philosophy that furniture should be simply designed and well made, a platform for beautiful materials. It didn't take long for the Heal's Building to become synonymous with elegant, modern living.

Recently the street has filled up with bog-standard competition. It pains me to write this, but on my last visit to Heal's I couldn't help feeling that the scourge of cheap imports had plagued this remaining bastion of quality. Browsing the voluminous ground floor (dedicated to everything for the home except furniture), I was stunned by contradictory product displays that constantly switched from good-quality brands to cheap, disposable imports. The sight of a pink-flocked chandelier made me scurry to the first floor furniture department.

The contrast couldn't be more acute. Calm and ordered, this floor could be a different store entirely. Some great designs hold true here, from talents like Matthew Hilton, Benjamin Hubert, Lee Broom and Kay + Stemmer. But there's also plenty of ubiquitous blandness. It strikes me that Heal's may have over-analysed its market, tried to appeal to everyone and ended up wowing too few.

Before entering this British institution it's worth taking a moment to admire the majesty of the architecture: a 1924 purpose-built Tudor revival Arts and Crafts gem with a regal street presence. Arthur Lasenby Liberty was the gentleman behind the business, which he established in 1875 to sell ornaments, fabrics and miscellany from Japan and the Far East. Over the years, the retailer has become famous for welcoming designs contemporary and traditional into its grand environment, and for supporting new and established talents throughout the store.

Such intricately crafted interiors are a rare sight today. The Liberty building is punctuated by three light wells and each floor is panelled in wood with lookouts over the voids. Both limited and blessed by such ornate surroundings, Liberty has nonetheless managed to remain modern and relevant in these competitive times. It offers avant-garde fashion, accessories, beauty products and home furnishings to a discerning audience.

The furniture and lighting department spans the top storey and prides itself on not offering the identikit choices seen in other stores. Indeed, the mix is downright unusual, with contemporary accents alongside Arts and Crafts and vintage pieces with rich patina. Frustratingly, Liberty's layout doesn't do this section many favours. Some items seem squashed by the limited floor space. On a recent visit, Liberty seemed to have over-embraced the trend for all things nostalgic and British – but with their heritage, perhaps they're the only ones who can pull it off.

10 LIGNE ROSET WEST END
📍 23-25 MORTIMER STREET W1T 3JE
📞 020 7323 1248
🔗 LIGNE-ROSET-WESTEND.CO.UK
🕐 MON-SAT 10-6, THU 10-8, SUN 12-5
⊖ GOODGE STREET

French brand Ligne Roset began in 1860 when Antoine Roset began manufacturing walking sticks and umbrellas. A century and a half later, contemporary furniture, lighting and home accessories is what sustains this family-run business, which now boasts more than 850 stockists worldwide. This is one such stockist, located in Fitzrovia and run by the friendly and helpful Robert Hasty and his team.

The sizable showroom has a strong street presence thanks to its enormous floor-to-ceiling glass frontage, with light flooding the colourful window displays and the space within. Spread over two floors, the clean-lined showroom is a suitably fresh, modern backdrop against which Ligne Roset's extensive catalogue can shine. Even a space of this size can only ever show a smattering of available items, so it's worth having a chat with the staff, who can steer you in the right direction should you be looking for something specific.

And let me tell you, they cover all bases: sofas, beds, armchairs, tables, storage, home entertainment, tableware, lighting, textiles, rugs, curtains, accessories… It's impressive stuff and thrills many homeowners, who can choose to kit out their entire home here. Stylistically, though, I struggle to sum up the collections. They range from serious, slick and hard-edged to more soft, colourful and characterful.

In the 10 years I've been monitoring the brand, Ligne Roset has evolved from rather bourgeois to a European leader in contemporary. After interviewing the suave and sophisticated Michel Roset I got a good sense of the passion

that he and his brother, Pierre, have injected into the fourth-generation business. If they continue adding current talents – like Inga Sempé, the Bouroullec brothers, Noé Duchaufour-Lawrance and Philippe Nigro – to the existing roll call of French designers, I see no reason why the company's trajectory won't continue.

11 MINOTTI LONDON
- 77 MARGARET STREET W1W 8SY
- 020 7323 3233
- MINOTTILONDON.COM
- MON-FRI 9-6, SAT 10-5
- OXFORD CIRCUS

13 OUTLINE EDITIONS
- 94 BERWICK STREET W1F 0QF
- 020 8451 3400
- OUTLINE-EDITIONS.CO.UK
- TUE-SAT 12-6.30
- PICCADILLY CIRCUS

Minotti is a thoroughbred Italian brand producing sleek, modern decor. The company began at the end of the Second World War as a small craft workshop in Italy and has grown significantly over the years under the careful direction of second-generation brothers Renato and Roberto Minotti. After successfully partnering in the UK for more than 15 years with the European Design Centre (p.083), the two companies decided to open this own-brand showroom in 2009.

Minotti is celebrated for its modern living and bedroom furniture and textiles, the latest of which are displayed here. High-flying clients buy into the Milanese 'classic meets modern' aesthetic, which the brothers describe as a 'perfect balance between tradition and modernity, luxury and comfort'. Design-wise, I can't say I find it particularly exciting, but I can appreciate the high-quality craftsmanship and production.

Monochrome is dominant in the raised-level showroom, sectioned off with mirrored and glossy walls. It takes itself seriously, and I find myself craving a bit of clutter when I visit – splashes of colour or a simple injection of humour. But I've come to accept that simply isn't the Italian way.

Anyone passionate about graphic prints should seek out this hidden treasure. Outline Editions is a boon to Soho, a one-time second-hand record store that was replaced by a pop-up shop that, in October 2010, was made a permanent fixture.

Outline Editions's mission is to showcase, commission and sell work by graphic artists at the forefront of fashion, music and pop culture – and it fulfils this purpose to the full. Visitors will be delighted to discover an exciting mix of illustrative and typographic limited-edition screen prints by both established and emerging designers. When we visited the space was hosting its first show – entitled *Clear Your Head* – featuring poster art and installations by Anthony Burrill. But if you're looking for something a bit more novel, the shop is filled with the work of more subversive artists, some in runs of 100 prints, others one-of-a-kind framed prints by the likes of Noma Bar. And it's all priced affordably.

The space itself is informal and relaxed. It elevates design to the standard of fine art, yet in an approachable, unintimidating way. The challenge is resisting taking a print home. The selection extends to the basement, which seems to be a work in progress. Nevertheless, the layout is well considered, with a box room dedicated to the work of Beyond the Valley. Staff are engaging and passionate about the artists they represent.

LDG

Eat & drink

Great for... bar dining

BOCCA DI LUPO
Rustic Italian reworked with modern flourishes. Dramatic lighting, antique mirrors, marble-topped bar. Trattoria vibe with extra atmosphere. Ice cream lovers head across the road to Gelupo.
12 ARCHER STREET W1D 7BB
020 7734 2223 | BOCCADILUPO.COM

Great for... charcuterie platters

DEHESA
Charcuterie and tapas bar. Delicious range of Spanish- and Italian-inspired sharing dishes. Beautiful decor, bay windows and reclaimed-oak parquet floor. Good wine list.
25 GANTON STREET W1F 9BP | 020 7494 4170 | DEHESA.CO.UK

Great for... coffee and cake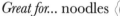

FERNANDEZ & WELLS
Deli, charcuterie and cheese room. Sister wine bar around the corner at 43 Lexington Street. Espresso bar a few streets away on St Anne's Court. Fresh, quality produce from reputable suppliers.
73 BEAK STREET W1F 9SR
020 7287 8124 | FERNANDEZANDWELLS.COM

Great for... caffeine hit

KAFFEINE
Stylish daytime haunt with loyal following. Chilled-out antipodean atmosphere. Tasty market-inspired food. Handy place to have in your Rolodex.
66 GREAT TITCHFIELD STREET W1W 7QJ
020 7580 6755 | KAFFEINE.CO.UK

Great for... noodles

KOYA
Small, stripped-back, canteen. Affordable Japanese serving noodles, soups, tempura and some rice dishes. Laidback addition to Soho scene.
49 FRITH STREET W1D 4SG
020 7434 4463 | KOYA.CO.UK

Great for... brunch

LANTANA
Small Australian café serving quality, no-nonsense food and proper coffee. Superb selection of super-salads. Ideal for breakfast, brunch or lunch. Eat in or takeaway. Gets busy, so off-peak times recommended.
13-14 CHARLOTTE PLACE W1T 1SN
020 7637 3347 | LANTANACAFE.CO.UK

Great for... sunny flavours

NOPI [PICTURED]
From the Ottolenghi founders, an all-day
brasserie offering sharing plates with
Middle-Eastern and Asian influences.
White interior with marble and brass
details. Some of the finest food in the area.
21-22 WARWICK STREET W1B 5NE
020 7494 9584 | NOPI-RESTAURANT.COM

Great for... Nordic delights

NORDIC BAKERY
Finnish café serving classic Scandi fare.
Clean, simple Nordic-inspired decor. Calm,
contemplative atmosphere. Great coffee
with savoury and sweet treats.
14A GOLDEN SQUARE W1F 9JG
020 3230 1077 | NORDICBAKERY.COM

Great for... pastries and cakes

PRINCI
Authentic Italian bakery-turned-canteen. Good
selection of fresh breads, pastries and pasta.
Designed by Claudio Silvestrin. Stone floors,
bronze fittings and one long, narrow communal
table. Buzzing from morning to night.
135 WARDOUR STREET W1F OUT
020 7478 8888 | PRINCI.CO.UK

Great for... casual dining

THE RIDING HOUSE CAFÉ
Brasserie from the owners of SE1
establishments the Garrison and Village
East. Destination venue in quiet location.
Mediterranean-inspired dishes served in
comfortable elegance.
43-51 GREAT TITCHFIELD STREET W1W 7PQ
020 7927 0840 | RIDINGHOUSECAFE.CO.UK

Great for... NY vibe

SPUNTINO
Small, relaxed restaurant with
distressed interior. Cracked-
glaze bricks, steel-topped bar,
old industrial fittings. American-
inspired dishes. No telephone,
no reservations. Gets busy.
61 RUPERT STREET W1D 7PW
SPUNTINO.CO.UK

Great for... informal meeting

TAPPED & PACKED
Popular café destination for those who take
coffee seriously. Knowledgeable baristas
advise on blends. Good selection of cakes and
sandwiches. Functionalist yet cosy interior.
Another location at 114 Tottenham Court Road.
26 RATHBONE PLACE W1T 1JD
020 7580 2163 | TAPPEDANDPACKED.CO.UK

Place to sleep?
DEAN STREET TOWNHOUSE   DEANSTREETTOWNHOUSE.COM

COLLECTNG

DESIGN

Collecting design, like all forms of collecting, is a bug that, once caught, is difficult to shake yet offers whole new worlds of knowledge and pleasure. Knowledge is key here. Without understanding why the object exists or what makes it covetable there is little value to the collection beside a monetary one. For most collectors, it is this hunt for knowledge that propels their collecting habits forward.

French philosopher Jean Baudrillard noted in his seminal 1968 text *The System of Objects* that among the various meanings of the French word *objet*, the Littré dictionary gives this: 'Anything which is the cause or subject of a passion; figuratively and par excellence – the loved object.' For Baudrillard, an avid collector, it is this appreciation of the 'loved object' that elevates something to the status of collectible.

As subjective as this might be, other catalysts that might tip an object from one to the other could be that the work was designed at a pivotal moment of a successful career; is an expression of an important socio-economic or political period; relates to a larger architectural or institutional power that imbues the design with a layer of 'scholarly' approval; is by a promising, influential or celebrated designer and/or is rare (due to limitations on its manufacture or that the existing examples do not get put back on the market); employs highly complex and atypical technologies, processes or materials that advance it beyond existing examples; has been validated by experts in an influential auction or exhibition; is simply appealing to the user.

From market stalls to galleries, designers' studios, fairs and auction houses, from obscure antiques to the debut creations of recently graduated, to one-off works from living legends, the opportunities to collect design are as varied as the types of design available to collect. Similarly varied is the nomenclature describing what we collect. 'Rare', 'unique', 'limited edition', 'prototype' and 'artist's proof' are among the

"While many collectors buy an object to serve its intended purpose, increasingly collectors are acquiring works with an agenda that goes beyond the needs of functionality or interior decoration."

many labels ascribed to collectible design, each one signifying something very different. Understanding these nuances of provenance, type and definition and the implications each one brings to a design collection is paramount.

Just as a museum curator follows an acquisition policy and assesses the value of a work before committing to it, so too do many collectors. It is a consideration of output, value and the contribution this designer or object has made to the contemporary culture – and what that could add to a collection. While many collectors buy an object to serve its intended purpose, increasingly collectors are acquiring works with an agenda that goes beyond the needs of functionality or interior decoration. Not only does this reflect an appreciation of design's dual role as both functional item and a vessel for expressivity (previously seen as the preserve of art), it is also symptomatic of the changes coming from within the industry: the growing tendency for design to be an observation on its own production, or its own environment. These are the critical and conceptual designs that are captivating an audience that wants more from their objects than high street goods can offer. Concomitantly there's been a shift away from the finite secondary (or second-hand) market towards a primary market, attracting newfound attention from designers, collectors and the industry alike.

Design infiltrates every aspect of our lives: from alarm clocks to tea kettles to the advanced technologies and infrastructures that facilitate both work and play. Can we talk of collecting design when, really, we all consume it on a daily basis in all manner of guises? Yet a mindful accumulation of designed objects that have been chosen to tell a story – of the makers, of the production or of its owner – does qualify as a collection. A curated collection of objects is larger than the sum of its parts and creates an environment or narrative that speaks both to us and of us.

LIBBY SELLERS IS THE OWNER OF GALLERY LIBBY SELLERS
libbysellers.com

de watchstore
zeen

Watches by boutique brands and named designers

www.dezeenwatchstore.com

Covent Garden
& Holborn

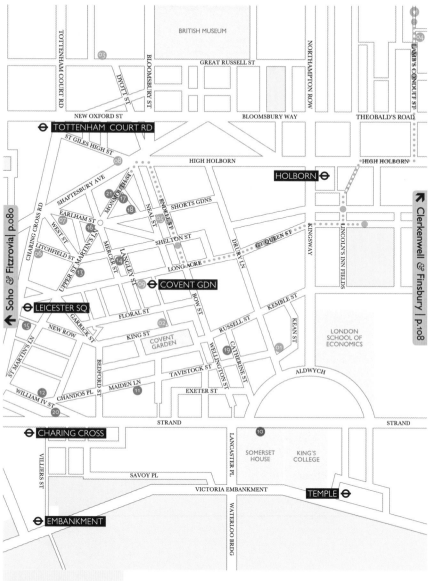

- Design galleries & institutions
- Design shops & C20th vintage
- Design bookshops

- Eat & drink
  (pp.102-103)

··· Take a walk route

01 ARAM
02 APPLE STORE
03 ARTEMIDE
04 DARKROOM
05 DO
06 KOENIG BOOKS
07 MAGMA
08 MOLTENI&C DADA
09 MUJI
10 SOMERSET HOUSE

Covent Garden
& Holborn

TAKE A WALK WITH

*Kit Kemp**

The characterful Lamb's Conduit Street, a haven for independent retailers, is a good place to start. Have a peek at Persephone Books at No 59, a charming shop specialising in reprinting forgotten 20th-century literature. At The French House you can pick up timeless crafts for the home. There's also family-run Schuller Opticians for brightly coloured frames. If you're looking for a bespoke suit, tailors Connock & Lockie are a little further down. Or simply order some food and watch the world go by on the terrace at Cigala, a Spanish tapas bar.

Head south along Lamb's Conduit Street, cross Theobald's Road and continue until you reach High Holborn. Cross over, turn right, all the while keeping an eye out for a small passageway on the left. Meander past a handful of shops until you reach Fleet River Bakery, a worthy pit stop. Continue into leafy Lincoln's Inn Fields. On the north side of the square stands the impressive Sir John Soane's Museum, formerly the studio of the neoclassical architect. It now houses his art, antiquities, drawings and models – and stages a schedule of popular temporary exhibitions.

Exit Lincoln's Inn Fields at Remnant Street, cross the Kingsway and jig over to Great Queen Street, which will take you into Covent Garden. You'll spot the striking Freemasons' Hall on the left and opposite is Bloomsbury Flowers, famous for its beautiful flower arrangements. Enjoy window-shopping a few doors up at the famous Stephen Jones Millinery – or ring the doorbell for a closer inspection of some fantastic hats.

At the corner, the road will turn into Long Acre. Continue along to Bow Street, and glance down for a view of the magnificent Royal Opera House. Then turn right into Endell Street, a mini-Mecca for vintage clothing, home to Rokit and Blackout II, both of whom carry exceptional pieces from decades past. To find Pop Boutique, one of my favourites, you'll need to bear left at the end of the street until you reach the start of Monmouth Street where it can be found at No 6. After hunting through the heaving racks, retreat to Brasserie Max in the Covent Garden Hotel for a cup of tea, cocktail or pre-theatre supper.

*Co-owner and design director for Firmdale Hotels firmdalehotels.com

01 ARAM

110 DRURY LANE WC2B 5SG

020 7557 7557

ARAM.CO.UK

MON–SAT 10-6, THU 10-7

COVENT GARDEN

When Zeev Aram launched his business on Chelsea's King's Road in 1964, he bravely introduced a new vocabulary to the furniture market in the UK. His modern, some might have said clinical, creations by the likes of Castiglioni, Le Corbusier and Breuer were pioneers at the time. But eventually Aram's patience with British tastes paid off and the modern vernacular began to gain traction. Today the situation is very different as the understanding of such design is much more mature.

Nearly 50 years on, the Aram family business is firmly rooted in London's design-retail establishment. And it's a treat to have the 1,800-square-metre showroom so conveniently located in the centre of London. Contemporary and classic furniture prevails here; it's accompanied by lighting, rugs and choice accessories, spread over four floors in a converted fruit and vegetable warehouse at the edge of Covent Garden.

All the established manufacturers are represented in store; the sizable floor space is given over to the likes of Cassina, Fritz Hansen, USM, Knoll, Carl Hansen and Vitra and gives prime placement to the complete range of designs by late legend Eileen Gray (for which Aram holds the worldwide license). More than 20 different sofa designs were on display the last time I visited – from Bauhaus classics to the latest creations from Milan. Browsing such a selection is a calming experience in this huge space, and at no point do you feel pressured to make a hurried decision. This attitude applies to all purchases here, big or small, as Aram's staff are well aware such investments are a big deal for most of us.

While many of the tried and tested classics we all know and love feature here, Aram continues its tradition of experimentation on the top floor. Here the Aram Gallery (aramgallery. org) is dedicated to a new and emerging crop of talented designers. It's worth checking out the rotating schedule of exhibitions to get a sense of the exciting new concepts, prototypes and experiments that could go on to inform our design environment.

02 APPLE STORE
- 1-7 THE PIAZZA WC2E 8HA
- 020 7447 1400
- APPLE.COM
- MON-SAT 9-9, SUN 12-6
- COVENT GARDEN

03 ARTEMIDE
- 106 GREAT RUSSELL STREET WC1B 3NB
- 020 7291 3853
- ARTEMIDE.COM
- MON-SAT 9-5 (CLOSED FOR LUNCH 1-1.30)
- TOTTENHAM COURT ROAD

The world's largest Apple outlet is a shiny declaration of the stature and prowess of the booming US computer and electronics brand. A soaring space in a stunning Grade II-listed colonnade facing old Covent Garden market, Apple's newest London addition profits from the top location and throngs of visitors to the area.

On a recent weekday morning the place was teeming with customers from all demographics contentedly sampling Apple's hardware. Each product – be it desktop computer, laptop, iPhone, iPod or the darling of the moment, the covetable iPad – is assigned its own corner of the store. And all are readily available to interact with.

Got a question? Fear not: this location employs more assistants than I've ever encountered in an Apple Store. Got a problem? Head to the Genius Bar for tech support, or to one of the regular training workshops. Wherever you happen to be looking, you'll feel the energy coming from the young, bright, dynamic team; it's contagious, and you'll soon get lured in further. The customer experience at Apple has been fine-tuned, with plenty of floor space, clean displays, smiling staff, chat and commotion, speedy service and heaps of people engaged with the devices.

But at the heart of all that revelry are the products, designs that are so damn refined. Sleek, understated, efficient, intuitive and technically pioneering, Apple is streets ahead of any competition. Without a doubt, visionary design and foresight put them there.

Founded by Ernesto Gismondi in Italy in 1960, Artemide is now widely considered one of the leading retailers of high-end residential and professional lighting. The business has grown steadily in half a century and can now boast a strong global distribution network with own-brand showrooms in most world-class cities.

The London location is uncharacteristically un-Italian – neither large nor flashy. Consequently, visiting this tiny townhouse off Tottenham Court Road is refreshingly unintimidating. The black-painted exterior frames a dazzling selection of lights, all crowded together for a warm glow that draws in people from the street.

Despite its enormous catalogue of sophisticated lighting systems for the office, this showroom highlights smaller-scale, domestic bestsellers – such as the versatile and ever-evolving *Tolomeo* series, a mid-'80s classic by Michele De Lucchi and Giancarlo Fassina. Indeed, many of Artemide's early offerings still prevail, including Vico Magistretti's *Eclisse* table lamp (1967), Gio Ponti's *Fato* lamp (1969), and Richard Sapper's *Tizio* articulated lamp (1972).

While the company continues to invest in design and innovation, its attentions have turned slightly towards energy efficiency and LED sources. Some of their more recent designs were created by top names like Ross Lovegrove, Zaha Hadid, Karim Rashid and Ora Ito (with often self-conscious results). Yet for lamps you can actually live with, my money rests on the consistent appeal of Italian legend Michele de Lucchi.

04 DARKROOM
52 LAMB'S CONDUIT STREET WC1N 3LL
020 7831 7244
DARKROOMLONDON.COM
MON–FRI 11-7, SAT 11-6, SUN 12-5
HOLBORN / RUSSELL SQUARE

Darkroom is often referred to as a 'concept store'. I have a bit of a problem with this term, which is often used to describe shops that actually have a point of view. It's not conceptual; it's very real. Since Darkroom opened at the end of 2009, the 'shop' has gone from strength to strength selling unusual, handmade, one-off and diverse accessories for men, women and the home.

It is truly independent, with a mission to communicate a passion for new, undiscovered and, yes, independent designers from around the world. Owners Rhonda Drakeford and Lulu Roper-Calderbeck come from backgrounds in graphic design and fashion, respectively, and without much prior experience in retail decided to take the plunge on Lamb's Conduit Street, a street known for its independents.

Darkroom's black-painted exterior perfectly frames the carefully composed window display: items that bridge the divide between fashion and interiors. Step inside and you're immediately struck by the confident visual presentation, whereby black walls and modular Cubist plinths provide a graphic backdrop to an intriguing mix of functional yet sculptural pieces.

Bold architectural shapes and striking colour palettes are prevalent here, and items are grouped to create tension and dialogue, enriched by the conflicting combinations of materials, scale and form. Handbags sit alongside jewellery, which may share their aesthetic or material with a vase or lampshade. This curated context is undoubtedly what helps to sell the pieces here – pieces which, I might add, are priced well within the reach of most people's budgets, making them

ideal for gifts as well as for personal treats.

Refreshingly, the owners play no lip service to brands and labels. The products – some established names mixed in with lesser-known designers and Darkroom's own expanding collection – are left to speak for themselves. They simply sell what they love. And they have personal relationships with many of their suppliers, which means they can fulfil specific customer requests.

Chances are you'll encounter either one of the owners on a visit here, and they'll be prepared with a friendly welcome and thorough answers to your questions. If you're unable to visit in person, be sure to browse the online shop.

05 DO

📍 34 SHORTS GARDENS WC2H 9PX

📞 020 7836 4039

🔗 DO-SHOP.COM

🕐 MON–SAT 10-6.30, THU 10-8, SUN 12-6

🚇 COVENT GARDEN

06 KOENIG BOOKS

📍 80 CHARING CROSS ROAD WC2H 0BF

📞 020 7240 8190

🔗 KOENIGBOOKS.CO.UK

🕐 MON–SAT 10-8, SUN 2-6

🚇 LEICESTER SQUARE

Do originated in the heart of Soho in 2006 before relocating to the Seven Dials area of Covent Garden last year. From a modest corner shop it sells a range of contemporary accessories, tableware, kitchenware and stationery, with the odd piece of furniture and lighting.

The ground level, you'll find, is lined with shelving, on which most of the smaller items are displayed. These items vary, though you may spot playful home accessories from London-based brands black + blum and j-me; conceptual creations from Dutch company Droog; or ceramics from the ubiquitous Italian manufacturer Seletti. Furniture is reserved for the cosy basement, where a small selection of chairs and benches from French furniture cooperative Alki are lit with a range of lights from Danish designer Tom Rossau and leading Italian brand Diesel.

Do does its part for emerging designers with the DoMasters programme, through which it selects the most promising products from design graduate shows worldwide and sells them, returning most of the profit to the designer. Such talents include Custhom, with its patterned teapots and jugs, and Sena Gu, whose collection of folky ceramics would cheer up any tabletop.

I find it difficult to put my finger on what it is about Do that doesn't quite do it for me. There is a disparity between the product genres, styles and prices, giving the store a sort of randomness that I can't help feeling could be more directional and coherent.

Koenig Books operates from corner premises on busy Charing Cross Road, amid an array of specialist bookshops. Koenig's focus is art, art theory, architecture, design and photography, and many of the titles it carries are obscure and hard-to-find. Such an edited selection comes courtesy of Walther Koenig Books, Germany's most established and reputable bookshop of this genre.

The shop builds on the success of its first London outlet at the Serpentine Gallery (p.027) by offering a diverse range of books from independent to large, established publishers. Art tomes are often beautifully designed and certainly worth celebrating, which is why, here, the jackets and not the spines are displayed facing towards the customer – a technique that makes a striking statement against the stylish all-black interior. Your curiosity will be piqued and you'll find yourself picking up and perusing all sorts of titles, some of which will, inevitably, make their way with you to the till.

Such tomes – limited edition, printed on high spec – can get pricey. Knowing this, Koenig offers a large sale department in the basement.

Along with this and the Serpentine Gallery location, Koenig runs the gorgeous bookshop at the Whitechapel Gallery in Aldgate.

07 MAGMA

- 8 EARLHAM STREET WC2H 9RY
- 020 7240 8498
- MAGMABOOKS.COM
- MON–SAT 10-7, SUN 12-6
- LEICESTER SQUARE

08 MOLTENI&C DADA

- 199 SHAFTESBURY AVENUE WC2H 8JR
- 020 7631 2345
- MOLTENIDADA.CO.UK
- MON–WED & FRI 10-6, THU 10-8, SAT 10-5
- TOTTENHAM COURT ROAD

If there's one place niche independent retail is showing its colours, it's at Magma. All credit to Marc Valli and Montse Ortuno, who spotted a gap in the market for books and magazines about illustration, graphics, typography, photography, architecture and design. In the face of growing online competition, they nonetheless opened this tiny Covent Garden store in 2000, hoping to inject something new beyond practiced retail conventions. They targeted 'creative types' with a penchant for tomes with beautiful typography, imaginative content, lavish photography and alluring cover art. With very little space to play with, they made full use of the walls, building floor-to-ceiling shelving on which most of their titles are displayed, covers facing out. After they opened, their impact was instant: punters lapped up their directional uptake of printed matter.

As soon as you walk in you feel the visual impact, too. Your attention grabbed, you'll start playing against type, reaching for cultish magazines and chunky coffee table titles. You may even snap up a print, T-shirt or tote.

A few doors down is Magma's multipurpose accessories shop (16 Earlham Street) with its range of graphic stationery, cultish games, toys, gifts and eco-design. If you happen to be in Clerkenwell, check out Magma's marginally larger sister store on Clerkenwell Road (p.112).

Heading along Shaftesbury Avenue from Piccadilly Circus, you'll eventually be greeted by the striking façade of Molteni&C Dada, with its immense glass windows that offer an excellent view into the flagship's interior. The established Italian furniture producer opened this 400-square-metre showroom in 2008, finally bringing its slick domestic designs to the attention of greater London. Inside, you're immediately met with a friendly welcome and an offer of help.

The furniture carried here is mostly designed by reputed international names such as Patricia Urquiola, Jean Nouvel, Arik Levy, Hannes Wettstein, Rodolfo Dordoni, Ferruccio Laviani and London's very own Foster + Partners. On the whole, the collection possesses a quiet elegance that's come to characterise a lot of high-end Italian design today. It'll appeal to those of you who appreciate quality without feeling the need to make a grand statement.

Browsing the space you quickly get a feel for the preferred palette of materials and colours, with pale and dark wood tones, tactile leathers and soft upholstery taking precedence with glossy, lacquered finishes, shiny aluminium and glass. You can't help but touch things, as a lot of the subtle details are concealed inside and behind wardrobes, shelving systems, tables, chairs, sofas and beds. If you're easily impressed by the gentle whooshes of sliding doors and the softened clunks of closing drawers, Molteni&C is likely to impress. Tactile kitchen displays from its sister brand, Dada, share the space.

09 MUJI
- 37-38 LONG ACRE WC2E 9JT
- 020 7379 0820
- MUJI.CO.UK
- MON-SAT 10-8, SUN 12-6
- COVENT GARDEN

10 SOMERSET HOUSE
- STRAND WC2R 1LA
- 020 7845 4600
- SOMERSETHOUSE.ORG.UK
- DAILY 10-6
- COVENT GARDEN/CHARING CROSS

Known and loved for its functional, reasonably priced and universally appealing products, Japanese super-retailer Muji has developed a global following and enjoyed huge success since it launched in 1980. Of course, that decade gave rise to the phenomenon of heavily branded goods. Muji's 'no brand' approach continues to buck that trend. After all, it's short for mujirushi ryohin, meaning 'no-label quality goods'.

Refreshingly, the value of a Muji product is in what it is, not who designed it. Furthermore, because Muji strives to introduce simple, basic, functional products for everyday living, the collections are removed from the vagaries of trends or marketing-driven 'premium-isms'. Remarkably, the chain manages to sell the same understated products year after year, and I believe it's this consistency that draws customers back. At Muji you know what you're in for.

From simple, unadorned furniture, storage and kitchenware to understated accessories, stationery and clothing, Muji embraces utilitarian materials and rational production processes, avoiding decorative flourishes and unnecessary packaging. It operates in an environment of white, grey and beige and favours materials such as opaque polypropylene, blond wood, brushed aluminium and stainless steel. Whatever you favour, it will certainly be reasonably priced.

There are ten Muji locations in London and their interior design adheres to the aforementioned Muji principles, unchanged for over three decades. Ironically, after more than 20 years in London the no-brand business has grown into one of the city's most widely recognised brands.

Somerset House is a platform for visual and performing arts housed within an impressive neo-classical gem. Under the arched entrance by the Strand is the Courtauld Gallery, famous for its art collection spanning from the early Renaissance to the 20th century. Beyond the arch you discover an expansive courtyard peppered with dancing fountains and flanked by regal architecture. Throughout the year the outdoor space plays host to installations by artists like Ai Weiwei; open-air films; music concerts; Fashion Week catwalk shows; and an ice skating rink come winter.

Across the courtyard is the main entrance, leading to the River Terrace from which Italian painter Canaletto once captured the breathtaking views along the Thames. At this level a number of rooms are ideal for solo retrospectives of artists and designers. If you're hungry, Tom's Deli and Tom's Kitchen serve up British fare overlooking the river. Otherwise, browse the Rizzoli bookshop. On the lower level, the 750-square-metre Embankment Galleries stage an ever-changing mix of exhibitions. Here you can enjoy shows with contemporary cross-disciplinary content like graphics, fashion, design, art, photography and architecture. There's something for every taste, including free tours for discovering the beauty and the mystery behind this illustrious historic landmark.

LDG

Eat & drink

Great for... meatballs

DA POLPO

Casual osteria serving Italian/
American comfort food. Interior
from reclaimed materials: salvaged-
tin ceiling from New York, Dutch
school chairs, chemistry-lab benches
and church pews.
6 MAIDEN LANE WC2E 7NA
020 7836 8448 | DAPOLPO.CO.UK

Great for... classic French

LES DEUX SALONS

Grand Parisian brasserie with robust
French cooking. Unique, traditional interior
comprising dark-green leather banquettes,
globe lights and mosaic flooring.
40-42 WILLIAM IV STREET WC2N 4DD
020 7420 2050 | LESDEUXSALONS.CO.UK

Great for... Indian snacks

DISHOOM

Popular all-day café drawing on faded
elegance of Bombay's diminishing Irani cafés.
Tactile interior: bentwood chairs, tiled floor,
marble-topped tables. Vibrant atmosphere.
12 UPPER ST MARTIN'S LANE WC2H 9FB
020 7420 9320 | DISHOOM.COM

Great for... aged steak & burgers

HAWKSMOOR SEVEN DIALS

Revamped basement brewery on a side street.
Textured interior of reclaimed materials with
New York vibe. Steak-lover's heaven with perfectly
cooked, aged cuts.
11 LANGLEY STREET WC2H 9JG
020 7856 2154 | THEHAWKSMOOR.CO.UK

Great for... institutional appeal

J. SHEEKEY

Legendary oyster bar and spanking bivalve bistro.
Art Deco mini-palace. Smoky mirrors with orange
sconces, monochrome photos of faded actors,
Orient Express-style table lamps. Glamorous, chic
and charming enough to almost forget about the
great food. Exemplary service.
28-34 ST MARTIN'S COURT WC2N 4AL
020 7240 2565 | J-SHEEKEY.CO.UK

Great for... fusion flavours

KOPAPA [PICTURED]

All-day restaurant and café from chef Peter Gordon serving some of the best food in the area. Casual dining experience for every occasion with high-calibre flavours. A treasure in a tourist area.

32-34 MONMOUTH STREET WC2H 9HA
020 7240 6076 | KOPAPA.CO.UK

Great for... selection of coffees

MONMOUTH COFFEE COMPANY

Small, personal coffee house roasting and retailing coffee since 1978. Tiny seating area for sit-in customers. Range of pastries and cakes to complement the finest coffee. Popular for takeaway.

27 MONMOUTH STREET WC2H 9EU
020 7379 3516 | MONMOUTHCOFFEE.CO.UK

Great for... the best of British cheese

NEAL'S YARD DAIRY

London's foremost British farm cheese retailer with enviable reputation. Cheese-lovers paradise.

17 SHORTS GARDENS WC2H 9AT | 020 7240 5700 | NEALSYARDDAIRY.CO.UK

Great for... Iberico ham

THE OPERA TAVERN

Popular Spanish- and Italian-inspired tapas bar. Ground-floor charcoal grill for meaty treats. Formal dining room upstairs. Relatively undiscovered by tourists.

23 CATHERINE STREET WC2B 5JS
020 7836 3680 | OPERATAVERN.CO.UK

Great for... French wine list

TERROIRS

New take on the classic French artisan wine bar. Offers 'natural' wines made from relatively small quantities of handpicked grapes. Noisy, informal place with great charcuterie.

5 WILLIAM IV STREET WC2N 4DW
020 7036 0660 | TERROIRSWINEBAR.COM

Place to sleep?
COVENT GARDEN HOTEL FIRMDALE.COM

COMMUNICATING DESIGN

Anything can be promoted with the right approach. People aren't stupid, but they tend to lap it up – whether it's the Olympic Games or every hyped anniversary you can think of. For PR masterminds it's all about money and exposure. And it can be one hell of a game.

Warhol and Dali were maestros in the world of PR – albeit with tongue wedged firmly in cheek. Le Corbusier and Frank Lloyd Wright were tireless self-publicists. Today's 'design art' dealers don't appear to have needed any tuition from the likes of Malcolm McLaren or Simon Cowell. The biggest reason for promoting anything these days is the return on one's investment. While hip publicity can signal 'hype' (which can equal 'crap'), the soft sell is dead. A maelstrom of marketing missives lays waste across our magazines, newspapers and blogs.

More than 60 years ago the organisers of the 1951 Festival of Britain initiated a PR campaign to attract visitors from all over the world. Leaflets were produced in eight languages and four red double-decker buses were dispatched to the Continent. The branding of Britain was also the launch pad for public awareness of design.

Meanwhile, across the pond, the great industrial designer Raymond Loewy hired a PR consultant to get him on the cover of *Time*. Loewy's career was based on the sheer force of personality, and he was brilliant at presenting himself as glamour personified, posing on one of 'his' streamlined locomotives for the Pennyslvania Railroad and building a replica of his studio in the Metropolitan Museum of Art.

In the 1930s, the design, PR and advertising industries were busy persuading the public to consume its way out of the Depression. In today's economically challenged climate, it is not hard to see how design will again be called upon to persuade us to buy things we don't necessarily need.

We may consider our generation too sophisticated to succumb to hype, but we've

> "…a plethora of lifestyle publications are only too happy to create a faux glamour around designers. Hungry for the finished product and, preferably, a celebrity link, the approach is inevitably misleading…"

never been so deluged with stuff that's calculated to seduce us. Nobody does it better than Apple, which achieves what most companies can only dream of: an avalanche of media coverage and worldwide buzz – before it's announced a thing.

Understanding and appreciating good design was a key remit for the Design Museum, which I helped launch in 1989. At that time media interest in design was exploding and a wealth of design publications and commentators were born. This has since morphed into a plethora of lifestyle publications that are only too happy to create a faux glamour around designers. Hungry for the finished product and, preferably, a celebrity link, the approach is inevitably misleading, simplifying the whole design process. This is further perpetuated by DIY programmes, with their quick-fix, staple-gun interiors, and those Get the Look pages so widely detested by architects and designers.

As award-winning writer Naomi Klein points out, we now live in a branded world, and commodities – be it furniture, food or fashion – are increasingly known by their brands. In today's cluttered marketplace, brands must resonate more than ever with consumers. Thus designers, whether they like it or not, must team up with brands, which can help clinch commissions. Developers and manufacturers seek out high-profile designers and brands that will add currency to their projects.

In today's brand-savvy culture the message and the method are crucial to the survival of designers. A PR strategy will help a design studio formulate its future goals while establishing its profile. Defining its USP is also key.

Editorial coverage remains the Holy Grail, and as the media landscape becomes increasingly fragmented, positioning a company in the minds of journalists takes a particular set of skills – plus large doses of persistence. But PR aside, design is a personable business, and success is often down to face-to-face relationships and networking. That and good work. In the words of Knoll: good design is (still) good business.

YVONNE COURTNEY IS A DESIGN WRITER AND PR STRATEGY CONSULTANT *designtastic.net*

Bauhaus:
Art as Life

Opening May 2012

**barbican
artgallery**

CITY
LONDON

The City of London
Corporation is the
founder and
principal funder of
the Barbican Centre

Clerkenwell
& Finsbury

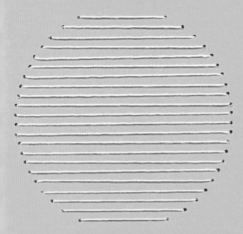

↑ Islington | p.124

KING'S CROSS ST PANCRAS

ANGEL

Shoreditch & Brick Lane | p.138

🔍

● Design galleries & institutions
● Design shops & C20th vintage
● Design bookshops

● Eat & drink
  (pp.118-119)

••• Take a walk route

01 BARBICAN ART GALLERY
02 KNOLL
03 KOLEKSIYON
04 MAGMA
05 MODUS
06 MOROSO/FLOS
07 POLTRONA FRAU GROUP
08 TIMOROUS BEASTIES
09 TWENTYTWENTYONE
10 VIADUCT

11 VITRA

Clerkenwell
& Finsbury

Patrick Clayton-Malone

I love London, and the Barbican Centre is a perfect place to begin your experience of it. The area around here is ideal for cyclists, so collect a bike at a Cycle Hire docking station if you fancy. Head down Long Lane, past the brilliant café Dose and the Rising Sun pub, then turn left into Cloth Fair, site of the church of St Bartholemew the Great and home to the late John Betjeman. Turn right and walk through the Victorian splendour of the Smithfield Market.

Follow Cowcross Street past Farringdon station, and walk straight up Greville Street to Hatton Garden, heart of London's jewellery trade since the Middle Ages. Continue up the hill, turning right into Leather Lane's weekday market. When you hit Clerkenwell Road you'll find Magma bookshop, which is great for a browse of design titles.

Make your way to Exmouth Market along Rosebery Avenue. You could spend the better part of an afternoon in Exmouth Market, visiting shops and galleries, and having an excellent brunch at Caravan or something small at Morito, one of the capital's best tapas restaurants.

Rest a while at Rosoman Place Park, then continue down Northhampton Road and zigzag down Clerkenwell Close, past Clerkenwell Kitchen, the charming Peabody Trust estate and the vintage Horseshoe pub, through Jerusalem Passage to St John's Square. The Modern Pantry is a hot lunch spot; together with the Zetter Townhouse Bar it's a welcome addition to this historic square.

Go east now, along Albermarle Way, over St John Street to Great Sutton Street and Modus, a stalwart of Clerkenwell's Design District. The strip of Old Street past Goswell Road is coming up in the world. Check out Look Mum No Hands!, a brilliant café, bike workshop and meeting place. Retrace your steps back to Goswell Road and turn left. Eventually you'll come upon the landmark Golden Lane Estate. This postwar housing project was designed by Chamberlin, Powell and Bon, architects of the Barbican, which is just a few metres south. Now you've come full circle… in more ways than one.

*Founder of Canteen and Very Good and Proper canteen.co.uk

01 BARBICAN ART GALLERY

SILK STREET EC2Y 8DS
020 7638 4141
BARBICAN.ORG.UK
MON, TUE, FRI, SAT, SUN 11-8, WED 11-6, THU 11-10
BARBICAN/MOORGATE

A looming presence east of Clerkenwell on the cusp of the City, the concrete Barbican landmark is an enormous complex and London's finest example of British brutalist architecture. It went up in the 1960s and '70s in an area that had been badly bombed during the Second World War and, ever since, its imposing architecture has sparked controversy and divided opinion (particularly after it gained Grade II-listed status). Whatever your thoughts about the aesthetics, there's no escaping the fact that Chamberlin, Powell & Bon's Modernist design remains a pioneer of urban master planning and architectural composition.

The Barbican Centre is housed within the complex, operating as one of the largest multi-arts centres in Europe with two theatres, three cinemas, a concert hall, exhibition halls, a public library, conference suites and several restaurants. With so much going on, the ground-level foyer is often heaving with visitors. So escape the hubbub and take a lift to the relative calm of the third floor, where the Barbican Art Gallery resides.

Throughout the year the gallery presents an international mix of art, architecture, design, fashion, photography and animation. Sometimes the focus will be on an individual, such as the recent shows featuring 20th-century architecture legend Le Corbusier; controversial Dutch fashion designers Victor & Rolf; design maestro Ron Arad; and the influential architecture practice OMA. Other shows take a broader look at movements and genres, such as *Future Beauty*, celebrating 30 years of Japanese fashion, or *The Surreal House*, which looked at the significance of surrealism for architecture. In 2012 look out for

Bauhaus: Art as Life, which will explore the impact of the most famous art school of the 20th century.

Adjacent to the exhibition space is the gallery shop, which changes its stock according to the exhibition content. Other retail ventures are dotted around the building, and the refurbished Barbican Foodhall on the ground floor is ideal for a casual meal. A big treat is the free Curve gallery and its programme of site-specific commissions by leading contemporary artists.

02 KNOLL

🚩 91 GOSWELL ROAD EC1V 7EX

📞 020 7236 6655

🔗 KNOLL-INT.COM

🕐 MON–FRI 9–5.30

🚇 BARBICAN

Knoll is one of the few truly legendary 20th-century furniture producers that maintain their strong global footing today. Founded by Hans Knoll in 1938, it began as a simple vision: that modern architects would need modern furniture to make their buildings livable. The fact that many of Knoll's Modernist designs remain steady sellers today is testament to the clear vision of Hans and his wife and business partner, Florence.

The duo nurtured and championed the most talented designers of their time, which resulted in the creation of some enduring classics, including Mies van der Rohe's *Barcelona* chair, Eero Saarinen's *Tulip* chair and table, Warren Platner's *Platner* tables and chairs and Harry Bertoia's *Diamond* chair. With such legends in the mix, the company has nevertheless gone on to embrace contemporary designs by the likes of Ross Lovegrove, Don Chadwick and Jehs + Laub. Such gems take pride of place in Knoll's smart London showroom, which houses the largest collection of KnollStudio designs in Europe.

Spread across two floors, the expansive showroom was designed by the eminent Italian architect and designer Piero Lissoni. The ground level is dedicated to items suitable for both home and office, while the first floor focuses more seriously on office systems.

Continuing in the spirit of the company's founders, Knoll is keen to support the exchange of ideas and occasionally hosts exhibitions and provocative debates that are well worth attending. Also good to note is the super-popular one-day sample sale in November.

03 KOLEKSIYON

📌 9 BREWHOUSE YARD EC1V 4JR
📞 020 3405 1885
🔗 KOLEKSIYON.CO.UK
🕐 MON–FRI 9–5.30
⊖ FARRINGDON

04 MAGMA

📌 117–119 CLERKENWELL ROAD EC1R 5BY
📞 020 7242 9503
🔗 MAGMABOOKS.COM
🕐 MON–SAT 10–7
⊖ FARRINGDON

It started in 1972 in Ankara as a humble iron workshop. But Koleksiyon has enjoyed considerable growth supplying items for contract and office interiors as well as the home. Its success is in its strong sales network across Turkey and in its impressive 86,000-square-metre production facility, which employs more than 500 staff. It was only a matter of time before the company would extend its reach to the UK. In May 2011 Koleksiyon opened an 800-square-metre showroom in the heart of Clerkenwell to showcase Koleksiyon products to architects, designers and end users.

It was as the latter that I hoped to experience this place. Clerkenwell is a hub for furniture trade showrooms, and so it would be interesting to see if Koleksiyon would hit the mark to an individual punter. Alas, after slowly completing a lap of the spacious showroom I remained unconvinced that the place – though professionally presented – was really geared for the likes of you and me.

Indeed the products on show were clearly aimed at professionals. And although there were displays of soft furnishings, task lighting and warm woods, none of it felt particularly inviting or even suitable for the home. I'm prepared to see past this – perhaps the style simply wasn't to my liking – but what was off-putting was that I managed to leave the place without being acknowledged by a single member of staff. Regardless of all else, this is a customer service faux pas I struggle to accept.

For culture lovers and hunters of the latest creative compendiums, Magma is a one-stop reference extravaganza that'll whip you into frenzy. Magma stocks a choice selection of current publications on design, architecture, art, photography, fashion and style, as well as a comprehensive collection of niche magazines from around the world. If you ever needed assurance that the printed page still carries a huge appeal, Magma proves it's alive and kicking.

The store, located on Clerkenwell's busiest thoroughfare, is a slightly larger yet younger sibling of the Covent Garden original (p.100). Paper is not the only thing on offer here; smaller design-related items like games, tote bags, T-shirts and prints also enter the mix, each with a considered graphic sensibility that appeals to Magma's regular design-hungry clientele.

The independently-owned business is a browser's paradise, with every publication displayed face-out to entice you to pick it up and explore, even if you weren't planning to. More often than not, I end up buying something I didn't come looking for, but I'm grateful for the curated selection of quality reads. Judging by the shop's popularity, it would seem I'm not alone.

05 MODUS

- 28-29 GREAT SUTTON STREET EC1V 0DS
- 020 7490 1358
- MODUSFURNITURE.CO.UK
- MON-FRI 10-6
- FARRINGDON

Modus is a British brand launched in 2000 by the entrepreneurial duo Jon Powell and Ed Richardson with all the ambition and vision needed to succeed in this competitive marketplace. Their determination, coupled with an expanding contemporary collection designed by leading British and international designers, has deservingly propelled Modus onto an international platform.

The London showroom is strategically situated in the heart of Clerkenwell, home of the capital's highest concentration of architects. Unlike many of the area's more formal office furniture showrooms, Modus boasts a product range that sits comfortably in both public and domestic settings. While most of Modus's business comes from contract orders, individual customers are welcome and shouldn't feel intimidated browsing the collections of seating, tables, storage and sofas.

The space, designed by the company's art director Michael Sodeau, embraces contrast with a combination of exposed brick, wood panelling, white plaster and architectural details accented in fluorescent orange. Due to space restrictions, only a small selection of designs is on display at any one time – normally the newer collections. The look, once overwhelmingly slick, more recently has begun to embrace a slightly softer, warmer sensibility. Favourites on my visit were the comfortable wooden *PLC* chair by PearsonLloyd; the graphic *Noughts and Crosses* stools by Michael Sodeau; and the *Gecko* table with lizard-like feet by Claesson Koivisto Rune.

⓪⑥ MOROSO/FLOS

🏠 7-15 ROSEBERY AVENUE EC1R 4SP
📞 020 3328 3560 / 020 3328 5140
✎ MOROSO.CO.UK / FLOS.COM
🕐 MON-FRI 9-5
⊖ FARRINGDON

⓪⑦ POLTRONA FRAU GROUP

🏠 150 ST JOHN STREET EC1V 4UD
📞 020 7014 5980
✎ POLTRONAFRAUGROUP.COM
🕐 MON-FRI 8.30-5.30
⊖ FARRINGDON

A few years ago, two leading Italian companies, furniture producer Moroso and lighting manufacturer Flos, came together to open an enormous London showroom to join the myriad others in Clerkenwell. It operates essentially for the trade, but members of the public who wish to view the products are nonetheless welcome to visit and experience the high-spec environment. Buzz for entry and ask for a look, and you'll be given full access to the ground floor and basement.

Moroso has a strong vision and its collections boast characterful details rarely seen in other Italian furniture brands. This is no doubt encouraged by the art direction of Patrizia Moroso. Her energy inspires the designers to express themselves to the fullest: talents such as Patricia Urquiola, Doshi Levien, Ron Arad, Tord Boontje and Edward van Vliet use colour, pattern and texture in refreshing amounts.

The bright white showroom hosts a diverse cross-section of their creations, which are complemented by lighting designs from Flos – classics by Achille and Pier Giacomo Castiglioni, Tobia Scarpa and Paolo Rizzatto, plus newer hits from Philippe Starck, Barber Osgerby and Jasper Morrison. The two brands are ideal partners, displayed to best effect clustered together in the mammoth, high-ceilinged basement.

Staff seem very busy behind their computer screens, but don't feel too intimidated to ask any questions you may have. Be aware, however: as they handle only trade orders here, all individual orders will be referred to a retail partner.

When this showroom opened in 2009 it signaled the arrival of the Italian design establishment in Clerkenwell. The Poltrona Frau Group is the holding company for a number of high-end furniture brands: Poltrona Frau (established in 1912); Cassina (1927); Cappellini (1946); and Gebrüder Thonet Vienna, Gufram and Nemo.

The six brands, along with furniture producer Alias, are united in this immense 650-square-metre showroom on St John Street. Transformed by Universal Design Studio, the bright, post-industrial space is spread over two floors and houses a variety of new, iconic furniture designs from each label. The monumental matt-black steel staircase that descends from the centre of the ground floor contrasts with the oak-slab stair treads; this helps draw your attention to the basement space and provides a stage-like display from which to highlight key pieces.

Even with this much room Poltrona Frau can only showcase a snippet of the group's offerings – each brand boasts a distinctive style and an enormous catalogue. If only each brand would share some information on their unique heritage. It's a wasted opportunity given their collective cultural calibre. Instead, the flagship seems to concentrate on contract sales. I can't help feeling that a rather businesslike formality takes precedence and slightly hinders what could be our active engagement with some stunning examples of Italy's finest contemporary design.

08   TIMOROUS BEASTIES
- 46 AMWELL STREET EC1R 1XS
- 020 7833 5010
- TIMOROUSBEASTIES.COM
- MON-THU 10-6, FRI 10-5, SAT 11-4
- ANGEL

09   TWENTYTWENTYONE SHOWROOM
- 18C RIVER STREET EC1R 1XN
- 020 7837 1900
- TWENTYTWENTYONE.COM
- MON-SAT 9.30-5.30
- ANGEL

Timorous Beasties represented a new wave in wallpaper and fabric when it arrived on the design scene in 1990. Glasgow artists Alistair McAuley and Paul Simmons eschew traditional florals and toiles in favour of a distinctive, some might say surreal and provocative style. In fact they've developed a knack for subverting traditional patterns and heritage illustrations with more sinister, contemporary imagery. Their fresh take has earned them plaudits, and their business has grown steadily.

The company's growing success gave them grounds to open a London showroom in 2007 among the independent traders of Amwell Street. The distinctive white frontage and pristine interior provides a calming backdrop to the sumptuous, colourful and playfully patterned designs. It's a small space, but its shrewd layout enables the team to display its entire collection of wallpapers and hand-printed and digitally printed fabrics. Head downstairs to the tiny basement for further displays of fabrics, wallpapers and rugs.

Take your time exploring your options here. Inspect the goods closely and you'll discover mischievousness in the patterns and colourways – designs vary from the subtle and subdued to the vivacious and iconoclastic. What comes across is the founders' playful imagination. They manage to inject a dose of waywardness into this traditional metier, without ever losing sight of the quality that distinguishes them from their more conservative competitors. Opening hours are sporadic, so call ahead before your visit.

Quiet courtyard spaces in central London are rare and should be cherished. This one, off a residential street, is home to design showroom twentytwentyone and is a welcoming haven of calm that I never tire of visiting. Unusually here, 'tranquility' and 'shopping' are two words that marry perfectly in the same sentence.

Benefiting from more space than the Upper Street location (p.131), this former dairy is home to a well-edited selection of contemporary furniture and lighting from the finest producers, as well as a few choice vintage items. Indeed, owners Simon Alderson and Tony Cunningham began their careers selling 20th-century originals until their interest in contemporary design took the front seat in the late '90s.

They've since developed a loyal following of customers in search of high-quality additions to their interiors and nurtured a knowledgeable, friendly and intelligent staff. A smile and offer of help greets you on arrival here, making you feel instantly welcome to browse the mix of 20th-century and future classics.

Whether contemporary or vintage, the array of chairs, sofas, tables, storage and lighting collectively adhere to Modernist ideals where honesty of materials and construction are paramount. Thankfully, the team sidesteps the starkness that can often reign in contemporary showrooms, meaning there is nothing uptight or pretentious in the presentation here. The warmly lit space is homely – ideal for contemplating the appealing blend of livable design from the comfort of a timeless sofa. Take your pick: they have some of the best choices in town.

10 **VIADUCT**

- 1-10 SUMMERS STREET EC1R 5BD
- 020 7278 8456
- VIADUCT.CO.UK
- MON-FRI 9.30-6, SAT 10.30-4
- FARRINGDON

Contemporary furniture and lighting showroom Viaduct established its presence in Clerkenwell long before the influx of furniture showrooms to the area. It converted a 1930s printhouse, just steps from Clerkenwell Road, into a calm, double-height showroom and has been attracting architects, interior designers and private clients ever since – for more than 20 years.

Viaduct serves as the UK agent for a handful of furniture manufacturers on show here: E15, Montis, Zeus, Maruni, Aiki, Pastoe and Bensen. Its other stock hails from some of the finest brands and designers in Europe. It can't possibly display everything from its partner suppliers, despite the size of its showroom. Instead it uses the space to showcase a snapshot of its offerings.

The long, voluminous ground-floor space greets you with set displays of sofas, tables, armchairs, storage and lighting, all perched confidently on the warm, textured-wood floor. At head height a row of chairs runs along the length of the space, acting as a sort of catwalk for some of the finest contemporary choices by the featured designers. The displays continue on the cosy mezzanine level, an excellent vantage point from which to survey the main floor. Behind a partition are the Viaduct offices.

The appeal here is clear: this is a single destination for the best in design-led furniture and lighting – coupled with well-informed and friendly service, by the way. A best-kept secret, the space is seldom swarmed with people; you'll be properly tended to here (and that's not a given; service is a basic premise that many competitors fall short of addressing). If I am going to spend

hundreds or thousands of pounds on high-end design, I'd like to do so knowing my requirements will be scrutinised and I'll be counselled accordingly. Describe what you're after and the knowledgeable staff will tap into the extensive product database and present the options.

On top of all this, it's worth pointing out that several times a year owner James Mair curates exhibitions in the space that explore a certain theme, material, genre or brand. These presentations tend to capture the design zeitgeist and are always representative of Viaduct's modus operandi: confident, composed and directional.

11 VITRA

- 30 CLERKENWELL ROAD EC1M 5PQ
- 020 7608 6200
- VITRA.COM
- MON–THU 9–5.30, FRI 9–5
- FARRINGDON

The design and architecture spheres have long held Vitra in the highest regard. The pioneering German manufacturer produces some of the finest examples of classic modern furniture designed by 20th-century masters such as Jean Prouvé, Charles and Ray Eames, Verner Panton and George Nelson and their contemporary counterparts. Their output has furnished interiors across the world, be they commercial spaces or the most discerning households.

It's been more than 50 years since the company began producing furniture for the office, public spaces and the home. And now it hopes to transcend the traditional home/work paradigm with a host of new developments – versatile products that work hard to accommodate our changing lifestyles. This is no mean feat, yet Vitra manages to hit the mark consistently with its new arrivals, pieces that combine genuine character with functional appeal.

Unlike many other successful manufacturers, Vitra launches only a few new products each year. Meanwhile, it invests properly in research and development and is unafraid to take risks in the process. The label has worked with some of the world's best designers – names like Antonio Citterio, Alberto Meda, Jasper Morrison, Barber Osgerby, Erwan & Ronan Bouroullec and Hella Jongerius – each of whom bring personality, ethics and wisdom to new matter. Consequently, each new launch is an innovation, an event and a success that feeds the Vitra reputation.

Vitra has built a strong global network of retailers, but it operates its own London showroom to display its *Home Collection* and office systems. The David Chipperfield-designed space in Clerkenwell is focused on trade commissions, though members of the public are also welcome to visit. You'll have to deal with a receptionist, but it's worth it for the experience. Be aware, however, that all private sales are directed to one of Vitra's retail dealers.

LDG

Eat & drink

Great for... brunch & coffee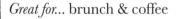

CARAVAN
Popular restaurant, bar and roastery run by
a friendly New Zealand team. Superb coffee,
hearty brunches, imaginative, Kiwi-inspired
tapas and unusual wines.
11-13 EXMOUTH MARKET EC1R 4QD
020 7833 8115 | CARAVANONEXMOUTH.CO.UK

Great for... quiet lunch

THE CLERKENWELL KITCHEN
Canteen-style café in a quiet enclave.
Ethical, sustainable fare incorporating
fresh ingredients from local producers.
Reasonably priced. Booking advisable.
27-31 CLERKENWELL CLOSE EC1R 0AT
020 7101 9959
THECLERKENWELLKITCHEN.CO.UK

Great for... hearty gastro dishes

THE EAGLE
Claims to be the first gastropub. Serves up original
dishes in generous portions. Great energy, often
busy. Open kitchen with North African influences.
Decent prices.
159 FARRINGDON ROAD EC1R 3AL | 020 7837 1353

Great for... simple British

HIX OYSTER & CHOP HOUSE
Elegant space in an old London sausage factory.
Wood floors, tiled walls, marble oyster bar, linen
tablecloths. Best of the season's oysters and
tender cuts of meat any time of day.
36-37 GREENHILL RENTS, COWCROSS STREET EC1M 6BN
020 7017 1930 | HIXOYSTERANDCHOPHOUSE.CO.UK

Great for... casual lunch

J&A CAFÉ
Modern British cafeteria hidden in a yard
off Clerkenwell Road. Wholesome, home-
spun dishes. Simple, textured, canteen-
like aesthetic with peaceful atmosphere.
4 SUTTON LANE EC1M 5PU
020 7490 2992 | JANDACAFE.COM

Great for... bicycle lovers

LOOK MUM NO HANDS!
Casual café/bar serving bike enthusiasts seasonal
food and great coffee. On a thoroughfare
busy with cyclists, complete with workshop for
punctures and general repairs.
49 OLD STREET EC1V 9HX
020 7253 1025 | LOOKMUMNOHANDS.COM

Great for... original flavours 18

THE MODERN PANTRY [PICTURED]

Exciting fusion menu with a touch of antipodean exotica. Light-filled corner location great for brunch. Fresh interior warmed by copper lighting by Piet Hein Eek. Enjoyable, relaxed and informal at all times of day.

47-48 ST JOHN'S SQUARE EC1V 4JJ

020 7553 9210 | THEMODERNPANTRY.CO.UK

Great for... Spanish bites 19

MORITO

New sister to fantastic Moro next door. Intimate, informal space with bright-orange Formica bar overlooking open kitchen. Delicious small plates complemented by choice sherries.

32 EXMOUTH MARKET EC1R 4QE

020 7278 7007

Great for... the perfect coffee 20

ST. ALI

Bustling café and roastery. Exposed-brick walls, wood floors, industrial furniture and fittings make for a relaxed vibe. Open evenings Thursday to Saturday.

27 CLERKENWELL ROAD EC1M 5RN

020 7253 5754 | STALI.CO.UK

Great for... no-nonsense cuisine 21

ST. JOHN

Wood floors, whitewashed walls and vaulted ceilings. Daily-changing menu. Comfortable atmosphere; gutsy snout-to-tail eating focused on meat from the local market.

26 ST JOHN STREET EC1M 4AY

020 3301 8069 | STJOHNRESTAURANT.COM

Great for... eccentric Britishness 22

THE ZETTER TOWNHOUSE

Recently opened sister venture to the Zetter Hotel. Maximalist English country-house look. Cosy cocktail lounge at the entrance nice for an evening drink.

49-50 ST JOHN'S SQUARE EC1V 4JJ | THEZETTERTOWNHOUSE.COM

COCKTAIL LOUNGE: 020 7324 4545

Place to sleep?
THE ZETTER TOWNHOUSE THEZETTERTOWNHOUSE.COM

GOOGLING DESIGN

The Internet. The World Wide Web. The Net. Whatever you call it, it's about connections, networks, interaction. The days of design in isolation are gone, and for every downside of that, there's an upside.

The designer now has the entire universe at his fingertips. He can research new production methods, search for inspiration and stay connected to a global community without ever setting foot outside the studio. Digitisation has removed the boundaries between designers and users. Ideas no longer stay hidden behind studio walls until they emerge as finished products – the consumer can now offer feedback at every stage. Meanwhile, open design platforms like OpenIDEO and Local Motors take that idea further, opening up the entire process – not just for feedback but for contribution.

'To become a place where good ideas gain momentum, OpenIDEO depends on participation – your inspirations, his comments, her concepts, our design process,' says a passage on www. openideo.com. 'It's these efforts, these big and small moments of sharing and collaboration, that make this platform a dynamic resource. It's a place where people design better together.'

But then public involvement in design has meant more than just feedback for some three decades now. The advent of desktop publishing and the widespread availability of the Internet turned everyone into a designer.

New designers no longer need the big producers and retailers; they can take their products to market themselves. With access to a global audience for online sales, and marketing made easier through social media, who needs a middleman?

Design discourse is no longer limited to a few trade titles, either. Social media doesn't just connect designers to audiences, it has democratised design criticism resulting in an explosion of varied content. But these connections take as well as give. The would-be imitator has the universe at his fingertips,

"Everyone is now a designer or critic. The market is flooded with poor-quality copycats, and too many blogs are limited to photos appropriated from other websites, presented without credit or analysis."

too. Big brands with low-cost labour can scout independent designers' websites for ideas to steal and undercut.

Globalisation provides not only a wider audience for British products, but also a wider range of products for British consumers. The proliferation of 'Inspired By' furniture creates consumers who cannot discriminate between originals and copies or simply don't care. There's a lot of talk about investing in quality in a recession, but the challenges facing the High Street suggest otherwise – it's used all too often as a testing ground before we seek cheaper prices online.

But while marketing and e-commerce connect designers and audiences, they also create distance. Products need to be touched and seen to be appreciated. It's difficult to differentiate quality from churned-out junk on a computer screen. And with all that eye candy, sometimes it's easier to buy nothing at all.

The conversations that arise over a face-to-face transaction add value, too. They give provenance to a product and user insight to the designer. The Internet might allow designers to market their products themselves, but those skills don't always come naturally. A designer's time is better spent designing. In fact, when asked during his Design Museum Twitter takeover 'How would you improve Twitter for designers?' Wim Crouwel said: 'Don't tweet anymore. It saves time for designing.'

Democratisation of design and design discourse is a mixed blessing. While it widens the talent net, it lowers the common denominator. Everyone is now a designer or critic. The market is flooded with poor-quality copycats, and too many blogs are limited to photos appropriated from other websites, presented without credit or analysis.

Like it or not, the Internet, Web 2.0 and whatever comes next are here to stay. The question is not: Do we like it? But: What will we do about it? The designers who flourish will be those who embrace the side of the coin that works for them and find ways to use the other side as a driving force for change.

KATIE TREGGIDEN IS THE AUTHOR OF DESIGN BLOG, CONFESSIONS OF A DESIGN GEEK *confessionsofadesigngeek.com*

Contemporary
Craft
Furniture

Another
Country

Islington

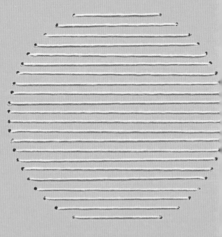

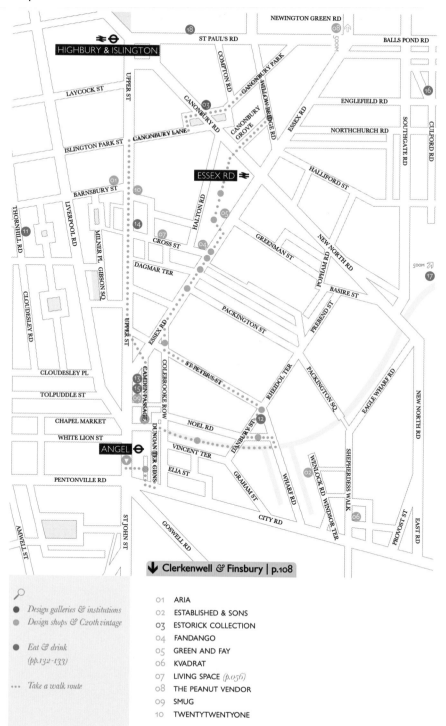

⬇ Clerkenwell & Finsbury | p.108

🔍

● *Design galleries & institutions*

● *Design shops & C20th vintage*

● *Eat & drink*
  (pp.132-133)

••• *Take a walk route*

01	ARIA
02	ESTABLISHED & SONS
03	ESTORICK COLLECTION
04	FANDANGO
05	GREEN AND FAY
06	KVADRAT
07	LIVING SPACE *(p.056)*
08	THE PEANUT VENDOR
09	SMUG
10	TWENTYTWENTYONE

Islington

*Hannah Martin**

From Angel tube, head left and immediately veer up a gentle slope to the left. Cut through the courtyard of the Angel Square building, taking a moment to read the memorial inscriptions to revolutionary Thomas Paine. Opposite the courtyard exit is the Candid Arts gallery and café, perfect for a pit stop. Pick up a bike from the Cycle Hire scheme here, if you wish.

Take a left onto City Road and again into Duncan Terrace Gardens. Enjoy the wild planting and search for a public artwork called Spontaneous City in the Tree of Heaven. Turn right out of the garden and head through the gate opposite, and you'll access the towpath of the Regents Canal, an escape from the city bustle. At the Wharf Road exit, turn left into Noel Road and pass the Island Queen pub, its interior reminiscent of an old gin palace. Then to residential Danbury Street, so typically Islington and home to the Duke of Cambridge, Britain's first certified organic pub.

Follow St Peter's Street up onto Colebrooke Row, taking you to the art-supplies source Cass Art. Turn right onto noisy Essex Road, a good source for antiques at Criterion Auctions and bric-a-brac at Past Caring. Straight ahead, at the bottom of Cross Street, you'll find Steve Hatt, one of London's finest fishmongers, and Get Stuffed, stuffed with taxidermy.

Further along Essex Road, after the South Library and just shy of the bus stop, turn left into Asteys Row Rock Garden and meander past the children's playground to access pretty Canonbury Garden. At Canonbury Road, zigzag left, then right onto Canonbury Grove, where you'll spot The Marquess Tavern, another fine Islington pub boasting an elegant dining room. Follow Willow Bridge Road into Canonbury Place, taking in the mysterious Masonic Research Centre on the left before continuing through Canonbury Square to Upper Street.

Turn left down this busy street, a rather mixed bag. Where it meets Essex Road, snake to your left into Camden Passage where you can enjoy the small antique and vintage market on Wednesdays and Saturdays. From here, you're close to where you first started.

*Owner of Hannah Martin Ltd hannahmartinlondon.com

01 ARIA

BARNSBURY HALL, BARNSBURY STREET N1 1PN

020 7704 6222

ARIASHOP.CO.UK

MON–SAT 10–6.30, SUN 12–5

HIGHBURY & ISLINGTON

For more than 20 years Aria has been a mainstay of upstart Islington, selling a comprehensive mix of contemporary homewares from well-known brands. Located just off busy Upper Street, the modern façade on this building deceptively conceals the voluminous structure of the original 1850s Barnsbury Hall. Inside are displays of newness – everything from furniture and lighting, tabletop and kitchen utensils to bathroom accessories, handbags and jewellery to contrast with the hall's stripped-back period features.

Aria has always embraced those more lighthearted European manufacturers: Italian giants like Kartell, Driade, Magis, Casamania and Kristalia are highlights here. Lighting follows in a similar vein, with select designs from Flos, Artemide, Foscarini adding a colourful glow to the cavernous shop. Making up the majority of stock are smaller goods exhibited in vitrines, which attract casual browsers from the neighbourhood. Then there's the annex with its sizable selection of tabletop designs from Alessi, displayed alongside a small café serving light refreshments, should you find yourself flagging. The basement focuses on assorted lighting, bathroom accessories and fine branded toiletries.

This destination has gained a reputation for affordable, well-designed accessories for the home, many of which are suitable for gifts. Opportunities for impulse purchases are aplenty here, and the store manages to create an accessible environment in which to push their design-led lifestyle mix.

02 ESTABLISHED & SONS

- 5-7 WENLOCK ROAD N1 7SL
- 020 7608 0990
- ESTABLISHEDANDSONS.COM
- MON–FRI 9.30–5.30
- OLD STREET/ANGEL

03 ESTORICK COLLECTION

- 39A CANONBURY SQUARE N1 2AN
- 020 7704 9522
- ESTORICKCOLLECTION.COM
- WED, FRI & SAT 10-6, THU 10-8, SUN 12-5
- HIGHBURY & ISLINGTON

You'd be excused for thinking you were in the wrong part of town when heading down Wenlock Road, home to contemporary British interiors brand Established & Sons. Despite being centrally located, the area is a retail desert. Add to that the fact the showroom has no street frontage and you'll really be confused. But persevere. You'll reach a discreet doorway that accesses an altogether different environment: the Established HQ. Mention to the receptionist that you're here to view the collections. You'll be led through the offices to the main showroom, a bunker-like double-height shell where the latest designs are handsomely displayed.

Established & Sons operates at the high end of the market, its objective to work with leading designers, architects, artists and artisans in the creation of quality original designs. The brand proves itself over and over in the strength of its diverse portfolio, featuring the likes of Barber Osgerby, Jasper Morrison, Terence Woodgate, Industrial Facility, Alexander Taylor, Klauser & Carpenter, Luca Nichetto, Jaime Hayon, Sylvain Willenz and Erwan & Ronan Bouroullec, to name just a few. Designs are exhibited to best effect in the immense showroom, backed by an imposing, curved exposed-concrete wall. The look is both strikingly stark yet wonderfully theatrical. You'll want to buy, but you can't here: this isn't a traditional retail shop. Make an enquiry and a staffer will provide you with a list of Established's partner retailers.

These days Italian design is widely understood to embody quality and ingenuity – values that flourished in 20th-century Italy as the country emerged as a modern, industrialising nation. Flicking through the pages of this guide, you'll notice a lot of Italian design, most of it from companies that established themselves during the postwar years. Of course, we'd do well to remember that other creative talents were part of Italy's great cultural heritage of the last century.

The country's art scene, for instance, was particularly robust. The acclaimed Futurist movement of the first half of the century captured the imagination of American sociologist and writer Eric Estorick (1913-1993). He spent a lifetime collecting drawings, paintings and sculptures by such luminaries as Amadeo Modigliani, Giacomo Balla, Umberto Boccioni, Giorgio Morandi and Mario Sironi. Prior to his death, the collector donated his entire Italian art collection to the Eric and Salome Estorick Foundation, and in 1998 an elegant Georgian building in Islington opened its doors to showcase the collection to the public. It is still Britain's only gallery devoted to modern Italian art.

A programme of temporary exhibitions runs throughout the year, celebrating fine art as well as design, fashion, photography and architecture. The quaint building also houses a small Italian-run café, and a bookshop and library with a collection of noteworthy titles covering Italy's significant contribution to 20th-century culture.

04 FANDANGO

- 2 CROSS STREET N1 2BL
- 07979 650 805
- FANDANGOINTERIORS.CO.UK
- WED–SAT 11–6
- ESSEX ROAD RAIL / HIGHBURY & ISLINGTON / ANGEL

05 GREEN AND FAY

- 137–139 ESSEX ROAD N1 2NR
- 020 7704 0455
- GREENANDFAY.CO.UK
- TUE–SAT 10–6
- ESSEX ROAD RAIL / HIGHBURY & ISLINGTON / ANGEL

Many dealers in antiques and 20th-century originals are moving their businesses online – such is the Internet's cost-effective allure and global reach relative to the high price and high risk of London retail space. Thankfully, Fandango is not one of them. Owners Henrietta Palmer and Jonathan Ellis recognise the importance that customers touch and feel original furniture before buying. Occupying a small and rather awkward triangular showroom in Islington, the duo manages to sustain a physical presence, to the delight of their customers.

In an area full of well-manicured shops I welcome the down-to-earth feel of Fandango. No two visits are ever the same as stock levels in the tiny space fluctuate constantly; sometimes it feels empty, others it's stuffed. If the weather agrees, pieces make it out onto the street, which attracts new custom and the attentions of passing drivers.

Classics by big name designers occasionally pass through the doors, but so, too, do anonymous gems, such as old French café tables and chairs and post-industrial lighting and storage. There's an emphasis on postwar European design, but if you're after something particular, chat to the owners: they may have something suitable in the restoration warehouse, a 10-minute walk away at 6A Rosemary Works, Branch Place, N1 5PH.

Roy Griffiths, owner of upmarket kitchen brand Harvey Jones, sold up in 2007 and embarked on a new family venture selling design and interiors, culminating in Green and Fay. On its website, the store trades as 'a unique furniture design and lifestyle store encouraging and promoting interior diversity and style'. I'm often wary of such statements, as they tend to under-deliver on their promise. Since its inception, I've monitored this store's evolution and seen improvements as it has gathered pace. However, while there are normally pieces that appeal in this sizable space, there are equal amounts that don't hit the mark. I'm often confused by the combination of products: beautiful vintage furniture alongside ubiquitous ceramics, or handmade sofas by British studio James Design alongside odd, inflatable Chesterfield-esque seating.

My issue is that it feels incoherent, as if too many people have contributed to the buying and then had to compromise on how the ensuing collections sit together. It's like they're trying to offer too much choice, from small-ticket items to full-fledged investment pieces. A full kitchen installation occupies the window space (no doubt a nod to the owner's past) and confuses the message further. While there are many valid contenders on the product roster, I can't help thinking that the team here needs to stop, stand back and embrace a more aligned point of view.

06 KVADRAT
- 10 SHEPHERDESS WALK N1 7LB
- 020 7324 5555
- KVADRAT.DK
- MON-FRI 9-5
- OLD STREET

68 THE PEANUT VENDOR
- 133 NEWINGTON GREEN ROAD N1 4RA
- 020 7226 5727
- THEPEANUTVENDOR.CO.UK
- TUE-THU 10-7, FRI-SAT 10-6, SUN 12-6
- CANONBURY/DALSTON JUNCTION

Danish fabrics and textile producer Kvadrat has established a global reputation since it was established in 1968, and recently it has gone even further, building significant stand-alone showrooms in several major cities. London is no exception, and in 2009 architect David Adjaye and graphic designer Peter Saville transformed this disused Victorian factory into the company's UK headquarters and showroom.

An imposing black door meets you upon arrival. But don't let its slightly intimidating appearance deter you: all visitors have to buzz for entry. Once you're welcomed inside, you should stand in the entrance area for a moment and take in the dramatic hall-like space. There's an immense wooden staircase faced with light-refracting glass panels in a variety of colours that invites you down to the lower-ground display area, where you're met by concrete tables and little else. Then the confusion sets in: where, exactly, do they keep the textiles? Eventually it'll be revealed that Kvadrat's catalogue of textiles is kept cleverly hidden in tall, narrow pullout units concealed along one wall. Whatever your requirements, a well-informed staff member will retrieve some large samples from the units and lay them out for your consideration.

You aren't likely to come here unless you're in the market for a top fabric to use as furniture upholstery or for curtains. But if you do find yourself here, you'll be in good hands. Kvadrat is universally embraced by the furniture industry as masters of upholstery fabric. And by the time you're finished, there's little you won't know about the company's high-quality portfolio.

Wedged between hardware shops and newsagents on Newington Green Road, The Peanut Vendor is a pleasant space filled with all manner of furniture and ephemera from times gone by. Blink and you'd miss this shoebox shop, if not for the striking red façade and savvy window displays that make it hard to ignore.

Stock here is sourced from antiques fairs and auctions and rotated on a weekly basis so no two visits are the same (though some prove more fruitful than others, depending on the whims of the market). From steel cabinets and wooden chairs to letterpress wood blocks and old metal keys, the shop hosts a wide range of items, each with a charm of its own. The focus here is not on excavating collectibles, but it wouldn't be unusual to stumble upon an original Anglepoise lamp or something equally as iconic. Still the shop is free of pretentious attitude; instead it's a place to bring together a collection of everyday pieces with midcentury charm.

You won't find flea-market junk, kitsch or retro tack. I came across a couple of unusual wooden First Aid boxes alongside an assortment of glass measuring beakers, a stack of weathered industrial chairs and an old set of dominoes. On the whole, pricing is reasonable which makes this a great destination for budget-conscious neighbours. But if you're planning a special trip from across town, call in advance –opening hours can be hit and miss, particularly earlier in the week when owners Becky Nolan and Barny Read are sometimes away on buying trips.

09 SMUG
🚩 13 CAMDEN PASSAGE N1 8EA
📞 020 7354 0253
🔗 IFEELSMUG.COM
🕐 WED, FRI & SAT 11-6, THU 12-7, SUN 12-5
🚇 ANGEL

Billed as a 'concept boutique', Smug opened on this quaint passage in 2009 and is curated by the cheerful graphic and interior designer Lizzie Evans. Expanding over three floors of a rickety, old terrace house, the narrow premises were totally reworked and now feel like a welcoming and somewhat retro home. In case you're wondering, the name refers to the 18th-century definition of 'smug', which meant 'to smarten up' – it's a far cry from today's connotation.

Evans introduces a treasure trove of new and vintage homewares, with a distinct bias for anything mid-century. An intriguing window lures you into a ground-floor displayed with unusual accessories, prints, cards, stationery and toys, many of which are ideal for gifts or impulse purchases. In the light-filled basement, melamine and vintage kitchenware prevails, with colourful glassware, muted ceramics and some candy-coloured accessories in abundance. The top floor is dedicated to 'living', its texture-rich scrap-wood floor a warm, earthy complement to cushions, woven textiles, vintage furniture and artwork. Evans's Top Ten Gift Ideas is an ever-changing display of her favourite finds.

Evans's passion is clearly the force behind Smug's sass. She supports young designers and niche producers and is true to her conviction that her wares should be affordable and, as often as possible, unique to the shop.

10 TWENTYTWENTYONE SHOP

274 UPPER STREET N1 2UA

020 7288 1996

TWENTYTWENTYONE.COM

MON–SAT 10-6, SUN 11-5

HIGHBURY & ISLINGTON

The retailscape of Upper Street changes just as rapidly as any other thriving shopping street in London, so it's no mean feat for twentytwentyone to have sustained a successful footing here since 1996. Simon Alderson and Tony Cunningham, the duo behind this neighbourhood institution, have evolved from selling 20th-century originals into the contemporary furniture and lighting market.

In 2009, what had been a rather small shop more than doubled in size to incorporate a new basement. The bright white rooms with textured grey flooring show a wider selection of homewares, many perfect for gifts. My favourites include sleek alarm clocks by plusminuszero, cast-iron candleholders by Normann Copenhagen, porcelain by Japanese producer Hakusan and stainless kitchen utensils by Sori Yanagi. On the lighting front, slender floor lamps by Örsjö and Santa & Cole get top billing along with table lamps by Wästberg and pendants from Flos. Furniture is available but fairly limited by space – a more extensive selection is displayed at the larger showroom down the road (p.115). The team has a reputation for stocking Europeans (in particular Scandinavians), but dig deeper and you'll spots pieces from Africa, America and the Far East.

There's no such thing as settling here. twentytwentyone manages to consistently introduce high-quality contemporary items without force-feeding customers with the garishly modern. Any stark, modern forms are softened with warm fabrics and colour, which appeal to customers transitioning to contemporary at home. Many people find the notion of 'design' to be intimidating, but the staff here does well to diffuse any discomfort with their knowledge, patience and friendliness.

LDG

Eat & drink

Great for... lunch in the garden

THE ALBION
Old pub with modern gastro vibe and Old English look. British comfort food cooked well. Friendly and informal. Large, leafy garden packed on a sunny day. Great for late Sunday lunch.
10 THORNHILL ROAD N1 1HW
020 7607 7450 | THE-ALBION.CO.UK

Great for... seasonal, local, organic

DUKE OF CAMBRIDGE
One of UK's first certified organic gastropubs. Sunday-brunch haunt on a quiet corner close to Regent Canal. Organic food made from seasonal local ingredients. Bright, lofty interior. Very laidback.
30 ST PETER'S STREET N1 8JT
020 7359 3066 | DUKEORGANIC.CO.UK

Great for... cosy gatherings

THE ELK IN THE WOODS
Popular pub with warm, British/Scandinavian ski-lodge interior. Rustic wood floors, vivid wallpapers, iron fireplace and mounted elk's head. Unpretentious and well-priced with great atmosphere.
39 CAMDEN PASSAGE N1 8EA
020 7226 3535 | THE-ELK-IN-THE-WOODS.CO.UK

Great for... colourful taste explosions

OTTOLENGHI [PICTURED]
Seriously popular revolution in food. Inventive, flavoursome dishes made from top-quality ingredients to eat in or take away. Tantalising food displays. Daily-changing menu. Sleek, white interior. Pricey but irresistible (especially the meringues in the window).
287 UPPER STREET N1 2TZ | 020 7288 1454 | OTTOLENGHI.CO.UK

Great for... pub grub

THE SCOLT HEAD

Revitalised old pub in residential area. Excellent food in an environment that hasn't been gentrified. Peaceful in the day, busier at weekends.

107A CULFORD ROAD N1 4HT
020 7254 3965 | THESCOLTHEAD.CO.UK

Great for... truffles

PAUL A YOUNG CHOCOLATES

Fine artisan chocolaterie on picturesque pedestrian walk. Decadent chocolates made by hand on site each day. Some unexpected ingredients, including Marmite.

33 CAMDEN PASSAGE N1 8EA
020 7424 5750 | PAULAYOUNG.CO.UK

Great for... canalside brunch

TOWPATH

Soulful, small-scale canalside café decidedly off the beaten track. Open during the day, only in warmer months. Serves flavourful top-quality café favourites and great coffee. Peaceful treasure in London.

42 DE BEAUVOIR CRESCENT N1 5SB | 020 7254 7606

Great for... rustic Italian

TRULLO

Excellent local on grim stretch of road. Warm, intimate interior serving up robust Italian dishes packed with flavour. Must book – otherwise, try the tapas-style offerings in the basement.

300-302 ST PAUL'S ROAD N1 2LH
020 7226 2733 | TRULLORESTAURANT.COM

LVNG
WITH
DESIGN

Living with design is not a choice but an inevitability, because everything man-made (and indeed woman-made, though hopefully not child-made) has been designed. Behind every product – from light fittings to dining tables, bus stops to bollards – someone, somewhere had an idea and then made a series of decisions as to how that idea could best be realised. That the same process applies to both the brilliant and the dodgy can sometimes come as a surprise.

What this means is that 'design' is neither a rarefied commodity nor a glossy cherry on top but an integral aspect of all of our lives. The vital distinction we need to make as consumers is not between the designed and the un-designed but between good design and bad. Like the girl with the curl: design, when good, can be very, very good. But when it's bad, it's horrid.

So what is good design? Well, obviously something that works, that fulfils its practical purpose with logic and fluency. But it's also something that can make the everyday pleasurable, something that even in daily use can delight, a sensation the Italian designer Gio Ponti described as 'a useless thing, but as indispensable as bread'.

Yet this is where value judgements of 'good' and 'bad' can get tricky, where we venture towards the quicksand of taste, because one person's delight can be another's disaster. Perhaps a more pragmatic way to evaluate an object, to decide whether something deserves your money and the space in your home, is to ask not only 'Does it work?' but also: 'Is it made to last?' 'Where was it made?' 'What's it made of?' 'Who made it?' 'How was it made?' 'Is it value for money?' 'Do you really love it or is it just a passing crush?' 'Is it easy to maintain?' 'To repair?' 'Does it come with a guarantee?' 'Might it be worth a few bob or two in years to come?' 'And does that really matter?' And to avoid the worst kind of design no-no: 'If it's pretending to be something it's not, is it doing so with a cheeky wink or is it just

"…design is neither a rarefied commodity nor a glossy cherry on top but an inescapable and integral aspect of all of our lives."

laughably serious?' In this way you'll not only avoid the faux pas of ersatz but you'll also catapult yourself around the tyranny of trends – while proving you are truly European.

To be fair to trends, when contemplating decor they are not the worst starting point. They act as a kind of stimulant to the design parts of your brain. Then again, trends are all well and good on the catwalk but buying a nice sofa is not the same as buying a nice top. For a start, it's quite difficult to move around wearing a sofa. On a more serious note, a good sofa is much more of a financial and emotional investment than a T-shirt.

Acquiring beautiful, comfortable and practical things for our home need not be a serious business, though, and the hunt can and should be as joyful as the acquisition itself. In fact the more you hunt the more you'll learn what works for you and what doesn't, and you'll avoid expensive mistakes.

The graduation shows at Britain's design colleges are excellent places to look for the unique and affordable. Or why not commission a more established designer or furniture-maker – many of whom emerge from their workshops to exhibit during London's Design Festival – to make something special for you, that fits perfectly into your home? You may well be surprised how their prices are often commensurate with the ready-made market, and the process can be extremely enjoyable.

On the subject of fit: if you're buying a larger piece, do always measure the space you have available – including entry points and turns on any staircases. When it comes to fit of the aesthetic type, don't be too shy to take samples along with you when you shop, so you can be sure all will harmonise. Though if you buy something you love, that's as good a guarantee of harmony as any.

NAOMI CLEAVER IS A DESIGN CONSULTANT, INTERIOR AND PRODUCT DESIGNER, TV PRESENTER AND WRITER *naomicleaver.com*

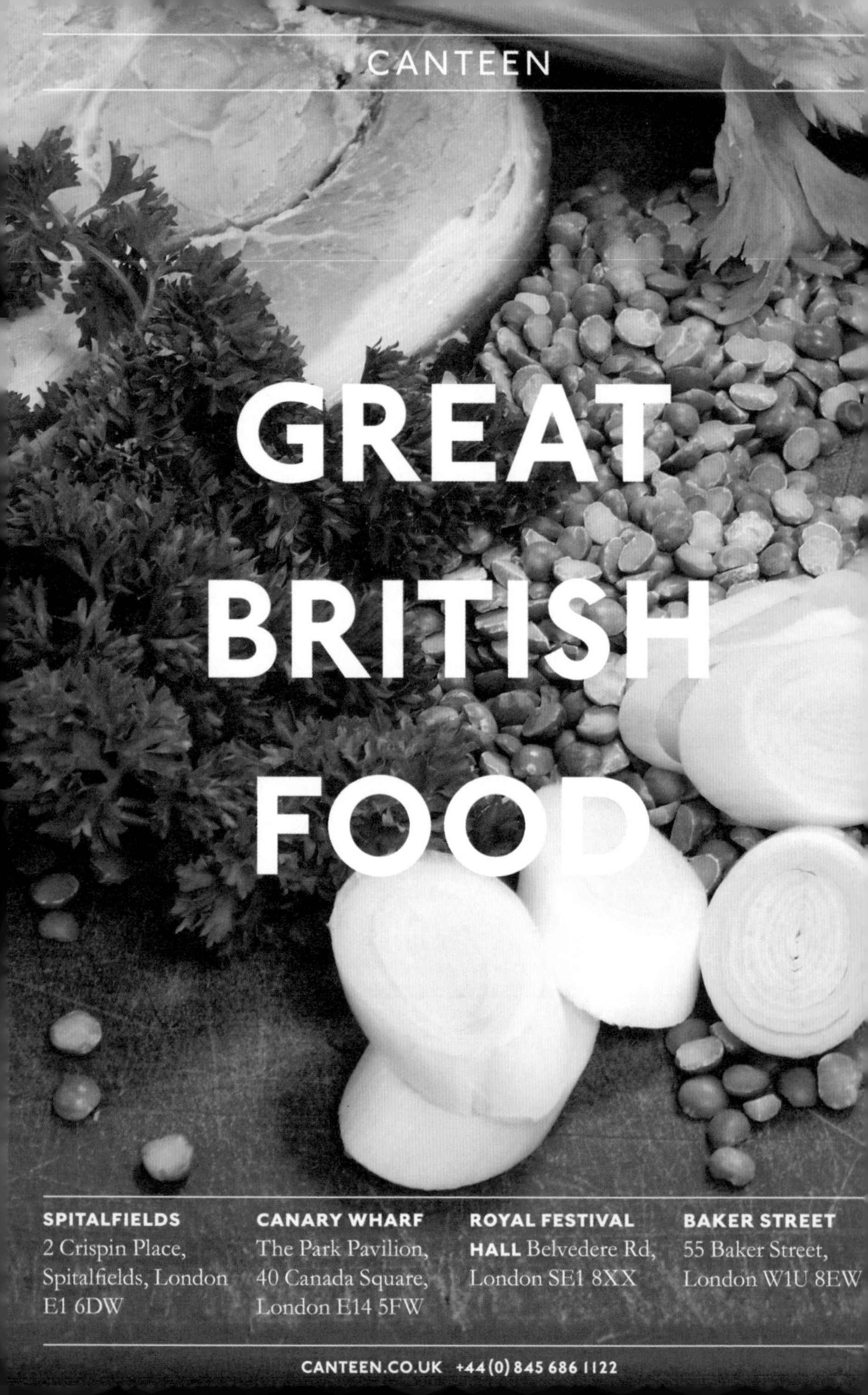
CANTEEN
GREAT
BRITISH
FOOD
SPITALFIELDS
2 Crispin Place, Spitalfields, London E1 6DW
CANARY WHARF
The Park Pavilion, 40 Canada Square, London E14 5FW
ROYAL FESTIVAL HALL Belvedere Rd, London SE1 8XX
BAKER STREET
55 Baker Street, London W1U 8EW
CANTEEN.CO.UK +44(0) 845 686 1122

Shoreditch
& Brick Lane

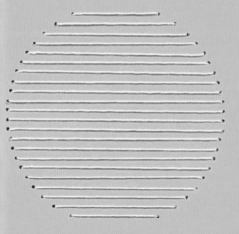

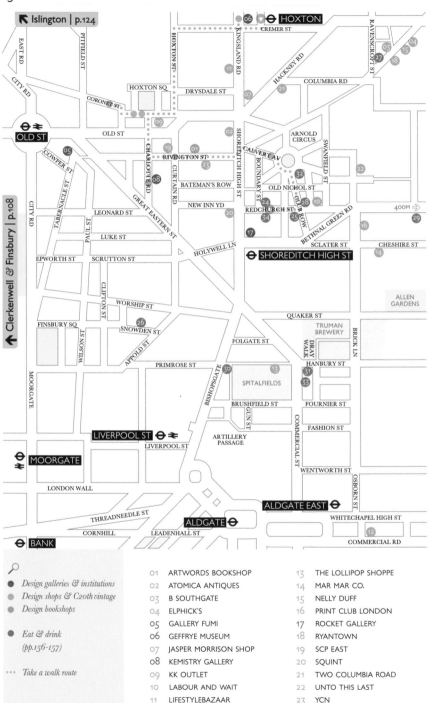

↖ Islington | p.124

HOXTON

← Clerkenwell & Finsbury | p.108

OLD ST

SHOREDITCH HIGH ST

LIVERPOOL ST

MOORGATE

BANK

ALDGATE EAST

ALDGATE

400M ⇒

🔍

● *Design galleries & institutions*

● *Design shops & C20th vintage*

● *Design bookshops*

● *Eat & drink*
  (pp.156-157)

··· *Take a walk route*

Shoreditch
& Brick Lane

TAKE A WALK WITH

*Sheridan Coakley**

The long, spacious carriages of the East London overground line lead to Hoxton station, which is a good place to start. The exit is behind the Geffrye Museum on Geffrye Street. Take a peek through the back gates at the period gardens and the elegant Arts and Crafts-inspired building extension.

Turn left onto Cremer Street, then take a right, cross over Kingsland Road and you'll reach Hoxton Street, which still holds an East End-style market on Saturdays. Walk down Hoxton Street to Hoxton Square and visit the White Cube art gallery or Daniel Blau Ltd, a new photography space. For something different, walk towards Coronet Street and Circus Space, London's only circus school. A viewing area in reception offers you a glimpse of the students at work. You'll likely admire the Electric Light Company Building (1896), in which the school is housed – it originally generated power from burning refuse.

At the south side of Hoxton Square, cross over Old Street and head down Charlotte Road, where artists moved into vacant warehouses in the late-'80s and '90s. No 44A was home to the enigmatic Joshua Compton, who brought together a group of young British artists. He hosted groundbreaking happenings – like the *Fete Worse Than Death* – and staged experimental exhibitions at his space, the *Art of Factual Nonsense*. Compton's death at 25 is commemorated in two plaques on the building, which now houses Counter Editions, a limited-edition print shop.

Double back along Charlotte Road and turn right onto Rivington Street. On Curtain Road, see if you can find the mystery site of the original Globe Theatre, whose curtain gave the road its name. Then cross over Shoreditch High Street to Calvert Avenue. Stop for a bite to eat at Leila's (No 15). Take the third right around Arnold Circus and you'll hit Old Nichol Street, site of a 19th-century slum once described by *The Illustrated London News* as 'one painful and monotonous round of vice, filth, and poverty'. It's all change on Redchurch Street, which is now a hub of galleries, cafés, shops, restaurants and media offices. If you just fancy a pint, hit The Owl & Pussycat and its secluded beer garden.

*Owner of SCP scp.co.uk

01 ARTWORDS BOOKSHOP
- 69 RIVINGTON STREET EC2A 3AY
- 020 7729 2000
- ARTWORDS.CO.UK
- MON–FRI 10.30–7, SAT 11–7
- OLD STREET/HOXTON/SHOREDITCH HIGH STREET

02 ATOMICA ANTIQUES
- 125 SHOREDITCH HIGH STREET E1 6JE
- 020 7739 5923
- ATOMICA.ME.UK
- TUE–SUN 11.30–5.30
- SHOREDITCH HIGH STREET

In a neighbourhood teeming with individuals working in design, fashion, art and media, it's hardly surprising that an independent bookshop specialising in contemporary visual culture would succeed. And Artwords's owner Ben Hillwood-Harris deserves to succeed: he dedicates tremendous amounts of energy to stocking a diverse and comprehensive cross section of titles, from the obscure to the popular.

The old adage 'never judge a book by its cover' is blown out of the water when it comes to creatives who instinctively react to a cover's visual stimuli. Well aware of this reality, Hillwood-Harris displays his books in an outward-facing manner to entice browsing. It certainly works. On a recent visit I found myself picking up books I'd never normally track down. This place always leaves me with renewed faith that the world of print publishing is well and truly alive – despite the much-hyped threat of digital. When it comes to visual culture, nothing beats the reproduction quality and tactility of print.

That tactility is increasingly present in the myriad high-end art, fashion, graphics, design and architecture magazines produced around the world. Thankfully Artwords is one of the few shops that remain in London with an extensive selection of these niche publications.

Artwords has another branch at 20-22 Broadway Market, E8 4QJ.

'I look for pieces that might have come out of an artist's studio or a strange movie,' says the owner of Atomica Antiques, William Simms. What, exactly, this means I'm not too sure. But looking at the shop contents, it would seem that midcentury sofas and lighting prevail, mixed in with some industrial designs, older antiques and... vintage kilims.

The shop's black-painted façade makes it discreet, despite its position at a busy Shoreditch junction. Compared with some of the area's more self-conscious offerings, Atomica is a low-key haven in which the serene Simms goes about his business. Nothing is 'merchandised', as stock comes and goes too frequently. Nor is specific emphasis placed on the more iconic collectibles. There is nothing of the snobby antique dealer here.

With the furniture, lighting and *objets* sourced from across Europe, there is sometimes some restorative work required, which takes place either in a separate warehouse or right in the shop. When there's a need for new upholstery, this is handled around the corner by Simms's skilled partner at 7 Upholstery (1A Boundary Street).

Believing people should visit the shop rather than buy online, Simms takes a relaxed approach to e-commerce. I'm also a believer in experiencing an item before purchase, but if you choose to make the trip to Atomica, ring in advance: the store's official opening hours are not always honoured.

03 B SOUTHGATE

📍 4 THE COURTYARD, EZRA STREET E2 7RH
📞 07905 960 792
🔗 BSOUTHGATE.CO.UK
🕐 SUN 9-3
🚇 HOXTON

04 ELPHICK'S

📍 160 COLUMBIA ROAD E2 7RG
📞 020 7033 7891
🔗 ELPHICKSSHOP.COM
🕐 SAT 12-5, SUN 9-4
🚇 HOXTON

It's quite remarkable for a shop to open for only six hours a week, but such is the trading reality for Ben Southgate, an antique and vintage furniture dealer who feeds off the traffic generated by the Sundays-only Columbia Road flower market nearby. Tucked away in a small courtyard off Ezra Street, B Southgate offers a welcome respite from the crowds and the opportunity to browse a fine collection of sofas, armchairs, storage and display pieces, lighting, toys and collectibles.

Most of the items here date back to the 1900s through the 1950s and, rather refreshingly, tend to steer away from the usual 20th-century icons. All items are sourced by Southgate himself and restored in his East Sussex workshop if necessary. In fact restoration is his speciality, an activity that takes up the rest of his time.

Stock varies from week to week. On my last visit, my eye was drawn towards a French leather daybed with comfy linen cushions and, beside it, a sizeable polished-aluminium studio lamp. Utilitarian stackable chairs worked nicely with a 1950s French Formica-topped bistro table and 1930s medical trolley. Vintage enamelled lampshades cast a warm glow onto a gleaming 1940s British Art Deco aluminium wardrobe, which was no doubt snapped up later that day. The larger items are accessorised with an intriguing supply of vintage games, toys and curiosities. And Southgate can explain the origins and recount the stories behind each piece.

Visiting Elphick's has become a ritual for regulars at Columbia Road's Sunday-morning flower market, and an unexpected treat for a new guard of shoppers and tourists alike. The charming, boutique-like space brings together an interesting collection of linocuts, giclée and screen prints by unknown, emerging and established artists and seems to attract quite a varied crowd.

There's something for most tastes in this range of artworks both framed and unframed, plus a well-edited selection of contemporary greeting cards, stationery and arty books, all suitable for gift giving. Animals, for some reason, are having a moment among the artists featured at Elphick's these days. Birds, especially, are enjoying their day in the enchanting illustrations of Americans Charley Harper and David Weidman as well as locals Claire Hartigan and Clifford Richards.

Most of the prints here are affordable, so fans of the artists above may find themselves with a brand-new illustration of a pigeon they didn't know they needed. But despite the fact the prints are not necessarily the stuff of an art collection, you can't really go wrong at Elphick's, whether you're treating a friend or yourself. The staff is warm and friendly and there's a good chance you'll spot Sharon Elphick herself, a practicing artist who sells a selection of her own prints on the adorable walls.

05 GALLERY FUMI

87-89 TABERNACLE STREET EC2A 4BA

020 7490 2366

GALLERYFUMI.COM

TUE-FRI 10-6, SAT 11-7

OLD STREET

You've got to have strong nerves to enter the market for contemporary collectible design in London, not least because that market is still relatively youthful. Indeed, the design-meets-art gallery scene gambles on the future collectibility of young design talent. A duo who wholeheartedly champion this movement are Valerio Capo and Sam Pratt, who opened their Shoreditch gallery in 2008, just as their high-rolling City customers were becoming anxious in the face of economic uncertainty.

And hats off to them as they soldier on with a strong schedule of exhibitions showcasing one-off and limited-edition furniture, lighting and accessories from talents like Max Lamb, Thomas Lemut, Paul Kelley, Pieke Bergmans, Studio Glithero, Kranen/Gille and Tina Roeder.

Spread over two floors, this Shoreditch gallery is all exposed-brick, wood floors and muted paint colours. When there's a solo exhibition on, the gallery becomes a focused celebration of the individual's thought process and skill and at other times the space features an ensemble cast.

As Capo and Pratt continue to develop their reputation, Gallery Fumi succeeds in attracting the right clientele from the neighbourhood – as well as from more affluent areas of the capital and beyond. While some stock is eye-wateringly expensive, there are pieces that make Fumi more accessible to those hoping to acquire contemporary collectibles right now.

06 GEFFRYE MUSEUM

- 136 KINGSLAND ROAD E2 8EA
- 020 7739 9893
- GEFFRYE-MUSEUM.ORG.UK
- TUE-SAT 10-5, SUN 12-5
- HOXTON

This 18th-century almshouse has been open to the public since 1914 as the 'home of the home', a museum exploring middle-class English houses and gardens across four centuries. Concealed behind iron gates on a rather grotty section of Kingsland Road, the impressive estate is unusually surrounded by a picturesque and peaceful garden itself.

Following the stone-slab path from the street into the museum's permanent gallery is like stepping back in time. Inside, a long corridor is lined with illustrations and mock-ups of period rooms, providing examples of people's tastes throughout the eras and explaining how they've evolved over time. The atmosphere is cosy and authentic, and each room is accompanied by an overview that puts it in context. You're invited to touch, look and listen to the multimedia exhibits.

Perhaps the biggest draw here is the award-winning period garden, stocked accordingly with native plants that were available at the time the building took shape. Overlooking this and the acclaimed herb garden is the Garden Reading Room with its delightful mural, and a peaceful drawing room filled with relevant periodicals and books. Past the reading room the space opens up into a new sky-lit atrium, then a contemporary wing that houses the museum's temporary exhibitions, plus a shop and restaurant.

An East End gem, the Geffrye will introduce you to an oft-overlooked side to English heritage – a home for ordinary, rather than extraordinary, objects. It's nevertheless exceptional for its accuracy and its unparalleled content.

07 JASPER MORRISON SHOP
📍 24B KINGSLAND ROAD E2 8DA
📞 N/A
🔗 JASPERMORRISON.COM
🕐 MON–FRI 11–5
🚇 HOXTON/OLD STREET

In 2009, leading British furniture and product designer Jasper Morrison opened this unassuming shop as an extension of his London design studio. Most passers-by would have no idea the shop even exists behind its unsuspecting black door at 24B Kingsland Road. Nestled among takeaway joints, brash bars and hip nightclubs is this peaceful atelier, which brings together a mix of Morrison's own designs and other household items the designer considers worthy examples of 'super normal' design.

What you'll find here is an intriguing anti-retail case study. Opening a shop with no street-facing window, no sign and only a buzzer to gain entry from the shabby stretch of road is arguably commercial suicide. That said the intimate space would not really work if it were swamped with punters. The charm of this place is its discretion, and, thankfully, its ethos goes beyond simply flogging stuff. Customers benefit from knowledgeable and passionate one-on-one attention. The staff, who pop out to greet you from the studio in the back, are full of information if you request it; otherwise they will quietly let you browse the offerings.

Reviewing this place, it's hard for me to wax lyrical about particular objects. I often tell friends that if they're looking to buy me a gift, I'm bound to love most things here. I become genuinely excited by Morrison's simple improvements to everyday objects. Every item here – be it a jug, pen, saucepan, bottle opener or stapler – is designed to perfection. A plain household tool can confidently blend all its material components

and appeal to the human senses in a beautifully subtle way.

Until you visit you will never believe it could be so exciting to contemplate such normality in design – such is the fashion-driven fanfare that pervades so much retail today. There are no references to the designer or manufacturer of each item, nor are there pretentious descriptions to accompany them. There's just the object displayed, almost vulnerably, with its price tag – leaving you to be the final judge of its merit.

08 KEMISTRY GALLERY
🢒 43 CHARLOTTE ROAD EC2A 3PD
📞 020 7729 3636
↖ KEMISTRYGALLERY.CO.UK
🕐 MON–SAT 10–6
⊖ OLD STREET/SHOREDITCH HIGH STREET

09 KK OUTLET
🢒 42 HOXTON SQUARE N1 6PB
📞 020 7033 7680
↖ KKOUTLET.COM
🕐 MON–FRI 9–6, SAT 12–5
⊖ HOXTON/OLD STREET

This independent space has been dedicated to exhibiting outstanding graphic designers since 2004, and all the while it's gained quite the reputation. Owners Graham McCallum and Richard Churchill believe graphic design is undervalued in importance next to its sister disciplines fine art and photography, and it's their mission to promote it to a wider audience. They've done so in style.

Kemistry's strong schedule of shows reflects its status as a space at the forefront of graphic design. Anthony Burrill, Daniel Eatock, James Joyce and Experimental Jetset are just some of the talents who have graced these walls. And recently the work of London-based artist and illustrator Paul Wearing was on show; his attention-grabbing work depicted human and animal silhouettes characterised with simple lines, patterns and bold blocks of colour.

Alongside the framed works of the seasonal exhibitions are limited-edition screen prints by a variety of contemporary design studios, all available for purchase. These bits provide a foil to the gallery's ostensible formality, as do the collections of books, ephemera and DVDs for sale.

The somewhat sombre atmosphere suits the purpose of elevating graphic design to fine-art standards; it gives the work a respect and reverence it deserves. Two caveats: staff are polite but hardly engaged; and the quiet, minimal space may make some visitors slightly uncomfortable.

KK is short for KesselsKramer, name of the dynamic Amsterdam-based communications agency that wanted its London studio to be more than just another anonymous office in the capital. The principals liked the idea of having a shopfront for various cultural escapades, and so they opened KK Outlet as an experimental extension of their commercial business (which operates from the basement).

Erik Kessels's love of books is indulged with a mix of intriguing, often hard-to-find titles and tomes he publishes under his own imprint, KK Publishing. The KK team also indulge their passion for found photographs, short stories and unusual artworks, which they hang on the walls to, apparently, energise their agency work and enable them 'to do things differently in the field of communications'.

Their passions take the form of rotating exhibitions, curated internally and, sometimes, by guest artists, designers and photographers. As the gallery component is essentially subsidised by the company's commercial activities, the shows here seem to embrace a unique set of criteria and are not afraid to be controversial, humorous, random or simply downright cool.

The friendly gallery manager Danielle Pender recently suggested KK may move to new and larger premises in the area, so it's worth calling ahead of any visit here.

10 LABOUR AND WAIT

85 REDCHURCH STREET E2 7DJ

020 7729 6253

LABOURANDWAIT.CO.UK

TUE-SUN 11-6

SHOREDITCH HIGH STREET

A nostalgic mood has swept the nation in recent years and it's alive and well at Labour and Wait, an east London store celebrating simple, honest and timeless products for our daily lives. First established on Cheshire Street in 2000, this store was among the first to get us to appreciate straightforward functionality, quality and quiet detailing in the everyday items we take for granted. Their outlook has been imitated (often badly) across London, but here you feel the integrity of the message prevails.

Now relocated to a green-tiled former pub at a light-filled corner location on Redchurch Street, Labour and Wait has been able to increase its evolving selection of artisanal household items, from hardware and kitchen utensils to tableware and clothing. It's the antithesis of cheap throwawayism and over-designed gadgetry that dominates today's consumer market. It seeks out specialist makers from around the world and endorses those who continue to manufacture with traditional methods. Everyday classics as well as less familiar treasures are displayed neatly in this tranquil space, which feels rather like a tidy, upmarket hardware store.

As much as possible, Labour and Wait turns its back on disposability in favour of hard-wearing materials and robust construction. It doesn't take a genius to work out that if we all invested in better quality products, we would be likely to hold onto items for longer and think twice before tossing them flippantly onto the growing garbage heap. In fact, many of the products at Labour and Wait will mellow and improve with age and retain their resale value – should you ever wish to replace them. Beyond their sustainable virtue, such products are actually beautiful and should be celebrated in the home rather than banished to the back of the cupboard. The Old World charm of enamel mugs, linen dishcloths, Japanese stainless-steel kettles, porcelain measuring spoons, cast-iron nutcrackers and aluminium dustpans are classics that go beyond their mundane utility.

Unfortunately, many of the words used to describe the ethos of this shop – 'simplicity', 'honesty', 'integrity', 'transparency' – are hijacked by untrustworthy bankers and politicians. At least at Labour and Wait there's no hyperbole.

11 LIFESTYLEBAZAAR

☞ 11A KINGSLAND ROAD E2 8AA

✆ 020 7739 9427

↖ LIFESTYLEBAZAAR.COM

🕒 MON–SAT 11-7, SUN 12-5

⊖ HOXTON

12 LIGNE ROSET CITY

☞ 37-39 COMMERCIAL ROAD E1 1LF

✆ 020 7426 9670

↖ LIGNE-ROSET-CITY.CO.UK

🕒 MON–SAT 10-6, THU 10-7, SUN 12-5

⊖ ALDGATE EAST

Years after its West End debut Lifestylebazaar moved east to this Shoreditch location in 2009 and soon became part of the area's burgeoning design scene. Housed in a converted Victorian boot factory nestled under the new railway bridge, the store has a feeling of Ye Olde London meeting its contemporary counterpart.

A two-storey emporium, it sells a mix of contemporary design and decorative objects for the home, including furniture and lighting. The common thread running through the product range is colour; bold primaries add fun and energy to everyday objects. Bright kitchen accessories from Joseph Joseph, Alessi and Koziol; glassware from LSA; cheery ceramics by Rob Ryan; and a handful of gimmicky items provide merely a snapshot of what's on display. Independent designers like ceramicists Andrew Tanner, Tina Tsang and the New English are supported here. Multihued acrylic furniture and lighting by Italian brand Kartell sits prominently alongside iBride's surreal, animal-inspired furniture – including the jolly *Bambi* table and drawers.

Owners Christopher Curtis and Laurent Nurisso are often present in the store and enjoy engaging in conversation with customers, revealing the stories behind many of the pieces. Good quality and affordability is the mantra they chant. They're adamant that their shop avoids being intimidating or overpriced – an understandable reaction against many of London's high-end design offerings.

You can't miss Ligne Roset's City showroom. It's spanned an entire block of this congested London artery since 2003. It's the French producer's largest UK showroom, with an impressive 750-square-metres of space in which a broad selection of the company's vast collections are spaciously arranged. The immense window displays are strategically located on the main route between the financial districts of the City and Canary Wharf, and the covetable furniture, lighting and occasional items no doubt catch the attentions of wealthy types commuting to work.

Walk in and you're immediately met with a colourful display of *Ruché* sofas by Inga Sempé. Her design unusually combines a linear wooden structure with soft, quilted upholstery that appears to be draped over the frame. Move beyond that and you'll see an arrangement of bulbous faceted armchairs, settees and footstools by Noé Duchaufour-Lawrance; they do help to soften the sharp corners of this bright space. Continue to browse the various displays and it'll be evident that the brand has gradually shifted away from its bourgeois yesteryear image and embraced a bolder creative direction. A new generation of designers can be thanked, in part, for injecting colour, joy and a fresh energy into today's collection.

As always, I would encourage you to visit in person and sample the furnishings yourself. If you tend to travel past by car, you'll know that street parking can be tricky in this neighbourhood. So you'll be relieved to hear that private parking is available upon request.

13 THE LOLLIPOP SHOPPE

10 LAMB STREET E1 6EA

020 7655 4540

THELOLLIPOPSHOPPE.CO.UK

MON–SAT 10–6, SUN 11–5

LIVERPOOL STREET / SHOREDITCH HIGH STREET

However you feel about the modernisation of Old Spitalfields Market, the renewal has certainly given rise to a flurry of new retailers. And The Lollipop Shoppe is a welcome addition. Owners Marco and Siobhan Di Rienzo named the design destination, which opened in 2010, after the 1960s psychedelic garage-rock band from Portland, Oregon. They sell a range of classic and contemporary pieces by new and established manufacturers.

They focus on 20th-century designs from well-known furniture brands including Vitra, Artek, Fritz Hansen, Knoll, Cassina, Ercol and Carl Hansen. That said, the contemporary producers also get an outing, among them Hay, Cappellini, Very Good & Proper and Established & Sons. There's a modernist sensibility here, characterised by purist forms, functionality and a respect for materials. And every piece is sourced for its quality and longevity – a rare thing in retail.

Tableware and accessories are thrown into the mix, too: Sori Yanagi cookware, Punkt cordless phones, Marimekko ceramics, iittala glassware and colourful cast-acrylic sculptures from Vasa Studio. In the basement you'll find choice lighting from Flos, Yamagiwa, Muuto, Bestlite, Louis Poulsen and Oluce.

Most pieces are arranged against smart black shelving; the black lets the design speak for itself while creating great contrast. It's also a welcome change from the all-white interiors that have become ubiquitous in London.

Leading architects Found Associates took this two-storey heritage market building and restored it to its former architectural glory, stripping the walls back to their original brickwork and keeping the Victorian pillars – which contrast nicely with the contemporary installations. As a result the space feels distinctly modern and fresh while retaining the integrity of the original building. In all, it's a well-groomed addition to London's design scene.

14 MAR MAR CO.

🏠 16 CHESHIRE STREET E2 6EH

📞 020 7729 1494

↖ MARMARCO.COM

🕐 THU-FRI 11.30-5.30, SAT 12-5.30, SUN 11-5

⊖ SHOREDITCH HIGH STREET

If there's one thing I like to see in every store I visit, it's a point of view. And Mar Mar Co. clearly has that. A far cry from the homogeneous and predictable nature of so much mainstream retail, this tiny Cheshire Street store opts for a curated gallery of products – without the gallery prices or the pomp.

The shop is run by Mark Bedford and Marianne Lumholdt, two graphic designers with an eye for design and an interest in the everyday things that surround us. There's a well-considered composition of items here. Textures are combined, patterns mixed and colours celebrated. The all-white space provides a fresh backdrop against which the products can shine. And because the stock is limited, your attention to each item becomes more focused.

Past the warm-grey threshold, you're greeted by a small table of accessories and tabletop items, like bright-yellow or red melamine sugar bowls; butter dishes from Portugal; Austrian stackable enamel storage containers with ash-wood lids; and red coffeemakers from Denmark. Cheerful textiles adorn the nearby shelves, including fluorescent teatowels by Danish designers Scholten & Baijings and wool blankets by Finnish talent Tina Ratzer.

Handmade pieces by independent designers sit easily beside mass-manufactured items from more established companies; but whatever the piece, the emphasis is on the product rather than the name. Prices for the relatively youthful clientele frequenting this characterful street remain affordable and conducive to an impulse purchase.

I've been visiting Mar Mar Co. for several years and have always been impressed that Bedford and Lumholdt have resisted the temptation to stuff their shop full of choice; that would inevitably water down their appeal. Instead they drip-feed new items into the mix and pay little heed to the fickle world of trends. It's a great challenge to remain unique amid the competition, but the friendly Bedford and Lumholdt manage to do it gracefully and on their own terms.

15 NELLY DUFF
- 156 COLUMBIA ROAD E2 7RG
- 020 7033 9683
- NELLYDUFF.COM
- SAT 12-4, SUN 9-3
- HOXTON

16 PRINT CLUB LONDON
- 214 BRICK LANE E1 6SA
- 020 7749 0750
- PRINTCLUBLONDON.COM
- SAT 12-7, SUN 11-6
- SHOREDITCH HIGH STREET

It's been several years now since Nelly Duff began offering up its appealing variety of graphic prints in London's East End. The shop's name, incidentally, references the local dialect of Cockney rhyming slang: 'duff' rhymes with 'puff', signifying breath, as in 'breath of life'. Stand around on the street long enough on a Sunday during the bustling flower market and you may be lucky enough to hear some authentic Cockney, though it's a fading tradition.

The worn wooden floorboards and exposed-brick walls of the shoebox gallery provide a textured backdrop against which Nelly Duff's handmade prints are displayed. The price range is broad, reflecting the variety of featured artists, which include emerging talents alongside hot graphic artists like Banksy, Mark Pawson and Anthony Burrill. You can pick up a print for as little as £25 or as much as several thousand, so both impulse purchasers and more serious collectors frequent the spot.

A lot of the works are printed locally through the shop, so the staff is knowledgeable about the skill that goes into each piece. They'll be on hand for a friendly chat about your favourite print, assuming they're not run off their feet by the steady flow of visitors on market day. Regardless, you're sure to find something here you can't leave without, whether it's a greeting card or a valuable limited edition.

Past a discreet entrance on Brick Lane, Print Club is a great space to discover today's contemporary print artists and start your collection of graphic art. Follow the luminescent sign into the basement to access the spacious white gallery, served by a friendly, passionate staff. The artwork – prints framed and loose alike – is the stuff of the gallery's own Dalston studio, which is used by a growing roster of member designers who lack their own print facilities.

An enticing mix of typographic and more abstract, painterly prints are on show. Visitors are invited to take a seat on one of the leather couches to contemplate which of the prints might best suit their own interior; otherwise they can browse through the portfolio of magazine articles and press releases about Print Club. There's also a bespoke wrapping paper business down here, featuring limited-edition, screen-printed papers that are like works of art in and of themselves for those without the means to give one of the larger prints a home.

Print Club is the perfect option for art-lovers without the budget for the lofty prices fine art commands. Prints are an affordable alternative – which may explain the surge in popularity of graphic art in recent years. If you end up leaving this shop empty-handed, you may well find the urge to pick up a squeegee and create a screen print of your own.

17 ROCKET GALLERY

TEA BUILDING, 56 SHOREDITCH HIGH STREET E1 6JJ

020 7729 7594

ROCKETGALLERY.COM

TUE-FRI 10-6, SAT 12-6

SHOREDITCH HIGH STREET

As the years have passed I've become more familiar with the splendour of Jonathan Stephenson's Rocket Gallery. Not only am I a fan of most things Stephenson selects, but I am also totally sold on the integrity that he brings to every subject he embraces – be it bold paintings by Peter Hedegaard, 1950s *Krenit* bowls by Herbert Krenchel, reissued classics from Jens Risom or contemporary furniture from Tomoko Azumi.

If these names aren't on your radar, I recommend visiting Rocket to familiarise yourself. Stephenson is a fountain of knowledge when it comes to the artists and designers he showcases, and he is happy to share his insights. He has both a passion for artistic methods and an acute understanding of materials, construction, composition and, above all, quality.

Rocket comprises two distinct spaces: one operates as a gallery while the other is more retail-focused. You enter directly into the former, a white post-industrial room illuminated by geometrically composed strip lights. This is where visitors come to see the programme of exhibitions, ranging from solo art and design shows to the occasional group show where Stephenson isn't afraid to mix design and art.

Beyond the gallery is the shop, which is constantly improving. A good portion is dedicated to specialist and rare books on design, art and photography. New and vintage furniture, lighting and accessories also have pride of place, all scrupulously sourced as per Stephenson's high standards. And when he sets his sights on something, he dedicates time and energy tracking

it down. His collection of midcentury furniture and prints (mainly Danish) is enormous, but more recently his interests have leaned towards 20th-century Dutch furniture from the likes of Martin Visser, Cees Braakman, Friso Kramer and Wim Rietveld, a change that will no doubt set Rocket down another intriguing path.

(18) **RYANTOWN**

- 126 COLUMBIA ROAD E2 7RG
- 020 7613 1510
- MISTERROB.CO.UK
- SAT 12–5, SUN 9–4
- HOXTON

Some may compare Rob Ryan's romantic paper-cut artworks to those of 19th-century Danish fairytale legend Hans Christian Andersen. In fact, Ryan has won himself a 21st-century following for his distinctive style of artworks, each infused with a story that often follows the tender interaction of people and the giving and receiving of love.

Ryan has gone beyond the role of artist diversified into mass-production on a modest scale, reproducing his own artworks onto functional and more modestly priced plates, mugs, teatowels, tiles and cards. He also takes on choice commissions that have broadened his market and his appeal.

I think it's fair to say that you either love or hate Ryan's work. Those who love it can purchase his singular style from this small east London shop, which he opened in 2008. Located on Columbia Road (the street famous for its Sunday flower market), the shop's wooden floor and white walls provide a simple backdrop against which a selection of his works can shine. On one wall his popular hand-painted tiles are arranged into a mural. Intricate paper cuts are exhibited alongside limited-edition screen prints and an ever-changing range of handcrafted goods that Ryan works on at his nearby studio.

19 SCP EAST

- 135-139 CURTAIN ROAD EC2A 3BX
- 020 7739 1869
- SCP.CO.UK
- MON-SAT 9.30-6, SUN 11-5
- OLD STREET

Shoreditch may be considered the beating heart of London's creative scene today, but back in 1985 the area was a neglected, post-industrial ghost town. That was the year the visionary owner of SCP, Sheridan Coakley, started his furniture business in an ex-upholstery workshop. It's remained faithful to the location ever since.

Coakley commissioned a new wave of design talent from humble beginnings – now legends like Jasper Morrison, Matthew Hilton and Konstantin Grcic – to create quality furniture for his fledgling brand. On that early strength to spot new talent he's gone on to become one of Britain's most highly respected manufacturers. It was a logical progression from his growing production and wholesaling business into retail. Today SCP is one of London's leading interiors stores, with a well-edited selection of useful and appealing products for anyone with a penchant for elegant and brilliantly considered stuff.

SCP's two loftlike sales floors accommodate those looking to furnish the whole home or those in search of smaller affordable items and gifts. On the ground floor is everything from clocks, books and hooks to clusters of lighting, textiles and tableware. Yet despite that overwhelming list, you're neither bombarded with too much choice nor blocked by intrusive branding and point-of-sale displays. Instead the products are simply left to speak for themselves.

Upstairs, a wide variety of SCP's new and bestselling furniture is arranged into enticing room configurations and easily accompanied by classics from myriad other leading suppliers, including Magis, Hay, Knoll, Kartell and Ercol.

The majority of stock adheres to Modernist values, but lately SCP has embraced a slightly softer, more tactile aesthetic and introduced more colour, pattern and texture. Acknowledging that warmth and comfort are paramount to a home (in contrast with the stark modernity often found elsewhere), SCP truly delivers what people want.

20 SQUINT

- 178 SHOREDITCH HIGH STREET E1 6HU
- 020 7739 9275
- SQUINTLIMITED.COM
- MON-FRI 10-6, SUN 1-5
- LIVERPOOL STREET/SHOREDITCH HIGH STREET

21 TWO COLUMBIA ROAD

- 2 COLUMBIA ROAD E2 7NN
- 020 7729 9933
- TWOCOLUMBIAROAD.CO.UK
- TUE-FRI 12-7, SAT 12-6, SUN 10-3
- HOXTON

A longtime passionate collector of antique textiles, former sculptor and painter Lisa Whatmough had the idea of combining her stash of fabrics with period furniture. That resulted in a collection of stunning sofas and chairs exuberantly upholstered in a patchwork of interesting fabrics. She opened Squint in 2005 and has since earned a loyal following among those looking to inject colour and surprise into their homes.

In its early days Squint reupholstered all manner of antiques. But Whatmough has since simplified things by offering a catalogue of shapes. During the consultation process customers discuss the look they're after: bold, plush and textural or calm, muted and restrained. Whatmough guides them from there, then takes over and begins putting all the ideas together. Whatever the order, customers can rest assured that the mix of contemporary and vintage fabrics will always be unique.

Squint's Shoreditch window display is a riot of colour and acts as a taster for what's inside. An enormous basement operates as a showroom, office and workshop, where you're free to walk around. It's here where you can witness Squint's 'maximalist' creations being skilfully handcrafted using traditional upholstery techniques. It's probably not the right kind of place for Minimalists.

Look out for a second Squint location, coming soon to west London. You may also be seeing a more affordable diffusion homeware range that will include fabric, wallpaper, ceramics and furniture.

Keith Roberts is the man in charge of Two Columbia Road, a leading light for collectors and lovers of 20th-century desks, tables, seating, storage, lighting, art and objects. Roberts – who was raised with the expertise of his father Tommy, in the same trade since the '60s – has been operating this corner store since 1995.

The prominent location benefits from the footfall along Hackney Road (particularly during the Sunday flower market), and the dark-grey frontage enticingly frames the rich pickings within. While familiar, iconic designs from the past century feature, the happy-go-lucky Roberts is aware that the vintage market has become saturated with such offerings and that now's the time to source a more unusual selection. It's his feeling that the roll call of Scandinavian masters has become expected of dealers, so only select Scandinavian pieces now make an appearance here. Similarly, the collection of trendy rosewood furnishings has been joined by Roberts's beloved warm-toned teak. Above all, Roberts just buys what he loves, confident that his customers will pick up on the rarity of his finds.

On some days the space feels earthy and warm, with plenty of woods and leather, and on others the pickings make a more colourful pop. Whatever your preference, Roberts emphasises the importance of visiting this space (and the overflow space across the road) in person. The website, an ever-important trading tool for dealers, is best used as a guide.

22 UNTO THIS LAST

- 230 BRICK LANE E2 7EB
- 020 7613 0882
- UNTOTHISLAST.CO.UK
- DAILY 10-6
- SHOREDITCH HIGH STREET

23 YCN

- 72 RIVINGTON STREET EC2A 3AY
- 020 7033 2140
- YCNONLINE.COM
- MON-FRI 10-6
- SHOREDITCH HIGH STREET

Unto This Last designs, produces and sells a variety of contemporary furniture, lighting and accessories. Big deal. So do a heap of other companies. Except the business model for this Shoreditch house is streets away from the others. This place marries the customisation potential of digital data with on-site production and machine efficiency, embodied by the inscription 'Less mass, more data' on the shop façade.

Set up in 2001, it represents the vision of founder Olivier Geoffrey, whose goal was to introduce 'local craftsmanship at mass-production prices'. Fed up with cheap, monolithic out-of-town warehouse stores, he was keen to offer a city centre alternative. In order to compete, Unto This Last would need to operate with military efficiency in time, materials and space, while also sidestepping complicated supply chains.

Its single location in an ever-evolving converted pub at the top of Brick Lane is where all the design, production and retail take place. Each item, designed in the upstairs studio with sophisticated software, is carefully conceived to suit the capabilities of the outfit's digitally controlled cutting machines. As each design is made to order, the customer can specify dimensions that suit their home, then collect it within weeks. The excitement comes in seeing everything produced, assembled and finished by craftsmen in the ground-floor workshop, made entirely visible from the showroom space. It's worth a visit just to take a look.

The latest comer on Rivington Street, YCN is petite, but it's got big personality. As one of the city's few illustration galleries, contributing illustrators come from across the UK, but the gallery benefits from the YCN creative agency and design studio situated upstairs; YCN member designers and illustrators regularly offer their framed screen prints for sale in the ground-floor gallery, the interior of which was designed by London-based furniture and product designers Peter Marigold and Oscar Narud.

There's a small selection of publications available for purchase, including the *YCN Students Awards Annual* and *Ideas Illustrated*, the quarterly celebrating new creative talent and ideas. And when I visited the gallery was on the cusp of introducing a small homeware and giftware range, described by manager Camilla Sundwall as 'playful utility'. This is in addition to some of the more unusual stock: decorative light-switch stickers by Henrietta Swift and characterful London maps by Herb Lester Associates.

One of the gallery's great assets is its library, which offers an intriguing mix of contemporary design publications available to borrow with a free-of-charge membership. The comprehensive selection of books is categorised by discipline, though visitors are likely to find the most unusual publications in the Lucky Dip section.

LDG

Eat & drink

Great for... British classics

ALBION

Bakery, grocers and café in one. Casual, stylish and nostalgically British in design and menu. Exposed brick complemented by white walls and harvest tables. Perfect for relaxed brunch. Open frontage in warm weather.

2-4 BOUNDARY STREET E2 7DD
020 7729 1051 | ALBIONCAFF.CO.UK

Great for... coffee break (25)

ALLPRESS

An antipodean favourite now in Shoreditch. Passionate café and roastery. Best for a caffeine hit but also a tasty sandwich or snack.

58 REDCHURCH STREET E2 7DP
020 7749 1780 | ALLPRESSESPRESSO.COM

Great for... finest Calabrian cooking (26)

L'ANIMA

Contemporary Italian with a focus on regional dishes: Calabria, Puglia, Sicily and Sardinia. Sleek, sophisticated design by architect Claudio Silvestrin. Stylish, comfortable dining.

1 SNOWDEN STREET EC2A 2DQ | 020 7422 7000 | LANIMA.CO.UK

Great for... cured meats and terrines (27)

BRAWN [PICTURED]
Sister to Terroirs in Covent Garden. Informal, pared-back interior. Plenty of honest dishes, including meaty and cheesy treats. Interest in provenance. Exciting list of natural wines.

49 COLUMBIA ROAD E2 7RG | 020 7729 5692 | BRAWN.CO

Great for... peace and quiet

CAFEAND
Café with discreet street presence and peaceful white interior. Combines food and drink with design, art and magazines for sale. Lovely cooking aromas encourage you to linger.

77 REDCHURCH STREET E2 7DJ | 020 3487 0980 | CAFEAND.CO.UK

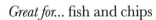

Great for... proper East End caff

E PELLICCI

Tiny, family-run Art Deco café with local appeal. Consistently rated by city magazines. Tasty, cheap, authentic British/Italian meals. Full British breakfast is a must.

332 BETHNAL GREEN ROAD E2 0AG | 020 7739 4873

Great for... dining in a church

GALVIN LA CHAPELLE

Michelin-starred restaurant from chef-brothers Chris and Jeff Galvin. Modern French served in a grand converted Grade II-listed church. Casual menu offered in the adjoining Café a Vin.

35 SPITAL SQUARE E1 6DY
020 7299 0400 | GALVINRESTAURANTS.COM

Great for... fish and chips

POPPIES OF SPITALFIELDS

Rejuvenated East End chippie serving since 1945. Adheres to traditional values and nostalgic style. Popular local with dine-in and takeaway options.

6-8 HANBURY STREET E1 6QR
020 7247 0892 | POPPIESFISHANDCHIPS.CO.UK

Great for... hidden lunches

ROCHELLE CANTEEN

One of Shoreditch's best-kept secrets. Canteen-style space in converted bike shed on the grounds of a onetime schoolhouse. Invisible from the street. Great homecooked food. Peaceful alfresco lunches in warm weather.

ROCHELLE SCHOOL, ARNOLD CIRCUS E2 7ES
020 7729 5677 | ARNOLDANDHENDERSON.COM

Great for... canteen style dining

ST. JOHN BREAD & WINE

Unpretentious, honest food in a pared-down environment opposite Spitalfields market. Simple, refreshing ivory walls, wood tables and industrial lighting. No-nonsense approach to ingredients and service. Packed at peak hours.

94-96 COMMERCIAL STREET E1 6LZ | 020 3301 8069 | STJOHNBREADANDWINE.COM

Place to sleep?
SHOREDITCH ROOMS SHOREDITCHROOMS.COM

APPRECIATING DESIGN

I was in a vast country estate in a hidden valley in the Chiltern Hills. Olde Englande to its core, but for an uncharacteristic modernist arrival, the thing I had come to see. The auditorium for Garsington Opera in the Getty-owned Wormsley Estate is a bespoke but entirely demountable structure. It's an incredible piece of design.

It is made of lightweight steel trusses, fabrics of various kinds including giant sliding shoji screens, a judicious dash of timber – and some fine, specially-designed auditorium seating. Architect Robin Snell worked with Race Furniture to produce special fabric-upholstered moulded-plywood ones. Race was one of the pioneering British furniture companies of the post-war years, still going strong today.

Why do I mention this? Durability. Because Garsington has a contract to stage its opera festival at Wormsley for 15 years. Every year the opera house will be packed away, to be brought out again the following summer. But both the building and the seating are designed to last up to 30 seasons. Parts can be easily replaced. The seating looks as if it would last for ever. High-tech meets traditional craft-based manufacturing skills. Good design, well made, lasts.

But it has got to be well made. I'd guess that just about everybody reading this, like me, has got the odd bit of dirt-cheap furniture from a certain Scandinavian edge-of-town retailer. It may well be quite well designed for its price point. But that's the problem. The price point means it is unlikely to last.

So you get clever. You buy certain things like these at very low cost, knowing and not caring that they are essentially temporary possessions. And you buy other things, if you can, which you know will last. And how do you choose those? Well, an item that has been in production for a long time is always a good clue, though not the only one. Something that is not devastatingly fashionable is another. Me, I'm by no means a design victim but I did make the decision some

> "Trust to your instincts. If you really like it, the chances are you won't regret shelling out a bit more to acquire it than you would for something high-street mainstream."

18 years ago to invest in a set of Arne Jacobsen-designed *Series 7* plywood chairs (first designed in 1955) and a *Super-Elliptical Table* by Piet Hein and Bruno Mathsson (designed 1968) made by the same company, Fritz Hansen. My children have grown up on these chairs and round that table, which have not only lasted fully intact, but actually improved in appearance with wear. If we wanted to replace them, however, we could – they are still in production. They were expensive. But 18 years later and counting, they seem very cheap.

Similarly, for 12 years now I have been gradually accumulating shelves, drawers and cabinets from the Vitsœ *606 system*, designed by Dieter Rams in 1960. Rams believes in the dictum "Less, but better." Very occasionally Vitsœ (a British company these days) introduces a new product, more usually it improves an existing one. If I move house, the shelves can move with me, along with the chairs and table. These things make me happy.

But away from the classics, don't be afraid to go for the new. In certain areas – lighting and furniture, especially chairs – there seems to be no end to the resourcefulness of designers. Is it well-made? Is it a reputable manufacturer? Is it by an up-and-coming designer? Trust to your instincts. If you really like it, the chances are you won't regret shelling out a bit more to acquire it than you would for something high-street mainstream.

Think of it this way. For a temporary summer opera festival, Garsington Opera could have hired some kind of events marquee and standard seats. But they didn't. They bought what's effectively a permanent building, using good designers and manufacturers – but one that can be packed away and brought out again, year after year. They see this as a good investment. I suggest you should think of the well-designed objects you crave in much the same way. Over time, they become a part of you. And with any luck you'll still love them, long after you've recycled the low-cost, short-life things you bought to plug a gap.

HUGH PEARMAN IS ARCHITECTURE AND DESIGN CRITIC OF THE SUNDAY TIMES AND EDITOR OF THE RIBA JOURNAL
hughpearman.com

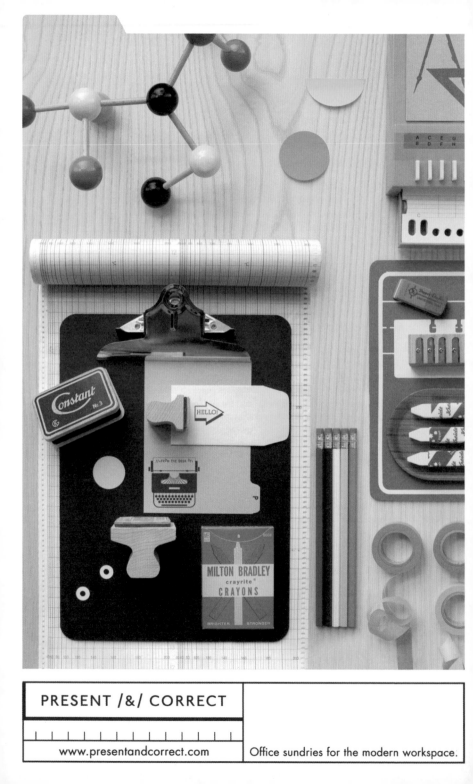

LONDON DESIGN GUIDE

presents

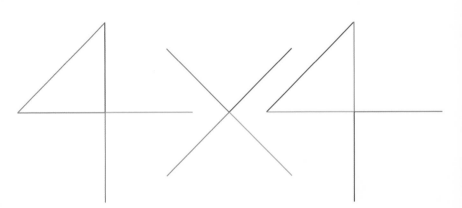

If there's one thing that really rattles me, it's superfluous and trivial 'stuff'. The world is awash with mediocre products that are not made to last and I'm not partaking. The attributes of quality and longevity have become my top criteria. Touring the design shops featured in this guide, I found it encouraging to encounter so many great products, and to see retailers sticking to their principles, not succumbing to 'cheap and cheerful' during this period of low consumer spending.

During my visits, I compiled a selection of products that stood out to me. Elegant, timeless, well proportioned, tactile, confident in both form and material composition – these were the qualities I was seeking. For all of us, these elements need to balance in a way that suits our own style and temperament. An interesting home is one that mixes up this balance to achieve intrigue. Whether it's new or old a design must have characteristics we can envisage fitting in with our lives, not dominating.

The name 4×4 is borrowed from the automotive industry. Indeed, 4×4s represent the pinnacle of engineering; they're designed for endurance, reliability, performance and precision. These may seem like grandiose words for a humble chair or kettle, but you'll find these qualities in each of the chosen products. The name 4×4 also informs the composition of this section: four products per page across four pages, a total of 16 designs in the categories of furniture, lighting and accessories.

The selections on the following pages are simply a snapshot of the items I picked up on during my travels, all of which are available from one or other of the shops in this guide. Whether or not you like or agree with the pieces I've selected for the coming pages, I would urge you to consider the principles that they embody – the ones I mentioned earlier. In a world swamped with choice, it's best to take a moment to reflect on what it is you're about to purchase. Aim to buy less and buy better.

Furniture

'DINING TABLE ONE'
Another Country
AVAILABLE FROM TWENTYTWENTYONE (PP.115 & 131)

'OSCAR' SOFA
Matthew Hilton for SCP
AVAILABLE FROM SCP (PP.043 & 153)

'BURNHAM WINDSOR' CHAIR
Matthew Hilton for De La Espada
AVAILABLE FROM EDC LONDON (P.083)

'C275' SIDE CHAIR
Jens Risom
AVAILABLE FROM ROCKET (P.151)

'PLC' CHAIR
Pearson Lloyd for Modus
AVAILABLE FROM MODUS (P.113)

'HEIDI' STOOL
Sebastian Wrong for Established & Sons
AVAILABLE FROM HAUS (P.186)

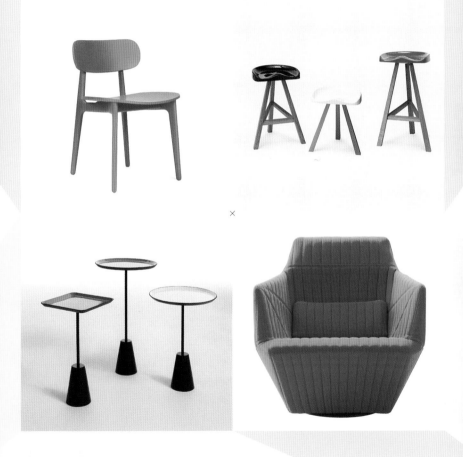

×

'SPOT' TABLE
Tom Dixon
AVAILABLE FROM TOM DIXON SHOP (P.044)

'FACETT' ARMCHAIR
Erwan & Ronan Bouroullec
AVAILABLE FROM LIGNE ROSET (PP.086 & 147)

'MONZA' ARMCHAIR
Konstantin Grcic for Plank
AVAILABLE FROM ARAM (P.096)

'SATELLITE' SIDEBOARD
Edward Barber & Jay Osgerby for Quodes
AVAILABLE FROM CHAPLINS (P.182)

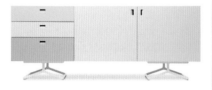

×

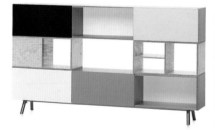

'PORTSMOUTH BENCH'
Edward Barber & Jay Osgerby for Isokon Plus
AVAILABLE FROM TWENTYTWENTYONE (PP.115 & 131)

'KAST' SHELVING UNIT
Maarten Van Severen for Vitra
AVAILABLE FROM VIADUCT (P.116)

'WILLIAM' SOFA
Damian Williamson for Zanotta
AVAILABLE FROM CHAPLINS (P.182)

'606 UNIVERSAL SHELVING SYSTEM'
Dieter Rams for Vitsœ
AVAILABLE FROM VITSŒ (P.059)

'SURFACE TABLE'
John Barnard & Terence Woodgate for Established & Sons
AVAILABLE FROM VIADUCT (P.116)

'LOW PAD' LOUNGE CHAIR
Jasper Morrison for Cappellini
AVAILABLE FROM THE LOLLIPOP SHOPPE (P.148)

Lighting

'LOUVRE LIGHT'
Klauser & Carpenter for Established & Sons
AVAILABLE FROM CHAPLINS (P.182)

'BALL LIGHT'
Michael Anastassiades
AVAILABLE FROM SIGMAR (P.027)

'RAIMOND' LIGHT
Raimond Puts for Moooi
AVAILABLE FROM TWENTYTWENTYONE (PP.115 & 131)

'ETCH SHADE'
Tom Dixon
AVAILABLE FROM TOM DIXON SHOP (P.044)

'ROMEO MOON' SUSPENSION LIGHT
Philippe Starck for Flos
AVAILABLE FROM SCP (PP.043 & 153)

'DOME' LAMP
Todd Bracher for Mater
AVAILABLE FROM PLACESANDSPACES (P.192)

'LIGHTHOUSE'
*Erwan & Ronan Bouroullec for Established & Sons
in collaboration with Venini*
AVAILABLE FROM VESSEL (P.045)

'LEAN' FLOOR LAMP
Jenny Bäck for Örsjö Belysning
AVAILABLE FROM TWENTYTWENTYONE (PP.115 & 131)

'CASTORE TERRA' FLOOR LAMP
Michele de Lucchi & Huub Ubbens for Artemide
AVAILABLE FROM ARTEMIDE (P.097)

'CARAVAGGIO' PENDANT LIGHT
Cecilie Manz for Lightyears
AVAILABLE FROM SKANDIUM (PP.028 & 058)

'TAB' TABLE LIGHT
Edward Barber & Jay Osgerby for Flos
AVAILABLE FROM SCP (PP.043 & 153)

'M2 OVAL' FLOOR LIGHT
Toyo Ito for Yamagiwa
AVAILABLE FROM THE LOLLIPOP SHOPPE (P.148)

'CLAESSON KOIVISTO RUNE W101' LED TASK LIGHT
Claesson Koivisto Rune for Wästberg
AVAILABLE FROM VIADUCT (P.116)

'HEAVY LIGHT'
Benjamin Hubert for Decode
AVAILABLE FROM HAUS (P.186)

'LE SOLEIL' SUSPENSION LIGHT
Vicente Garcia Jimenez for Foscarini
AVAILABLE FROM ARIA (P.126)

'UNFOLD' PENDANT LIGHT
Form Us With Love for Muuto
AVAILABLE FROM HAUS (P.186)

Accessories

CHAMPAGNE GLASSES
Michael Anastassiades & Ilse Crawford
AVAILABLE FROM SIGMAR (P.027)

'LA CINTURA DI ORIONE' POTS AND PANS
Richard Sapper for Alessi
AVAILABLE FROM ALESSI (P.068)

'KITCHEN MANAGEMENT' STORAGE BOXES
Dottings for Riess
AVAILABLE FROM TWENTYTWENTYONE (PP.115 & 131)

'HANG AROUND' COOKING UTENSILS
KiBiSi for Muuto
AVAILABLE FROM THE LOLLIPOP SHOPPE (P.148)

'TWIST A TWILL' BLANKET
Tina Ratzer for Silkeborg Uldspinderi
AVAILABLE FROM MAR MAR CO. (P.149)

'STORE' CONTAINERS
Estd for Established & Sons
AVAILABLE FROM HAUS (P.186)

'ZERO' MIRRORS
Hiroyuki Kato for Teori
AVAILABLE FROM TWENTYTWENTYONE (PP.115 & 131)

'HOMEGROWN BLUE' RUG
Edward Barber & Jay Osgerby for The Rug Company
AVAILABLE FROM THE RUG COMPANY (P.042)

'MY' TEAWARE
Anouk Jansen for Jansen+Co
AVAILABLE FROM SCP (PP.043 & 153)

'MOON' ESPRESSO CUP AND SAUCER
Jasper Morrison for Rosenthal
AVAILABLE FROM JASPER MORRISON SHOP (P.144)

×

'WATER KETTLE'
Sori Yanagi for Gateway Japan
AVAILABLE FROM DAVID MELLOR (P.021)

'TEEMA' MUGS
Kaj Franck for iittala
AVAILABLE FROM SKANDIUM (PP.028 & 058)

'THE BOWL'
Mogens Lassen for By Lassen
AVAILABLE FROM SKANDIUM (PP.028 & 058)

'CIOTOLINO' COPPER DISH
Donata Paruccini for ENO
AVAILABLE FROM DARKROOM (P.098)

'SURFACE' VASES
Achim Haigis for Rosenthal
AVAILABLE FROM VESSEL (P.045)

'HEIMA' CANDLESTICKS
Francis Cayouette for Normann Copenhagen
AVAILABLE FROM TWENTYTWENTYONE (PP.115 & 131)

For more 4x4 selections, keep an eye on the London Design Guide website throughout the year. We'll keep featuring products in a variety of specialist categories, from coffee cups and cushions to sofas and storage.

Citywide

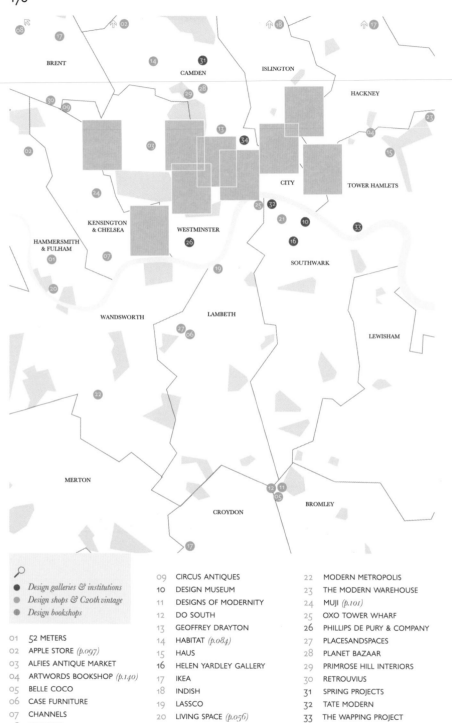

Citywide

INTRODUCTION

*Max Fraser**

This chapter is dedicated to London's most relevant neighbour-hood destinations – the ones that lie outside the city's major design hubs but are too important to overlook. Sure, there's a lot to be said for the power of association; a design quarter is often more than the sum of its parts. But these businesses are targets in themselves, reasons to explore a new area of town, embodiments of fresh points of view. That is what the Citywide chapter celebrates.

It's easy to forget just how vast a city London has become. Neighbourhoods are constantly in flux; they morph with gentrification, industrialisation, commercialisation, and shift demographically – not all for the better. Over the city's 600 square miles there are dozens of little villages that merge organically over time, making it extremely difficult to cover every base. Keeping on top of these changes has been an ongoing challenge for me while researching this guide – not least working on this chapter.

Then there's the challenge of getting around. London is a frustrating city for transport users. Since the introduction of the mayor in 2000 there have been some positive changes, yet the transport network is relentlessly plagued by its old infrastructure. Crossing the sprawling, disjointed city can eat up considerable chunks of time, which may explain why Londoners tend to be localised and somewhat insular. The age-old rivalry between areas north and south of the Thames is a stereotypical reminder of this. There's no obvious remedy, but public schemes like the Cycle Hire programme may help to relieve our anxiety over the neighbourhood divide – and the congestion that keeps us away.

I've been on many mini-adventures while researching this chapter. They've included some sub-standard places but several lovely ones, too. The more often I get outside my comfort zone, the more often I wonder how many hidden treasures I'm still missing out on. This edition includes significantly more Citywide entries than the 2010 guide, and I'm proud of that. Of course, if you know of any worthy contenders in your vicinity, please send your suggestions to info@londondesignguide.com.

*Editor of London Design Guide londondesignguide.com

01 52 METERS

- 291 LILLIE ROAD SW6 7LL
- 020 7381 1774
- 52METERS.COM
- MON-SAT 10-5:30
- WEST BROMPTON

03 ALFIES ANTIQUE MARKET

- 13-25 CHURCH STREET NW8 8DT
- 020 7723 6066
- ALFIESANTIQUES.COM
- TUE-SAT 10-6
- EDGWARE ROAD

It's on a stretch of road in Fulham known mostly for its serious antiques, yet 52 Meters is decidedly playful with its ever-changing mix of midcentury design. The nondescript exterior is deceptively so; inside is a bright, spacious showroom spread over two floors, including a basement and outdoor space in the back.

Walk in and you'll get the immediate impression owners Tom Stewart-Liberty and Henry Saywell work hard to source pieces that don't conform to a defined aesthetic, genre or period. Neither the stock nor the layout takes itself too seriously. You'll be intrigued by the eclectic mix of lighting that hangs from the ground-floor ceiling – a perfect complement to the collection of furniture sat below. I was amused to have found an original prototype of Tom Dixon's *Spiral Light* stood between a pair of snug Ico Parisi armchairs from the late 1940s. There's also a schedule of artist exhibitions here. The time I visited the shop was dotted with amusing porcelain figurines by artist Dan Weill, including a Charlie Chaplin dressed in Fred Flintstone's emblematic attire.

It's refreshing to find such an unusual collection in this calm corner of London – though you might feel you're rather in Milan, Paris or even Venezuela, via a 1920s desk or rocking chair from the '80s.

Bennie Gray opened Alfies on the site of the Edwardian department store Jordan's in 1976 and, ever since, the vintage market has won the admiration of collectors, designers, even those with a casual interest. With more than 75 dealers spread across 3,500-square-metres, Alfies is one of the country's largest indoor antique markets. The fact that the surrounding shops on Church Street are now occupied with antiques dealers is mostly down to Gray.

Behind the magnificent Art Deco façade is a maze of rooms spread over four floors, where dealers of furniture, lighting, glass, ceramics, jewellery, art and vintage clothing are crammed in. There's 20th-century design peppered throughout the building, with the largest concentration in the basement at Decoratum, with its tidy room sets arranged by era, emphasising pieces from the 1940s to the 1970s. Vincenzo Cafferella is another prominent name, offering an extensive collection of mainly midcentury Italian lighting, furniture and art.

There's an old-school vibe to Alfies, and its swirly carpets and fluorescent lighting strips it of any pretension. Strike up a conversation with any of the longtime traders to pick their brains. But be shrewd: many have the propensity to inflate their prices. Don't feel pressured to buy. If you fancy something special, mull it over at the Rooftop café and restaurant.

05 BELLE COCO

- 40 CHURCH ROAD SE19 2XE
- 02000 111 715
- BELLECOCO.COM
- THU–FRI & SUN 10–5, SAT 9–6
- CRYSTAL PALACE

06 CASE FURNITURE

- 189 STONHOUSE STREET SW4 6BB
- 020 7622 3506
- CASEFURNITURE.CO.UK
- MON–FRI 10–6, SAT 10–4
- CLAPHAM COMMON

The understated south London neighbourhood of Crystal Palace is home to a handful of vintage dealers, of which Belle Coco is one. The shop is located in one of a trio of streets that makes up the Crystal Palace Triangle – and carries a wide variety of furniture, lighting, ceramics, glass and other retro paraphernalia.

It's nestled among some other specialist dealers on the triangle, but Belle Coco is the best looking of the lot. It also puts the pavement outside to best use; the tight displays that spill out the door make Belle Coco an intriguing neighbourhood destination. Once you're inside, though, it becomes apparent the outdoor display is a practical matter – the small shop could never accommodate all that stuff.

Even the ceiling is an attraction, speckled by a spectrum of light emitted from the collection of sculptural retro pendant lamps. Otherwise the floor is stuffed with furniture – be it a black leather lounge chair by Robin Day, a wooden telephone bench from Ercol or a smoky-glass and chrome dining table by Merrow Associates. Yet despite any big-name items there is nothing intimidating about a visit here, thanks to the warm welcome you get from owners Helen and Ains – and the jolly music they pipe in for your pleasure.

As we go to press, Helen and Ains were about to open a second outlet on the same stretch of Church Road, to operate as their local repair and upholstery workshop. It's a necessary side to the business that ensures all originals here are sold in the best possible condition.

You might not expect to come across a contemporary furniture Mecca in a peaceful residential side street in south London, but that's the surprise that awaits you only a stone's throw from Clapham High Street. British manufacturer Case Furniture opened the space in 2010 to showcase its innovative collection and invite trade buyers and the local public to explore the full range of designs. A warm welcome comes courtesy of Case's dedicated and informed staff.

British furniture pioneer Paul Newman (he founded Notting Hill's Aero) established the company in 2006 to introduce fine collections by both established and emerging designers at an accessible price point. Though it's still a young business, the neighbourhood's enthusiasm would suggest Newman's goal is being achieved.

Case's solid roster of contributors tends towards designers with a timeless and functionalist approach. Leading British talent Matthew Hilton, for instance, has contributed several award-winning items to the floor, such as his *Cross* extending dining table and *Bridge* chair, table and armchair. Bethan Gray and Marina Bautier have created simple and versatile shelving along with Shin Azumi, who has also tackled a home-office desk with integrated storage. Other talents include Nazanin Kamali, William Warren and the late British master Robin Day.

The collections are well considered and sturdily designed, and side-step avant-garde flourishes in favour of commercial appeal. Newman is experienced enough to know what customers actually want to live with, and he proves it here.

07 CHANNELS

- 1-3 NEW KING'S ROAD SW6 4SB
- 020 7371 0301
- CHANNELSDESIGN.COM
- MON-SAT 10-5:30
- FULHAM BROADWAY

08 CHAPLINS

- 477-507 UXBRIDGE RD, HATCH END, MIDDX HA5 4JS
- 020 8421 1779
- CHAPLINS.CO.UK
- MON-SAT 10-6
- HATCH END RAIL

Furniture designer Samuel Chan's showroom and shop benefits from a high-profile space on busy New King's Road, right at the Chelsea-Fulham border. Here Chan marries his talent for traditional woodcraft with a flair for contemporary styling in a bright white, welcoming space. It's a treasure trove of wood in all forms and textures, from dining tables to letter-shaped candleholders. Honourable mentions include the *Motley* touch-sensitive stackable drawer systems and the *Hume* book tower, both timeless designs integrating simple, geometric forms. Chan's collaboration with graphic designer Anthony Burrill netted the *ABC Screen*, a room divider with geometric contours cut into the wood by hand.

The collections monopolise a full three floors of the double-width space. The basement is home to the *Cabinet of Last Things*, a selection of handmade and/or limited-edition accessories from past seasons, the last of their kind, at discounted prices. That alone is worth the trek to this unassuming stretch of the New King's Road, but Channels really offers the complete package.

Chan is one of those talented yet quietly inconspicuous designers who, refreshingly, don't shout about themselves. As such his achievements speak through the displays in his showroom. Sure, you'll find dotted around the space a few framed posters displaying his accreditations with the Design Guild Mark and his commitment to quality and craftsmanship – but all that is pure understatement.

Chaplins is one of the largest high-end contemporary furniture and lighting showrooms in the UK, occupying more than 2,500-square-metres over two floors and two buildings. The family-run business, now operated by Simon Chaplin, has been trading for about 20 years and enjoys steady growth – despite its rather odd suburban location in deepest northwest London. If you drive from central London (though I don't recommend it; take the train), the neverending sprawl of suburban houses provides a clue as to where Chaplins' customer base lies: the commuter wealth-belt with big homes to fill.

The premises make striking presence on this stretch of high street, the tidy window displays making a big style statement. Sure, some of it is bourgeois, leaning toward the gaudy, but the overall selection is fresh and contemporary. You'll spot designs from the contemporary canon, the likes of Vitra, Ligne Roset, Established & Sons, B&B Italia, Zanotta, Cassina and Moooi, to name only a few. Since my last visit two years ago the emphasis has shifted, happily, to more textural pieces made from natural materials and finishes; some of the old gloss and shine is disappearing.

You'll find furniture and lighting for any scenario here, but even with this much space it's impossible to come anywhere close to showing all that their 180 European suppliers have to offer. If you're hunting for something specific, be sure to ask the staff to advise, or visit the comprehensive website before visiting.

09 CIRCUS ANTIQUES

🏠 60 CHAMBERLAYNE ROAD NW10 3JH
📞 020 8968 8244
🔗 CIRCUSANTIQUES.CO.UK
🕐 TUE-SAT 10-6
Ⓔ KENSAL RISE

10 DESIGN MUSEUM

🏠 28 SHAD THAMES SE1 2YD
📞 020 7403 6933
🔗 DESIGNMUSEUM.ORG
🕐 DAILY 10-5.45 (LAST ADMISSION 5.15PM)
Ⓔ TOWER HILL / LONDON BRIDGE

The appetite for vintage collectibles is stronger than ever as more people choose to soften their modern interiors with texture and patina from the past – in part in rebellion against today's slick, contemporary aesthetic. Circus Antiques capitalises on this burgeoning market from its prominent corner in Kensal Rise.

While many dealers focus on midcentury furniture and lighting designed by the most popular Modernist masters, Circus owner Mark Slade prefers to widen his catch, bringing together 19th- and 20th-century beauties that don't command such hefty prices. Antique and vintage tables, desks, seating and storage blend with lighting, mirrors, artworks and *objets*, doing their damndest to attract both locals and enthusiasts from further afield.

When I browsed the relatively small space, the furniture highlights included a 1950s Italian sofa and matching armchair reupholstered in bright blue; a 1920s English camel-back sofa with ball and claw feet, upholstered in oatmeal linen; and a pair of 1940s American wooden school chairs. These were accessorised by a large 1920s English bleached-oak pharmacy cabinet, which housed a number of curiosities, and illuminated by a 1930s French Art Deco mirrored floor lamp and a pair of 1980s Italian Murano table lamps.

Such examples illustrate the diversity of pieces available at Circus. The website is always kept up to date, but I would recommend a visit to the shop to enjoy each piece up close. When you're in the area, you might also check out the collectibles at Niche (70 Chamberlayne Road) and Howie & Belle (No 52).

In 1982 the first phase of the Design Museum launched in the basement of the V&A (p.030) under the instruction of design's leading entrepreneur, Terence Conran. The museum matured into its own Bauhaus-inspired building at the end of the '80s, and since then it has showcased and commented on the ingenuity of furniture, graphics, architecture, fashion and industrial design throughout the 20th century and into the 21st.

The institution has developed a global reputation as a cultural beacon in the celebration of design excellence. Under the directorship of Deyan Sudjic, the museum has thrived with a schedule of retrospectives (featuring design legends living and late) and an annual showcase of trailblazing contemporary projects, plus a schedule of lectures and debates. Despite its spectacular riverside views, the museum has a drawback: its slightly awkward location in relation to public transport. This will likely be solved when the museum moves to new premises in the Commonwealth Institute building in Kensington in 2014.

Still, it's worth the trip. After a walk round the exhibitions you can relax in the ground floor café or take a more formal lunch at the Blueprint Café upstairs. The Design Museum Shop is one of the city's finest, a focused resource for design books and periodicals, as well as contemporary housewares, many of which have been specially commissioned by the shop.

11 DESIGNS OF MODERNITY

🛋 CRYSTAL PALACE ANTIQUES, JASPER ROAD SE19 1SJ
📞 07966 285 694
🔗 DESIGNSOFMODERNITY.COM
🕐 DAILY 10-6
⊖ CRYSTAL PALACE

12 DO SOUTH

🛋 2 WESTOW STREET SE19 3AH
📞 020 8771 0500
🔗 DO-SOUTH.COM
🕐 TUE-FRI 11-6, SAT 10-6, SUN 11-5
⊖ CRYSTAL PALACE

Designs of Modernity occupies the basement of the Crystal Palace Antiques & Modern warehouse, a four-storey former Victorian warehouse with a sort of crumbling charm about it. About a dozen dealers with different specialities sell furniture from the 17th-century onwards. The owner of Designs of Modernity, the knowledgeable Ben Adams, flies the flag for the Modernists, sourcing furniture, lighting, decorative objects and posters from 1950s to '70s with an emphasis on Danish originals.

Real beauties await you here. If I had space at home, I would have snapped up a number of chairs on my last visit – most notably a set of teak *Model 75* chairs with Danish cord seats designed by Niels O. Møller in 1954. Danish legend Hans J Wegner was well represented, as well as lighting by his contemporary Poul Henningsen. Original graphic posters from the 1972 Münich Olympic Games adorned the walls. That said, stock changes regularly and is updated weekly on the website, so call ahead if you're looking for something particular.

The warehouse operates as a sort of cooperative, whereby dealers come and go and sales are handled by a gentleman in a tiny 'cabin' by the front door. It's worth knowing that credit cards are not accepted. This can prove problematic if you intend to spend, but that's a small mercy in what is otherwise a pleasurable and relaxed destination.

Crystal Palace has become fairly self-sufficient in recent years, having lured in a growing number of independent businesses, which tend to establish themselves in the streets comprising the Crystal Palace Triangle. Do South is one such addition, occupying a bright corner space that benefits from plenty of passing traffic.

Introducing high-end contemporary European living-room and dining-room furniture to this part of the city was a brave move by owners Freddie Oke and Noel Douglas. With little prior retail experience, neighbourhood denizens Oke and Douglas (an ex-publisher and ex-advertising executive respectively) chose to open a new lifestyle store, hoping to change the status quo on the triangle.

They've done so by combining new and old furniture, lighting and accessories – all of which, presumably, are meant to reflect the diversity of styles found in most people's homes. The mix of products here can seem somewhat random. There are slick, big-ticket contemporary brands like Zanotta, Moroso and Sancal alongside reupholstered sofas, armchairs and cushions from the 1950s, '60s and '70s. But, where possible, there's also a good selection from local producers, like the *Made in Peckham* line of furnishings by Hendzel and Hunt, constructed from reclaimed, locally sourced waste materials. More affordable accessories and accents also join the displays.

Do South was fairly new when I visited. I'm a believer that such places take a bit of time to find their legs, and I suspect it will mature into a more coherent destination in line with the appetites and whims of its neighbours.

13 GEOFFREY DRAYTON
85 HAMPSTEAD ROAD NW1 2PL
020 7387 5840
GEOFFREY-DRAYTON.CO.UK
MON-SAT 10-6
WARREN STREET

In May 2012, Geoffrey Drayton celebrates 50 years since he opened his first shop, which sold quality contemporary European furniture and lighting out of a space in Walthamstow. Without question Drayton was a pioneering importer of the alternative modern lifestyle at a time when a new generation of Londoners was eager to embrace it. Since his debut the market has changed beyond recognition as increasingly more designers and manufacturers vie for our attention.

Drayton's current location on Hampstead Road, past the northern end of Tottenham Court Road, takes up almost the entire block and has recently expanded to a whopping 1,000-square-metres. The enormous windows that front the space give you a good glimpse of the vast quantity of stock. It doesn't take long to realise you'll be spoilt for choice inside.

Over the years the list of suppliers stocked at Geoffrey Drayton has grown to represent the cream of the crop in modern European design. Established furniture and lighting brands are its mainstay: Vitra, Knoll, Fritz Hansen, Cor, Montana, Poltrona Frau, Magis, Kartell, Flos, Artemide, Foscarini, Luceplan and Louis Poulsen are only representative of the wealth of names in store. In fact Drayton is the longest established dealer in the UK for both Cassina and B&B Italia, and carries the most comprehensive collection of the former. Another major element of the business is fitted furniture systems for living rooms and bedrooms, usually from Interlübke of Germany or Porro of Italy.

Their comprehensive roster of suppliers covers all the bases for classic and state-of-the-

art interiors. And, remarkably, the staff manage to showcase an example from every collection (though it can get rather crowded). Such abundance can be slightly overwhelming, but I'd encourage you to thoroughly explore. After all, the opportunity to see such a broad high-end selection in one place is unusual in central London, where space is at a premium.

With plenty of domestic settings to browse, it is inevitable you'll have some questions. To answer these and offer advice, Drayton and his team (including his son Guy) are always on hand. Indeed you'll need their knowledge and expertise to guide you when you're investing this much money in your home.

HAUS

- 39 MORPETH ROAD E9 7LD
- 020 7536 9291
- HAUSLONDON.COM
- THU–SAT 11-6, SUN 11-5
- MILE END / BETHNAL GREEN

Before the arrival of Haus in Victoria Park 'village', I think it's fair to say this area of east London was devoid of high-calibre contemporary design. But since its opening at the end of 2009 the shop has attracted a raft of other independent stores, making the area a real pleasure to stroll around – despite being slightly awkward to access by public transport.

The white-walled, clean-lined space is certainly inviting from the outside, the strategic lighting adding intrigue and casting a warm glow onto the merchandise, namely furniture and home accessories. Haus may be small but it stocks an extensive list of leading design brands like Vitra, Magis, Established & Sons, Swedese, Tom Dixon, Bestlite, Flos, Foscarini, Artek and more. Accompanying the big brands are items from smaller producers or individual talents, many of which are suitable for gifts.

With the warehouse nearby, the aim is to frequently rotate the stock to show off the breadth of the collection, while giving the locals a reason to return. Whatever happens to be on display when you visit, every item will possess those winning attributes: quality, functionality and longevity. There are no flippant or fashion-driven gestures here. This is hardly surprising. Haus is co-owned by Andrew and Jane Tye, a designer and sculptor respectively. On the whole, designers tend to be very hard to please when it comes to designs that are not their own, so you can rest assured that every item in the shop has been closely scrutinised and considered.

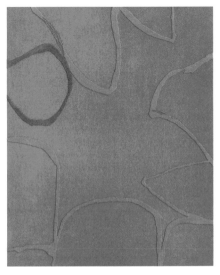

16 HELEN YARDLEY GALLERY

🏠 A-Z STUDIOS, 3-5 HARDWIDGE STREET SE1 3SY
📞 020 7403 7114
🔗 HELENYARDLEY.COM
🕐 WED-FRI 11-5 (OR BY APPOINTMENT)
⊖ LONDON BRIDGE

Rug designer Helen Yardley chose a modest
converted warehouse on a quiet Bermondsey
back street for her expansive studio and
showroom. Ring the buzzer, venture upstairs and
you're likely to be greeted by one of Yardley's
friendly assistants, if not the smiley Yardley
herself. This designer and producer of rugs,
carpets and wall hangings started her studio in
1983, and it has since evolved to attract a loyal
following of architects, designers and private
clients. The painterly style is her signature:
sweeping brushstrokes and swathes of colour
echoed in hand-tufted wool, hand-knotted
needlepoint and printed felt. There's also a
standard range of rugs called *The Collection*, most
of which are made to order.

The 200-square-metre showroom is calm,
whitewashed and naturally lit – a clean backdrop
against which the vivid palette of the rugs can
sing. Should you be after something bespoke, the
studio encourages one-on-one meetings to discuss
customer requirements. You can view samples,
sneek a peek into Yardley's creative hotbed and
watch new rugs taking shape in the workshop.
It makes sense, considering the bespoke
nature of the work, that customers get a better
understanding of the skill and craftsmanship
behind each item.

17 IKEA

🏠 CROYDON, EDMONTON & WEMBLEY
📞 0845 358 3364
🔗 IKEA.COM/GB
🕐 (SEE WEBSITE)
🚇 (SEE WEBSITE)

18 INDISH

🏠 16 BROADWAY PARADE N8 9DE
📞 020 8340 1188
🔗 INDISH.CO.UK
🕐 MON-SAT 10.30-5.30, SUN 12.30-4.30
🚇 CROUCH HILL RAIL

The vast majority of us have shopped at IKEA. The ubiquitous brand is the world's largest home-furnishing retailer with nearly 300 suburban stores attracting 626 million visitors and annual sales topping €23 billion. The Swedish flat-pack success story has introduced a sense of design to the masses – as well as incredibly efficient procurement systems. So clever, so fine-tuned… and jaw-droppingly cheap.

We all love a bargain, which is why we nearly always leave IKEA with more stuff than we intended. So much about coming here involves effort, so if you're going to go through it, you don't want to leave empty-handed.

All this stuff troubles me. According to its 2010 Sustainability Report, IKEA releases 30 million tonnes of CO_2 per year, directly and indirectly, across its total operations. Annually, 197 million catalogues are printed to alert us to what's in store. As most large corporations like to tell us, they are 'responding to consumer demand'; fair enough. But going forward, IKEA claims to encourage customers to adopt more sustainable behaviour at home. It increasingly takes responsibility for a product's demise by offering customers proper discard channels. The global brand is trying.

Unfortunately, we consumers are not very good at separating low prices from low value. We don't cherish cheap things. Because we paid little for something, it is somehow OK to discard it without much thought. It is this culture of flippant disposability that must change. That, however, will take a societal shift in mentality.

Crouch End is the North London branch of Indish, here since 1996. The neighbourhood brims with independent stores and possesses a village-like independence from London – heightened by its disconnect from the Underground network. Plenty of young families live in the area and there's no doubt this demographic makes up a large percentage of Indish's customers, attracted as they are to the colourful, playful mix of accessories, tableware, furniture and lighting. While there's a recession going on outside, Indish resolves itself to add brightness and joy to our homes.

The small, narrow space manages to pack in a wide variety of stuff. Many of the brands can be found elsewhere, but here locals are spared a trip into town to find them. Iconic and characterful items from Italian producers Alessi, Kartell, Magis and Flos meet calmer equivalents from Scandinavians like iittala, Muuto, Royal VKB, Marimekko, Eva Solo, Normann and Stelton. British names are also supported here: Thorsten van Elten, People Will Always Need Plates, black + blum, Donna Wilson, Hulger, Suck UK and Thelermont Hupton.

Whether or not these names mean anything to you, you can rest assured prices remain affordable, making Indish suitable for gifts or impulsive pick-me-ups.

19 LASSCO

BRUNSWICK HOUSE, 30 WANDSWORTH RD SW8 2LG

020 7394 2100

LASSCO.CO.UK

MON–SAT 10-5, SUN 11-5

VAUXHALL

Back in 1758 the Georgian mansion Brunswick House was home to the Duke of Brunswick and surrounded by three acres of lush riverside parkland. Things are somewhat different today, though the listed gem defiantly remains standing in Vauxhall Cross – albeit in the shadow of the ghastly St George Wharf complex and polluted by thunderous traffic. Don't let this put you off. Once on English Heritage's *Building at Risk* list, the house was saved by architectural salvage company Lassco in 2004 and incrementally restored over the years. Thankfully, this wounded architectural veteran has had its dignity reinstated.

While you can revel in the stateliness of the building, the immense variety of reclaimed items sold within it will soon divert your attention. Enter through the grand stone portico and roam around the panelled rooms, their creaky floorboards laden with a continually changing display of architectural antiques, salvage and curiosities.

Each room takes a different focus, be it hooks, doorknobs, hinges and handles or antique rugs and Victorian furniture. Even chimneys, entranceways, chandeliers and colonnades find space to shine anew. Venture down into the vaults, cellars and stone-flagged pantries to get your fill of cast-iron radiators, porcelain basins and ornate French brass taps. Or head outside for statues, old public and garden furniture, fountains, lanterns and lampposts.

The joy of visiting Lassco is in the exploration of this eccentric and slightly hotchpotch place. Even more amazing than the massive amounts of always-changing stock is the staff's ability to keep track of it all – and log it onto the website too.

As I was leaving, I discovered to my delight that the ballroom has been transformed into the laidback Brunswick House Cafe (brunswickhousecafe.co.uk), where you can take a break from trawling and grab a cup of coffee or a tasty and affordable lunch or dinner amid retro paraphernalia. Brunswick House defiantly enjoys its new lease of life. What a marvel, considering the intrusive modernisation that continues only spitting distance from its walls.

21 LOOPHOUSE

- 88 SOUTHWARK BRIDGE ROAD SE1 0EX
- 020 7207 7619
- LOOPHOUSE.COM
- MON–FRI 9.30–5.30
- BOROUGH

22 MODERN METROPOLIS

- 735 GARRATT LANE SW17 0PD
- 020 8971 9191 / 07811 956 698
- MODERNMETROPOLIS.COM
- MON, TUE, THU–SAT 10-6, SUN 11-4
- TOOTING BROADWAY / EARLSFIELD RAIL

When the trend for wood floors began to overtake the preference for fitted carpet, an energetic rugger called Lorraine Statham got in the game. She founded Loophouse in 1992, in the early days of an upward trajectory in rugs that sees no sign of stopping. All that unforgiving hardwood needs some softening, and Statham's contemporary rugs have become a popular choice.

Because her fine-quality, 100 per cent wool creations are all handmade, they're ideal for bespoke customers. Interior designers, architects and private clients are attracted to Loophouse for that reason – as well as for the warmth, tactility and wide range of styles, textures and techniques she incorporates in her craft.

But colour is Statham's main driver, and bold florals and geometric patterns stand out at the Southwark Bridge showroom. Yet while her portfolio offers something for everyone, it often inspires customers to bespoke – especially once her wool tuft samples appear and the discussion of 'pile heights' and 'weave textures' unfurls.

Statham's enthusiasm for her trade is contagious, but should you wish to discuss any bespoke options with her specifically, I advise making an appointment in advance. A visit to the studio will reveal a snapshot of what she's able to produce – cushions, beanbags, throws, wallpapers, tapestries and wall art included – but you'll have to stay longer for the full experience.

It once occupied a space on Brick Lane, but Modern Metropolis has been gracing Summerstown in southwest London for the past seven years. It's quite the treasure trove of postwar furniture, lighting and artworks. Formerly a more dainty, organised boutique, it has evolved into a cave bursting at the seams, styled by its owner to make it feel less intimidating to customers.

Yet it's so chock-a-block, you might have some trouble working your way around the floor – that's if you can even see the floor for all the stuff. Still it'll be worth your efforts to manoeuvre around the evolving range. Most of the stock is from Belgium, Italy and Germany, and it's quite exciting to see so many classics in one space. Eames chairs are aplenty, as well as more unusual (but still iconic) pieces, like the spherical, futuristic Keracolour television. The walls – lined with rows of chairs and other curiosities – showcase a gallery of framed posters and prints, ranging from music posters from Sony BMG to Hockneys and Peter Blakes acquired from art dealers.

There's something for everyone to admire here, and the slightly chaotic displays make you feel as though you might retrieve a hidden treasure. And there's a good chance of it. The experience is like rummaging through a relative's attic, but what you'll find will be collectible – and probably in better condition.

23 THE MODERN WAREHOUSE

🚚 3 TRAFALGAR MEWS E9 5JG
📞 020 8986 0740
↖ MODERNWAREHOUSE.COM
🕐 BY APPOINTMENT ONLY
⊖ HACKNEY WICK

24 OXO TOWER WHARF

🚚 BARGEHOUSE STREET SE1 9PH
📞 020 7021 1600
↖ COINSTREET.ORG
🕐 TUE–SUN 11–6 (STUDIOS)
⊖ BLACKFRIARS/WATERLOO/SOUTHWARK

While researching vintage dealers online (their preferred trading platform nowadays) I came across the highly polished website of the Modern Warehouse, with its up-to-date stock of covetable midcentury furniture, lighting and accessories from Scandinavia, the US and the UK. On closer inspection it appeared the outfit operates a London warehouse 'open by appointment daytime, evenings and weekends'.

I'm not a fan of shops with an appointment-only policy, and our remit at the *London Design Guide* doesn't cover such places. But I must say I was intrigued, so I went ahead and booked an appointment. When I arrived at the gated mews in Hackney Wick, East London, however, it became clear why the owners favour this system: this is not a location one simply stumbles upon, or one that would benefit from any passing trade.

I was met by David, who runs the business with Rob (they prefer to go by their first names). David welcomed me immediately and invited me to look around the current stock, which was displayed in tidy room-set displays over two floors. On this day the emphasis was on Danish design, including stunning armchairs by Hans Wegner, plus a rare rosewood desk and a teak and oak sofa by Arne Vodder, among other top-quality gems.

So don't be put off by the appointment-only policy – you're not obliged to buy anything when you make one. Though you could, alternatively, keep an eye on the website, which is updated fortnightly to include recent shipments. Or you could sign up to the mailing list to make yourself eligible for invitations to regular open-weekend and evening events.

Once the production facility for the famous OXO beef cubes, this 1930s riverside landmark fell derelict in the 1970s before development trust Coin Street Community Builders converted it into a mixed-use live-work-eat-shop site. With a tower of flats above, the plaza comprises ateliers, cafés, restaurants and an exhibition space.

More than 30 designers run their businesses from the first and second floors, their spaces doubling as retail showrooms for their wares. Their output spans furniture, lighting, ceramics, glass, home accessories, textiles, jewellery and fashion – the idea being that you can observe the designers at work and commission or purchase directly from them. Brands to look out for include Innermost, black + blum, j-me, Suck UK, Bodo Sperlein, Anne Kyyrö Quinn, Miranda Watkins, 95% and w2 Products.

Visitors access the studios from the adjoining walkway. When you peer in you may well hesitate before entering, for fear of interrupting the workflow. Yet it's worth pointing out that each studio is obliged to welcome visitors; it's part of their rent agreement.

Opening hours can be frustratingly sporadic. However a trip here is seldom wasted. There's often an exhibition in the ground-floor gallery@ oxo. Or you can enjoy a drink at the top-floor Oxo Tower restaurant and bar, which command some of London's best skyline views.

26 PHILLIPS DE PURY & COMPANY
HOWICK PLACE SW1P 1BB
020 7318 4010
PHILLIPSDEPURY.COM
MON–FRI 10–6
VICTORIA

27 PLACESANDSPACES
30 OLD TOWN SW4 OLB
020 7498 0998
PLACESANDSPACES.COM
TUE–SAT 10–5.45, SUN 12–5
CLAPHAM COMMON

Harry Phillips founded his London auction house under a different name in 1796. The company has morphed considerably over the years and today focuses on selling the finest contemporary art, design, jewellery, photography and editions. Within the category of design, two annual auctions bring together modern and contemporary furniture, lighting and *objets*. The events are much anticipated by collectors and the industry alike, and act as a barometer for the appetite for collectible design today.

Today the London headquarters is housed in a converted Victorian post-sorting complex on peaceful Howick Place, away from busy Victoria Street. Visitors check in at a generous reception area, and then (depending on the auction and exhibition scheduling; check prior to your visit) head up the central staircase into the impressive viewing space. The high ceilings, white walls and wood floor provide a serene backdrop for the myriad collectibles showcased here.

Across all its auctions Phillips de Pury has a more edgy, youthful, controversial bent compared to its more traditional, elitist competitors. It was one of the first to embrace collectible works by living designers, in addition to its stable of 20th-century masters. In addition to auctions, Phillips curates selling exhibitions and deals with private sales and corporate collections. Recently launched is a second, smaller Mayfair space (p.073), where the house stages highlight exhibitions for forthcoming auctions.

Located amid a small stretch of shops at one corner of Clapham Common, placesandspaces has managed to maintain something of a neighbourhood feel, despite the distinctly international slant to their stock. The beautifully curated windows – characterised by the colourful and rather playful furnishings and accessories that are a speciality here – are a lure to passers-by.

The room inside is modest, and visitors would be forgiven for thinking that what you see is what you get. But what's lacking in floor space is made up with a vast catalogue of suppliers. placesandspaces is a sourcing specialist, a hunter-gatherer in the design world, as owner Laura Slack likes to put it, so be sure to tap into their resources if you're after something specific.

Slack has always excelled at combining timelessly modern furniture with sculptural lighting and more playful, quirky touches. Over the past few years she has increasingly shifted away from ubiquitous design icons towards more distinct, individual ranges from lesser known yet fine-quality designers and brands. Her business operates as UK agent and distributor for Holland's Droog; Japan's kyouei; Denmark's Oficina Kreativa and Mater; France's Moustache; Spain's Merry; and Latvia's Mint – as well as other producers. She also oversees the manufacture of her own designs, in collaboration with London studio Arris. As such, the diversity here is refreshingly unexpected.

28 PLANET BAZAAR

ARCH 68, STABLES MARKET, CHALK FARM RD NW1 8AH

020 7485 6000

PLANETBAZAAR.CO.UK

MON-FRI 12-6, SAT-SUN 10-6

CHALK FARM

29 PRIMROSE HILL INTERIORS

115 REGENT'S PARK ROAD NW1 8UR

020 7722 6622

ESSENTIALVINTAGE.COM

TUE-SAT 11-6, SUN 12-5

CHALK FARM

Since Maureen Silverman, a former artist, established Planet Bazaar in 1997 it's grown to be one of London's most respected dealers in vintage furniture, lighting, lifestyle accessories and contemporary artworks from Europe, Scandinavia and the US. Its current incarnation in the Stables Market in Camden Town is relatively new, having relocated here from Islington in 2009.

For many Londoners the appeal of the market has waned since the one-time hippie Mecca underwent development and the ensuing gentrification changed the flavour of the neighbourhood. The constant influx of tourists buying no end of tacky imports is enough to put anyone off coming here, but true lovers of vintage should persevere and make a trip to Planet Bazaar – situated, fortunately, just off the main drag.

It operates out of a Victorian railway arch with an open frontage that lends intrigue and lures market shoppers into the long, narrow space. Myriad curiosities lie within, displayed in dense formations so browsers can happily hunt through the content. What you see is what you get.

These days Silverman is less focused on collectible names. Sure, you'll see some token Eames, Jacobsen and Nelson pieces, but the majority is generic vintage with an unusual twist. Furniture and lighting from the '50s to the '70s prevails, alongside clusters of ceramics and glass. The walls are lined with miscellaneous artworks and, further back, glass cabinets showcase odd bits of jewellery and old toys. Pricing is reasonable and Silverman's laidback attitude is refreshing. After all, she is simply selling what she loves.

Phil Cowan, the owner of Primrose Hill Interiors, has been in the design business for more than 15 years, selling midcentury furniture, lighting, accessories and art. He started out in Camden's Stables Market with more of a slant towards 1960s pop designs. Then, in 2002, he crossed the threshold of affluent Primrose Hill and the selection became, well, a bit more grown up.

While his selections are tastefully curated across the shop's two floors, Cowan is not afraid to have some fun. He'll mix and match classic Scandinavian rosewood pieces with quirks like a zebra-skin armchair, a '70s chrome and smoked-glass coffee table, an Op Art print or 20th-century oil paintings. More recently he has brought in vintage jewellery, candles and cushion ranges – although, frankly, I consider these an unnecessary frivolity that confuses the message.

The fact that Cowan offers an interior-design service may go some way towards explaining why the displays are kept so tidy and are styled to replicate areas of the home. This helps customers envisage how things may sit in their own homes, be it a Danish teak desk, Italian mahogany sideboard, German rosewood drinks cabinet or Murano-glass vase.

Whatever your impression of this place it's refreshing to see such character and a point of view expressed here; the shop is a reflection of its personable owner. Just check it's open before making a special trip.

30 RETROUVIUS

- 📍 2A RAVENSWORTH ROAD NW10 5NR
- 📞 020 8960 6060
- 🔗 RETROUVIUS.COM
- 🕐 MON–SAT 10–6
- ⊖ KENSAL GREEN

Partners Adam Hills and Maria Speake have a passion for the gems that lurk in buildings prior to their demolition. Since setting up Retrouvius in 1993 the duo have succeeded at salvaging these treasures and giving them a second lease of life.

Their shop, off a rather nondescript stretch of Harrow Road, is a subtle find. You'd be forgiven for walking straight past, given that it's nestled between a house clearance shop and a catering equipment supplier and has no obvious sign over the door. But now that we've helped you, just buzz and you'll be invited to enter Retrouvius's texture-rich world.

The staff are more than happy to help, but I prefer to explore the charming, higgledy-piggledy collection of rooms at my own pace, first taking stock of the shop itself, which was built from reclaimed materials.

Neither a showroom nor a warehouse, Retrouvius sits somewhere in between. Displays don't have that painstakingly 'considered' quality, as stock constantly fluctuates due to the serendipity of salvage. On any given day old school chairs, wood tables, cast-iron coat hooks, utilitarian stacking stools, factory lights, old signage, couture mannequins and oak library steps might be positioned together with architectural antiques like fireplaces, wall panels, columns, doors or windows. There's also an array of basic reclaimed materials. And every so often you'll encounter something totally off the wall – something the owners took pity on – beside something so desirable they had to fight for it.

The design studio is situated upstairs and is where Speake and her team work across a broad

variety of domestic and commercial interiors projects. This bespoke interiors work, all of which incorporates some salvaged material treated with a contemporary language, gives Retrouvius an edge over other salvage competitors. It's also where their goal, to 'bridge the gap between destruction and construction', comes to life.

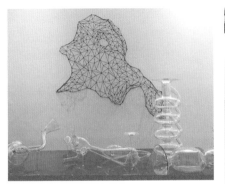

31 SPRING PROJECTS

- SPRING HOUSE, 10 SPRING PLACE NW5 3BH
- 020 7428 7159
- SPRINGPROJECTS.CO.UK
- TUE-WED 10-5, THU-FRI 12-7, SAT 11-4
- KENTISH TOWN

London photographers will be familiar with the illustrious photographic studios at Spring, located in a Kentish Town back street, where countless ad campaigns and fashion shoots are staged. The imposing brick Spring House also provides the stage for a 300-square-metre commercial gallery on the ground floor. The contemporary, custom-built space, curated by director Andrée Cooke, attracts all manner of artists, designers and fashion folk who come to witness the cross-pollination between the creative disciplines.

A receptionist will welcome you into Spring Projects at the entrance to the building and direct you to the high-ceilinged space. All white walls, it benefits from a gorgeous parquet floor, on which the exhibitions are arranged. One of the more extraordinary installations, *American Chateau*, came to the gallery in 2009 and comprised a collection of whimsical pieces by Spanish designer Jaime Hayon and his Dutch partner Nienke Klunder. The duo took inspiration from American pop culture and the 17th-century European opulence and produced a sort of Versaille-meets-Disneyland hybrid, overlapping high- and low-culture references from distant and more recent eras. A centrepiece of the show was a glossy table in the shape of a limousine, its legs twisted into the form of an infamous fast-food logo.

Past shows also include *B-side*, an exhibition of work by fashion designer Hussein Chalayan; *The Crate Series*, wherein Studio Makkink & Bey transformed ordinary shipping crates into domestic cabinets rich in detail; and *Escape Into the Upper Air*, newly commissioned work by designers El Ultimo Grito. Spring's exhibition programme rotates every few months, but there are periods of downtime in the gallery, so be sure to call ahead before planning a visit.

32 TATE MODERN
- BANKSIDE SE1 9TG
- 020 7887 8888
- TATE.ORG.UK/MODERN
- SUN-THU 10-6, FRI-SAT 10-10
- SOUTHWARK

33 THE WAPPING PROJECT
- HYDRAULIC POWER STATION, WAPPING WALL E1W 3SG
- 020 7680 2080
- THEWAPPINGPROJECT.COM
- MON-SAT 12-10.30, SUN 10-5.50
- WAPPING

Tate Britain's younger sibling took over the once disused Bankside Power Station in 2000 to house the major art movements of the 20th century. Exhibited over three levels are masterpieces that span from Matisse and Picasso to Dalí and Pollock. Special exhibitions exploring the works of individual artists, such as Miró, Rothko and Gauguin, complement the permanent displays. And the breathtaking Turbine Hall plays host to awe-inspiring installations by the likes of Anish Kapoor, Ai Weiwei and Tino Sehgal.

The bookshop ups the ante of traditional museum shops to present an exciting and diverse range of literature and ephemera. More than 10,000 publications line the wall: books on art theory and education, monographs and coffee table tomes. Magazines are a forte here too; there are plenty of hard-to-find art, design and architecture titles available. Added to this is a range of gifts created exclusively for Tate by contemporary designers like Grayson Perry and Takashi Murakami, and an interactive Art on Demand service allowing visitors to choose artworks to their specifications. All of this means it's not unusual to make a trip to the Tate Modern for the bookshop alone.

2012 sees the opening of Tate Modern's second phase of development. You'll see the existing building joined by an ambitious extension designed, like the main building, by architects Herzog & de Meuron. The new build will aim to increase the gallery's floor space and learning facilities while reaffirming the institution as a mainstay of London's South Bank.

The gates along a regenerated area of post-industrial London open onto what looks like a disused car park and redbrick factory, but it was once the Wapping Hydraulic Power Station. The distinguished theatre director Jules Wright transformed this derelict space and made it fit for unconventional artistic content, creating a cultural hybrid of contemporary art gallery, performance venue and fine-food restaurant.

Only upon entry do you get a sense of the sensitive conversion. The cavernous space still hosts the original decommissioned machinery of the pump house, and it serves as a centrepiece of this bygone era. Diners perch on minimalist furniture, which contrasts perfectly with the building's industrial fixtures: giant hooks, old fuse boxes, heavy chains and pressure valves. Artworks are exhibited on and around these existing fittings and diners are nestled among it all in this triple-height space, flooded with light.

Beyond the restaurant, in the former Boiler and Filter Houses, is the main gallery, a dark, cavernous space that has provided a raw canvas for exhibitions by photographer Guy Bourdin, bag designer Ally Capellino, United Visual Artists and, more recently, Yohji Yamamoto.

Before you leave be sure to pop into the tiny bookshop, housed in a glasshouse among the bamboo, bulbs and greenery on the lawn. This welcome addition to the space, run by journalist and editor Benjamin Eastham, carries a range of new and vintage style tomes, including special edition monographs and international magazines.

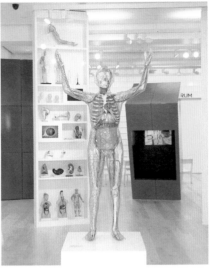

34 WELLCOME COLLECTION

- 183 EUSTON ROAD NW1 2BE
- 020 7611 2222
- WELLCOMECOLLECTION.ORG
- TUE-SAT 10-6, THU 10-10, SUN 11-6
- EUSTON SQUARE / EUSTON

This superb London institution explores the connections between medicine, history, art and life in the past, present and future in a way that's uniquely engaging. Wellcome's strap line is 'a free destination for the incurably curious', and it's entirely appropriate; the exhibitions staged here somehow make you confront things you may never have thought to confront before.

In his will, Sir Henry Solomon Wellcome instructed the formation of the Wellcome Trust, a charity to invest the profits of his pharmaceutical business in medical research. Sir Henry was an enterprising character, a scientist and businessman on the one hand and a collector and philanthropist on the other. Indeed, his passion for medicine led him to collect more than a million artefacts from around the world. These form the basis of the Wellcome Collection.

Throughout the year Wellcome stages popular, thought-provoking exhibitions exploring all manner of topics related to science and what it means to be human. The permanent galleries showcase fascinating snippets from the collection together with medical ideas that have emerged since Wellcome's death in 1936. Tours, events and lectures rotate regularly, and it's well worth checking out the library archive and the onsite bookshop – or simply enjoy a snack at the Peyton & Byrne café by the entrance.

It's entirely appropriate that this entry is the last in our publication, a final and perhaps humbling reminder that the application of design extends well beyond domestic niceties. Indeed the Wellcome Collection showcases the more pragmatic, potentially life-saving area of

product design: healthcare. It reminds us that civilisation has overcome extraordinary hurdles in the prevention and cure of disease and has intelligently invented every conceivable solution to aid and repair our bodies and minds. The objects in the Wellcome Collection expose mankind's primitive past while reminding us just how resourceful it can be.

Whatever you take away from your visit here, it's worth being reminded where human priorities should remain, and where designers would be wise to focus their energies.

DISCARDING

DESIGN

There's no question that, on a national scale, the vogue for vintage has saved a lot of furniture from landfill. Buying things second hand was once a resort of necessity; now it's a desired aesthetic. As with any fashion, though, the big question is what happens when it passes – if second hand, vintage and shabby chic are mere aesthetic fads, we'll eventually be back where we started, with unwanted goods heading back to landfill in a few years' time.

The big question is not so much how to dispose of design, but how to have less design to dispose of. Fashion is the enemy of sustainability. We become consumed by the constant cycle of desire, replacing our mountains of stuff with mountains of new stuff. The new stuff never stops coming. Observing the ranks of subtly tweaked, injection-moulded plastic chairs reverentially spotlit on pedestals at furniture fairs every year, it's hard not to wonder how many near-identical chairs are sitting unused in warehouses or office-clearance depots.

It may sound radical to suggest that no more chairs be made until a use has been found for all the existing chairs, but isn't the alternative – to keep manufacturing more chairs for a saturated market – genuinely perverse?

If it's the desire for ever-more fashionable objects that motivates us to replace a perfectly useful item with a newer model, it's also the power of fashion that makes those discarded objects difficult to dispose of. We tend to buy things when they're in fashion, at their most valuable, then discard them when they've become outmoded, thus at their least valuable. To escape the cycle we need to take a wider view on things and a moment of thought before making design decisions. Instead of being washed along on current trends we need to trust our aesthetic convictions and surround ourselves with things we have deeper connections with than the pages of a glossy magazine. The things we hold onto tend to be

> "When people move into a new home, the knee-jerk response these days is to gut it and make it their own. We need to ask ourselves whether this is necessary."

those objects that are knitted into our personal experience – connections we've built over time, pieces we found at a particular moment.

When people move into a new home, the knee-jerk response these days is to gut it and make it their own. We need to ask ourselves whether this is necessary. Besides the fact that gutting a house consumes tremendous amounts of resources, in the long term a house that's been kitted out all at once is much more susceptible to fads and fashions than an interior that's grown up around its inhabitants.

When it comes to disposing of stuff, the question of quality should come into the equation. Shabbily produced flat-pack furniture will not sustain years of hard use or bear much reselling. It makes sense to buy less and buy better. If something is well made, it'll retain some kind of value in reuse, even if it's damaged: a beautiful tabletop can be taken off broken legs to become a kitchen surface, for example. Old paving slabs, floorboards and fixtures given a second life as architectural salvage only retain that value because they were carefully produced in the first place. The architectural portal www.salvo.co.uk lists pretty much every architectural salvage company in Britain.

If you're disposing of furniture (and the packaging it comes in), you can always consider Freecycle, and there are plenty of house-clearance companies that will take things off your hands. The shortcomings of eBay seem to have stimulated a car boot renaissance, perfect for divesting yourself of more interesting pieces. For vintage and design objects, it's worth searching out dealers that specialise in the right area and understand the worth of a piece. Fashionable design does regain value if you can afford to bide your time in the right market. In the '90s you couldn't give away Memphis furniture, but in the past few years it's become the focus of specialist auctions the world over.

ADAM HILLS IS CO-DIRECTOR OF RETROUVIUS *retrouvius.com*
HETTIE JUDAH IS A WRITER AND CURATOR

ARCHI TONIC

THE INDEPENDENT RESOURCE FOR ARCHITECTURE AND DESIGN

WWW.ARCHITONIC.COM

www.architonic.com/PRODUCT CODE

DESIGN RESOURCES 📖 ↖

ABITARE ABITARE.IT
Italian magazine focused on architecture, interior design and innovative construction techniques. Features profiles of projects around the world, interviews with top designers and architects, information on new products and commentary.

APARTAMENTO APARTAMENTOMAGAZINE.COM
Fresh, simple independent magazine interested in real (ie unstyled) homes and design solutions. Born of the will to establish a connection with readers by positioning interior design as a means of personal expression.

ARCHITONIC ARCHITONIC.COM
Growing resource for architects, designers and private individuals hunting for the latest materials, products and fixtures, with a choice of tens of thousands of searchable items.

AZURE AZUREMAGAZINE.COM
Profiles international designers and architects; reports on major trade fairs across North America and Europe; and investigates design issues related to our changing society. Sources innovative projects, materials and products.

BLUEPRINT BLUEPRINTMAGAZINE.CO.UK
One of the leading magazines for architecture and design with a track record of more than 25 years. Takes a parallel approach to the different design disciplines, believing that fashion, product, furniture and architecture can share ideas.

COOLHUNTING COOLHUNTING.COM
Daily online update on ideas and products from the cultural intersection of art, design and technology. Regular video content gives an inside look at the work of various designers and artists.

CORE 77 CORE77.COM
Established online magazine dedicated to the practice and produce of industrial design. Practical resource for information as well as a venue for essays and reports on the topic of design in general.

CRAFTS CRAFTSCOUNCIL.ORG.UK
British bimonthly magazine for applied and decorative arts, and the only publication to celebrate all craft forms – from textiles to jewellery, architecture to furniture, plus ceramics, glass, metalwork and more.

CRANE CRANE.TV
Online video culture magazine with a cache of more than 500 videos showcasing the latest and best on its five channels: Art, Design, Fashion, Lifestyle and Travel.

CREATIVE REVIEW CREATIVEREVIEW.CO.UK
Leading magazine for visual communications, focusing on graphic design, advertising, digital media, illustration and photography. Also features video reports and interviews in its CRTV section.

DAILY ICON DAILYICON.NET
Online magazine featuring profiles of designers, architects and products as well as regular weekly posts on the latest happenings in architecture, interiors, art and travel. Special focus on furniture and accessories for home.

DAMN DAMNMAGAZINE.NET
Independent bimonthly publication reviewing international contemporary culture. Offers a diverse mix of articles for professionals and amateurs alike, with an emphasis on art, design and architecture.

DESIGN ADDICT DESIGNADDICT.COM
Extensive design portal and comprehensive source of information on 20th-century product design. Index of designers and manufacturers. Great design blog.

DESIGNBOOM DESIGNBOOM.COM
A leading online independent publication for key contemporary issues and critique of all aspects of art and design. Snapshot reports from international design shows, interviews and portraits of today's leading design protagonists. Plus design history and even a design shop.

DESIGN OBSERVER DESIGNOBSERVER.COM
Blog featuring critical writings on design, communications, arts and popular culture. Editorial by design connoisseurs Michael Bierut, William Drenttel and Jessica Helfand.

DESIGNSPOTTER DESIGNSPOTTER.COM
Online magazine dedicated to everything related to young, modern contemporary design, including product and interior design, fashion, residential architecture, exhibitions and publications. Offers a platform for publication and publicity for designer makers.

DESIGN WEEK DESIGNWEEK.CO.UK
Online news resource for design professionals. The latest features and exclusive commentary from the design industry. A regular must-read.

DETNK DETNK.COM
Online think tank dedicated to contemporary design and interiors, with a marketplace for the trade and acquisition of collectible design. Daily news accompanied by video interviews with leading designers from around the world.

DEZEEN DEZEEN.COM
Rapidly growing online design and architecture magazine providing a daily overview of the very latest news and projects from designers and architects around the world. Also includes Dezeen Screen, a design movie channel.

DOMUS DOMUSWEB.IT
Historically acclaimed Italian design and architecture magazine, first published in 1928. Bilingual, with articles printed in both Italian and English. Full of contemporary design and ideas, reviews of architecture, new products on the market and topical articles covering current events.

ELLE DECORATION
Monthly style magazine for luxury modern interiors. Showcases the leading designer trends and inspirational ideas in home furnishings, architecture and the decorative arts.

EYE MAGAZINE EYEMAGAZINE.COM
Quarterly international print magazine aimed at professional designers and students. Features critical, informed writing about graphic design and visual culture, and a stimulating lineup of interviews, profiles, history and polemic.

FORM FORMMAGAZINE.COM
Bimonthly architecture and design magazine with news from emerging talents in the industry.

FRAME FRAMEMAG.COM
Bimonthly review of interior architecture and design. Focuses on cutting-edge corporate and public interiors, particularly retail, exhibition, hospitality and workplace design.

GRAFIK GRAFIKMAGAZINE.COM
UK periodical for the creative and graphic-design industries. Delivers a bimonthly dose of news; editorials; launches from around the world; product reviews; and industry opinion pieces.

ICON ICONEYE.COM
UK design and architecture magazine tackling controversial topics with a critical edge. Website offers news and a selection of features from the magazine.

INTERNI INTERNIMAGAZINE.IT
Italian design magazine famous for selecting and documenting those works that are influential to Italian and international design culture.

INTRAMUROS INTRAMUROS.FR
Bimonthly and bilingual French/English magazine. Covers mainly French but also international design news and trends in the furniture, objects, interior design, fashion and new technology sectors.

LONDON DESIGN GUIDE LONDONDESIGNGUIDE.COM
Essential for anyone exploring the London design scene. Website acts as an extension of the printed publication, heralding events and exhibitions taking place across the capital.

MARK MARK-MAGAZINE.COM
Quarterly report on architecture and interior news. Another slick publication from the makers of Frame magazine.

METROPOLIS METROPOLISMAG.COM
US magazine examining contemporary life through design, architecture, interiors, product, graphics, crafts, planning and preservation.

MOCOLOCO MOCOLOCO.COM
A web magazine dedicated to modern contemporary interior design including furniture, accessories, lighting, floor and wall coverings, books, websites, audio and video, with online and retail stores.

MONOCLE MONOCLE.COM
A monthly publication from ex-*Wallpaper** editor Tyler Brûlé, covering international affairs, business, culture and design. Mainly targeted at wealthy cosmopolitan readers.

PLAZA PLAZAMAGAZINE.COM
Swedish magazine about fashion, design and interiors. Geared towards the rich and glamorous with a Scandinavian perspective. Includes a wide range of interviews with top designers, architects, industry executives, film stars and musicians.

SIGHT UNSEEN SIGHTUNSEEN.COM
Online magazine dedicated to design, art, fashion, food, photography and other creative disciplines. Features interviews, first-person accounts and behind-the-scenes documentation.

SURFACE SURFACEMAG.COM
American design, fashion and lifestyle magazine. Known for its creative inspiration, coverage of the burgeoning design world and cutting-edge design trends, and profiles of emerging designers.

TED TED.COM
Technology, Entertainment, Design. Non-profit event where the world's leading thinkers and doers gather to discuss design, entertainment, technology, business, science and other global issues. All talks uploaded onto the site and available to watch for free.

TL TLMAGAZINE.BE
Belgian quarterly focusing on innovative talent, materials and trends in the fields of design, fashion, retail and urban environments.

TREEHUGGER TREEHUGGER.COM
A prominent sustainability website offering the latest news, solutions and product information on green design.

WALLPAPER* WALLPAPER.COM
International design lifestyle magazine. Features the biggest developments in the worlds of interiors, design, architecture, travel and fashion. Published monthly. Also publishes travel guides.

YATZER YATZER.COM
Online design magazine featuring the very latest and most unique items from all the creative fields, including architecture, art, interiors, industrial design, graphics and fashion.

Tom Dixon
Shop.

Tom Dixon Shop
Wharf Building
Portobello Dock
344 Ladbroke Grove
London W10 5BU

Opening Times
Monday – Saturday 10am – 6pm
Thursday late night till 7pm
Sunday 11am – 5pm

Contact
Nina Hazlehurst
+44 (0)20 7183 9737
nina.hazlehurst@tomdixon.net

For more information please visit
www.tomdixon.net

SCP

SCP East
135–139 Curtain Road
London EC2A 3BX
+44 (0) 20 7739 1869
shopeast@scp.co.uk

SCP West
87–93 Westbourne Grove
London W2 4UL
+44 (0) 20 7229 3612
shopwest@scp.co.uk

www.scp.co.uk

Index

British Library Cataloguing-in-Publication data. A catalogue record for this book is available from the British Library.

The research for this publication was completed in 2011. Although the authors, editors, and publisher made every effort to ensure that the information contained in this publication is up-to-date and as accurate as possible at the time of going to press, some details are liable to change. The publisher accepts no responsibility for any loss, injury, or inconvenience sustained to any person using this book.

Printed in the UK by Butler Tanner & Dennis, Frome

Butler Tanner & Dennis uses paper products that are environmentally friendly, from well managed forests and mills that are FSC accredited.

Trade orders: Central Books, orders@centralbooks.com centralbooks.com. For further distribution details and advertising enquiries, visit: londondesignguide.com

ISBN: 978-0-9563098-1-5

Publisher's acknowledgements:
Spotlight Press would like to thank all contributing shops, galleries, institutions, designers, manufacturers, agencies and photographers for their kind permissions to reproduce their images in this book.

© ® Transport for London
Underground Roundel logo reproduced by kind permission of Transport for London

Photography credits: all images credited to the titled businesses unless stated otherwise. (18) right Eric Laignel (19) left Anthony Parkinson (22) left Marcus Peel (24) all Inge Clemente (26) left Jonathan Root (27) left The Serpentine Gallery, Photograph © 2007 John Offenbach (29) all Luke Hayes/ TASCHEN (30) left © Morley von Sternberg; top right www.alanwilliamsphotography.com; bottom right © Victoria and Albert Museum, London (31) all © V&A Enterprises (32-33) Lisa Linder (41) all Peer Lindgreen (43) left Pelle Crepin (44) all Morley von Sternberg (46-47) Ben Roberts (54) left Anthony Parkinson (56) right Marimekko

Corporation (58) right Khalid Bazzi (59) all © Vitsœ (60-61) Canteen (71) left and top right © Stuart Haygarth Courtesy Haunch of Venison; bottom right © Thomas Heatherwick Courtesy Haunch of Venison (73) all Courtesy of Phillips de Pury & Company (74-75) Tom Mannion for Tom Dixon (84) left Luisa Zanzani/ Gallery Libby Sellers; right Luke Hayes (86) left Stephen Jakub; top and bottom right Felix Clay (87) right Photograph by Kate Moross, 2011 (88-89) Keiko Oikawa (96) all Paul Raeside (98) all Peer Lindgreen (101) right Jeff Knowles (102-103) Jonathan Gregson (110) all Lyndon Douglas/ Courtesy Barbican Art Gallery (111) all Grant Smith (112) left philipvile.com (113) all Mark Whitfield Photography (115) right Mark Whitfield Photography (117) all © Jane Thompson (118-119) Jorge Monedero (127) left Gyorgy Korossy; right Courtesy of Estorick Collection of Modern Italian Art (128) right Paul Blease (129) left © Photography by Ed Reeve Courtesy of Kvadrat; right Rupert J Tapper (130) left and bottom right SMUG; top right Hilary Walker (131) all Mark Whitfield Photography (132-133) Antonio Cadoni (141) right Suzie Winsor (142) left Gallery FUMI; top and bottom right Maya Art (143) left © Geffrye Museum. Photo: David Clarke & Marcus Leith, top and bottom right: © Geffrye Museum. Photo: Chris Ridley (144) all Nicola Tree (146) all Andrew Moran (147) left Isabel Sierra Y Gómez de León; right Stephen Jakub (148) all Guy Archer (150) left nellyduff.com; right Fred Higginson (151) all Paul Tucker Courtesy Rocket (153) all Pelle Crepin (154) right T.C.R (156-157) Courtesy of Brawn (164) top left David Brook; top right SCP Ltd.; bottom right © Paul Tucker / Courtesy Rocket Gallery / Benchmark Furniture (165) top left Mark Whitfield Photography; top right Peter Guenzel; bottom left Tom Mannion for Tom Dixon; bottom right Jean Pierre Lemoine (166) top right Quodes from Chaplins; bottom left Dan Tsantilis; bottom right © Vitra (167) top right © Vitsœ; bottom left Peter Guenzel; bottom right www.cappellini.it (168) top left Peter Guenzel; top right Studio Michael Anastassiades; bottom left Nicole Marnati; bottom right Tom Mannion for Tom Dixon (169) top left www.flos.com; top right Mater Ethnical Living; bottom left Peter Guenzel; bottom right Örsjö Belysning AB (170) top left Artemide; top right Skandium; bottom left Courtesy of Barber Osgerby and Flos; bottom right Gateway Japan (171) top left Wästberg; top right Decode; bottom left Foscarini; bottom right Muuto (172) top left Studio Michael Anastassiades; top right Richard Sapper for Alessi, www.alessi.com; bottom left Christina Häusler; bottom right Muuto (173) top left Tina Ratzer; top right Peter Guenzel; bottom left Teori. Co. Ltd. (174) top left Kjell Postema; top right Jasper Morrison Studio; bottom left David Mellor Design; bottom right Skandium (175) top left Skandium; bottom left Rosenthal; bottom right Normann Copenhagen (181) left Ains Phillips (182) left Philip Vile / Channels; right Chaplins Furniture Ltd. (184) left Ben Adams; right James Balston (185) all Guy Drayton (187) all Matthew Hollow (188) left Inter IKEA System P.V. 1999-2011; right M Silgardo (189) all Stefan Lorett (190) left James Gardiner (191) right Peter Durant (192) left image courtesy of Phillips de Pury & Company; right Jessica Pinotti / placesandspaces (194) all Tom Fallon (195) all photographs by Noah Da Costa Courtesy Spring Projects (196) right Angus Bolton (197) left and bottom right Wellcome images; top right Rama Knight / Wellcome images.

LONDON
DESIGN GUIDE
.com

Register to receive monthly news updates,
promotions and special reader benefits
throughout the year.